MARVEL STUDIOS

ANT-MAN AND THE WASP

PRELUDE

MARVEL'S ANT-MAN AND THE WASP PRELUDE. Contains material originally published in magazine form as MARVEL'S ANT-MAN AND THE WASP PRELUDE #1-2, AVENGERS #195-196, AVENGERS ORIGINS: ANT-MAN
ND THE WASP and ASTONISHING ANT-MAN #1. First printing 2018. ISBN 978-1-302-90944-4. Published by MARVEL WORLDWIDE, INC., a subsidiary of MARVEL ENTERTAINMENT, LLC. OFFICE OF PUBLICATION: 135
Vest 50th Street, New York, NY 10020. Copyright © 2018 MARVEL No similarity between any of the names, characters, persons, and/or institutions in this magazine with those of any living or dead person or institution is
ntended, and any such similarity which may exist is purely coincidental. **Printed in the U.S.A.** DAN BUCKLEY, President, Marvel Entertainment; JOHN NEE, Publisher; JOE QUESADA, Chief Creative Officer; TOM BREVOORT,
xecutive Director of Publishing Technology; ALEX MORALES, Director of Publishing Operations; DAN EDINGTON, Managing Editor; SUSAN CRESPI, Production Manager; STAN LEE, Chairman Emeritus. For information
egarding advertising in Marvel Comics or on Marvel.com, please contact Vit DeBellis, Custom Solutions & Integrated Advertising Manager, at vdebellis@marvel.com. For Marvel subscription inquiries, please call 888-
11-5480. **Manufactured between 3/30/2018 and 5/1/2018 by LSC COMMUNICATIONS INC., KENDALLVILLE, IN, USA.**

0 9 8 7 6 5 4 3 2 1

MARVEL STUDIOS
ANT-MAN AND THE WASP
PRELUDE

BASED ON THE ANT-MAN SCREENPLAY BY
EDGAR WRIGHT & JOE CORNISH
AND ADAM McKAY & PAUL RUDD
STORY BY EDGAR WRIGHT & JOE CORNISH

WRITER: WILL CORONA PILGRIM

PENCILER: CHRIS ALLEN

INKER: ROBERTO POGGI

COLORIST: GURU-eFX
LETTERER: VC'S TRAVIS LANHAM
COVER ART: RYAN MEINERDING
EDITOR: MARK BASSO

FOR MARVEL STUDIOS
VP PRODUCTION & DEVELOPMENT: BRAD WINDERBAUM
PRESIDENT: KEVIN FEIGE

ANT-MAN CREATED BY STAN LEE, LARRY LIEBER & JACK KIRBY
WASP CREATED BY STAN LEE, ERNIE HART & JACK KIRBY

COLLECTION EDITOR: JENNIFER GRÜNWALD
ASSISTANT EDITOR: CAITLIN O'CONNELL
ASSOCIATE MANAGING EDITOR: KATERI WOODY
EDITOR, SPECIAL PROJECTS: MARK D. BEAZLEY
VP PRODUCTION & SPECIAL PROJECTS: JEFF YOUNGQUIST
SVP PRINT, SALES & MARKETING: DAVID GABRIEL

EDITOR IN CHIEF: C.B. CEBULSKI
CHIEF CREATIVE OFFICER: JOE QUESADA
PRESIDENT: DAN BUCKLEY

MARVEL'S ANT-MAN AND
THE WASP PRELUDE #1

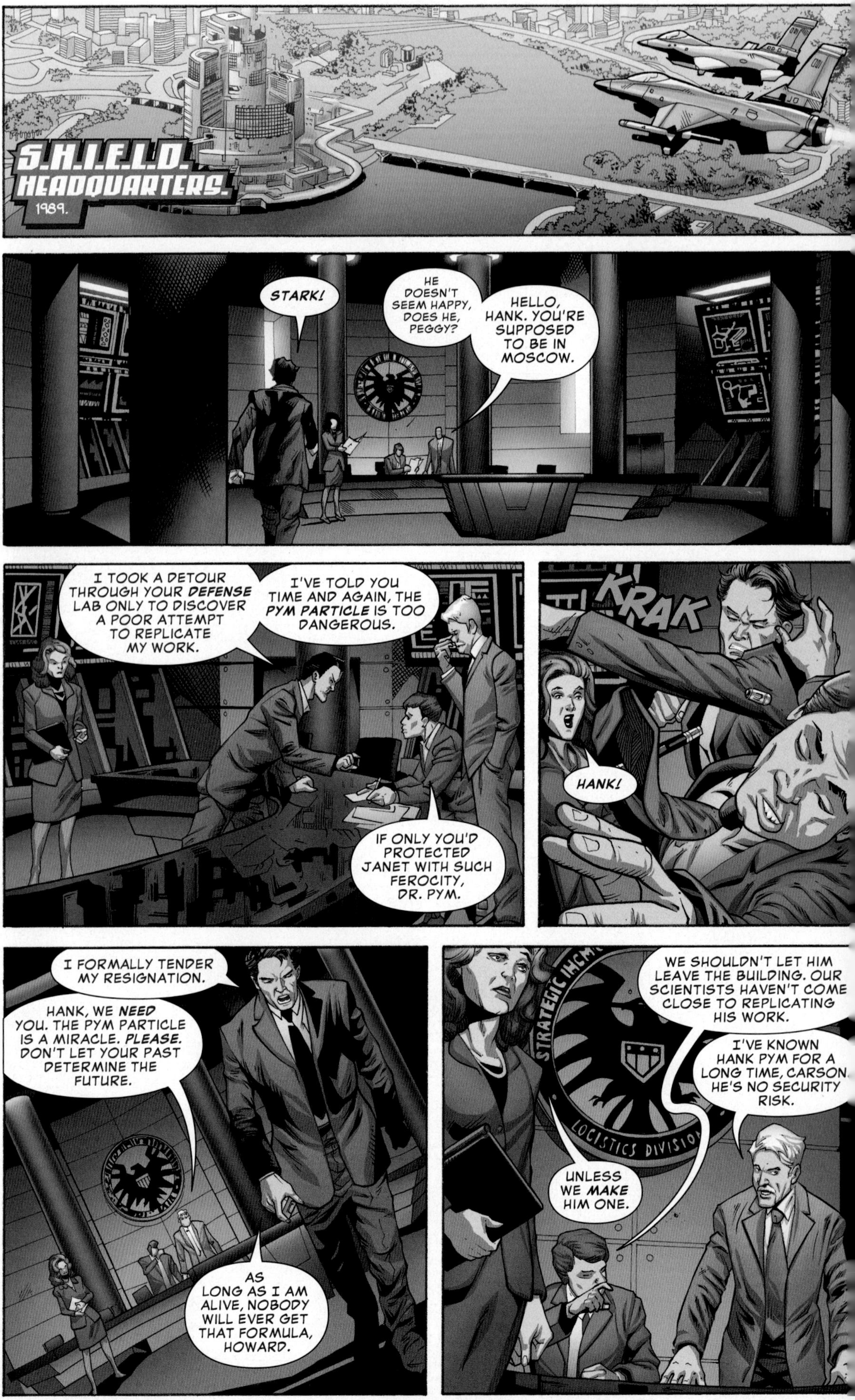
S.H.I.E.L.D. HEADQUARTERS.
1989.
STARK!
HE DOESN'T SEEM HAPPY, DOES HE, PEGGY?
HELLO, HANK. YOU'RE SUPPOSED TO BE IN MOSCOW.
I TOOK A DETOUR THROUGH YOUR DEFENSE LAB ONLY TO DISCOVER A POOR ATTEMPT TO REPLICATE MY WORK.
I'VE TOLD YOU TIME AND AGAIN, THE PYM PARTICLE IS TOO DANGEROUS.
IF ONLY YOU'D PROTECTED JANET WITH SUCH FEROCITY, DR. PYM.
KRAK
HANK!
I FORMALLY TENDER MY RESIGNATION.
HANK, WE NEED YOU. THE PYM PARTICLE IS A MIRACLE. PLEASE. DON'T LET YOUR PAST DETERMINE THE FUTURE.
AS LONG AS I AM ALIVE, NOBODY WILL EVER GET THAT FORMULA, HOWARD.
WE SHOULDN'T LET HIM LEAVE THE BUILDING. OUR SCIENTISTS HAVEN'T COME CLOSE TO REPLICATING HIS WORK.
I'VE KNOWN HANK PYM FOR A LONG TIME, CARSON. HE'S NO SECURITY RISK.
UNLESS WE MAKE HIM ONE.
LOGISTICS DIVISION

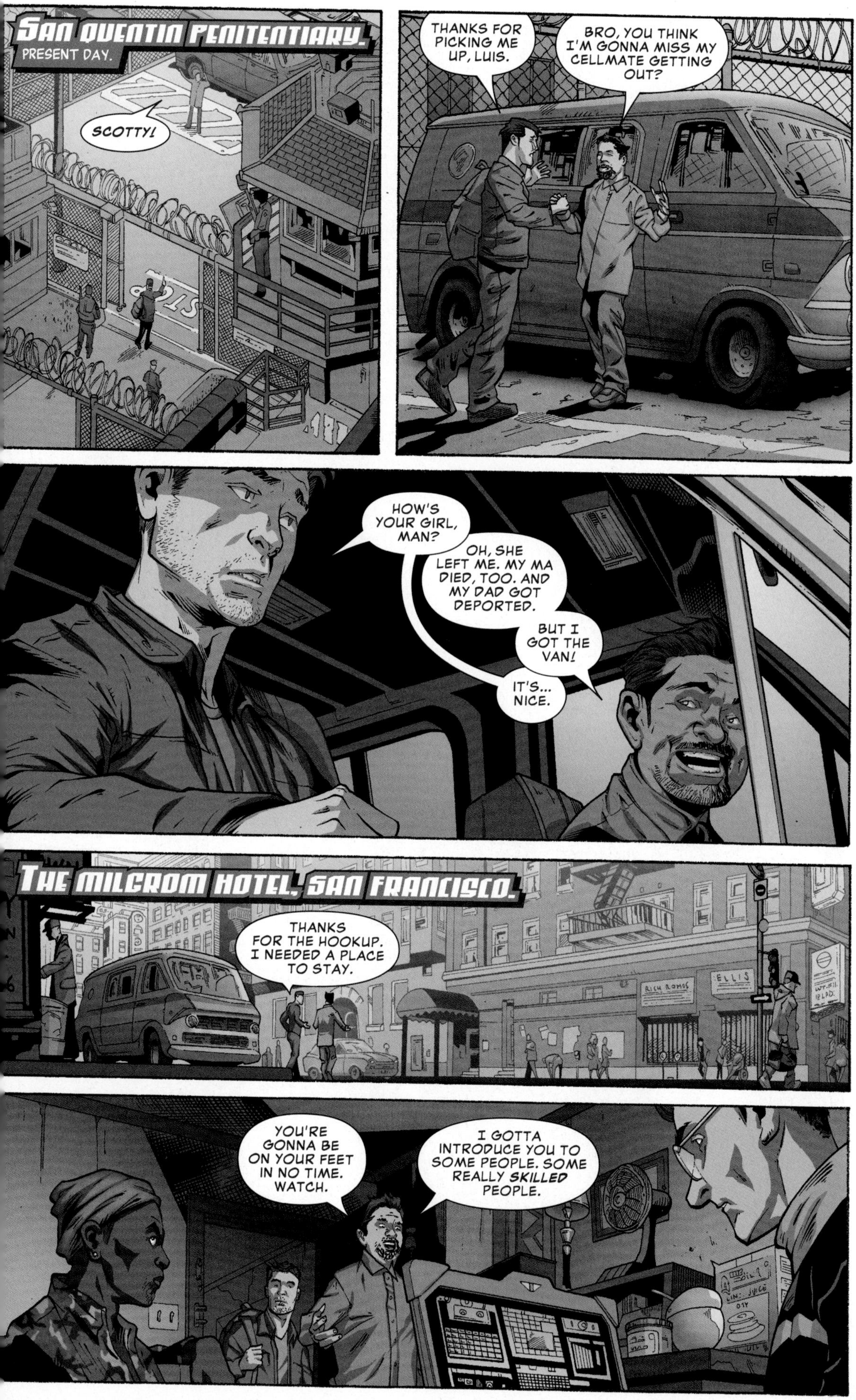
SAN QUENTIN PENITENTIARY.
PRESENT DAY.
SCOTTY!
THANKS FOR PICKING ME UP, LUIS.
BRO, YOU THINK I'M GONNA MISS MY CELLMATE GETTING OUT?
HOW'S YOUR GIRL, MAN?
OH, SHE LEFT ME. MY MA DIED, TOO. AND MY DAD GOT DEPORTED.
BUT I GOT THE VAN!
IT'S... NICE.
THE MILGROM HOTEL, SAN FRANCISCO.
THANKS FOR THE HOOKUP. I NEEDED A PLACE TO STAY.
YOU'RE GONNA BE ON YOUR FEET IN NO TIME. WATCH.
I GOTTA INTRODUCE YOU TO SOME PEOPLE. SOME REALLY SKILLED PEOPLE.

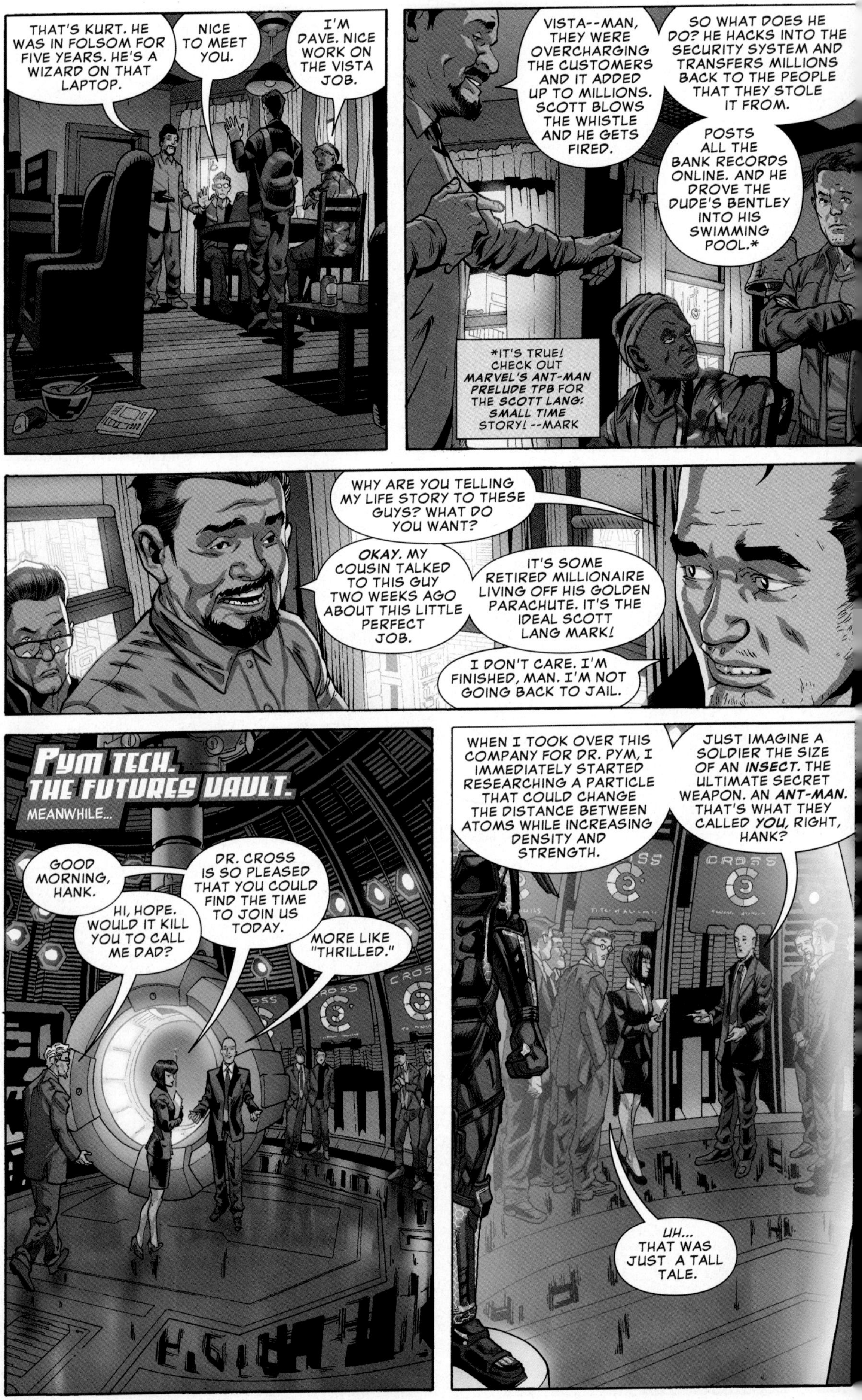
THAT'S KURT. HE WAS IN FOLSOM FOR FIVE YEARS. HE'S A WIZARD ON THAT LAPTOP.
NICE TO MEET YOU.
I'M DAVE. NICE WORK ON THE VISTA JOB.
VISTA--MAN, THEY WERE OVERCHARGING THE CUSTOMERS AND IT ADDED UP TO MILLIONS. SCOTT BLOWS THE WHISTLE AND HE GETS FIRED.
SO WHAT DOES HE DO? HE HACKS INTO THE SECURITY SYSTEM AND TRANSFERS MILLIONS BACK TO THE PEOPLE THAT THEY STOLE IT FROM.
POSTS ALL THE BANK RECORDS ONLINE. AND HE DROVE THE DUDE'S BENTLEY INTO HIS SWIMMING POOL.*
*IT'S TRUE! CHECK OUT MARVEL'S ANT-MAN PRELUDE TPB FOR THE SCOTT LANG: SMALL TIME STORY! --MARK
WHY ARE YOU TELLING MY LIFE STORY TO THESE GUYS? WHAT DO YOU WANT?
OKAY. MY COUSIN TALKED TO THIS GUY TWO WEEKS AGO ABOUT THIS LITTLE PERFECT JOB.
IT'S SOME RETIRED MILLIONAIRE LIVING OFF HIS GOLDEN PARACHUTE. IT'S THE IDEAL SCOTT LANG MARK!
I DON'T CARE. I'M FINISHED, MAN. I'M NOT GOING BACK TO JAIL.
PYM TECH. THE FUTURES VAULT.
MEANWHILE...
GOOD MORNING, HANK.
HI, HOPE. WOULD IT KILL YOU TO CALL ME DAD?
DR. CROSS IS SO PLEASED THAT YOU COULD FIND THE TIME TO JOIN US TODAY.
MORE LIKE "THRILLED."
WHEN I TOOK OVER THIS COMPANY FOR DR. PYM, I IMMEDIATELY STARTED RESEARCHING A PARTICLE THAT COULD CHANGE THE DISTANCE BETWEEN ATOMS WHILE INCREASING DENSITY AND STRENGTH.
JUST IMAGINE A SOLDIER THE SIZE OF AN INSECT. THE ULTIMATE SECRET WEAPON. AN ANT-MAN. THAT'S WHAT THEY CALLED YOU, RIGHT, HANK?
UH... THAT WAS JUST A TALL TALE.

YELLOWJACKET
CROSS
WELL, I WAS INSPIRED BY THE LEGEND OF THE ANT-MAN.
DISTINGUISHED GUESTS, I AM PROUD TO PRESENT THE END OF WARFARE AS WE KNOW IT: THE *YELLOWJACKET!* AN ALL-PURPOSE WEAPON OF WAR CAPABLE OF ALTERING THE SIZE OF THE WEARER FOR THE ULTIMATE COMBAT ADVANTAGE.
OH, NO...
DARREN, THERE'S A REASON THAT I BURIED THESE SECRETS. DON'T DO THIS.
WE COULD HAVE DONE THIS TOGETHER, HANK. BUT YOU RUINED THAT. THAT'S WHY YOU'RE THE *PAST* AND I'M THE *FUTURE.*
WE HAVE TO MAKE OUR MOVE, HANK. HE STILL CAN'T SHRINK A LIVE SUBJECT. JUST GIVE ME THE SUIT AND LET ME FINISH THIS ONCE AND FOR ALL.
OPEN
NO. IT'S TOO DANGEROUS. ANYWAY, I THINK I FOUND A GUY WHO CAN HELP US.
WHO?
DADDY!
PEANUT! HAPPY BIRTHDAY! I'M SO SORRY I'M LATE. I DIDN'T KNOW WHAT TIME YOUR PARTY STARTED.
WHAT ARE YOU DOING HERE, LANG? YOU HAVEN'T PAID A DIME OF CHILD SUPPORT. RIGHT NOW, IF I WANTED TO, I COULD ARREST YOU.
IT'S GOOD TO SEE YOU TOO, PAXTON. THE CHILD SUPPORT IS COMING, ALL RIGHT? IT'S JUST HARD FINDING A JOB WHEN YOU HAVE A RECORD.
SCOTT, YOU CAN'T JUST SHOW UP HERE. YOU KNOW THAT.
I'VE MISSED SO MUCH TIME, MAGGIE, AND I WANNA BE A PART OF CASSIE'S LIFE.
GET AN APARTMENT. GET A JOB. PAY CHILD SUPPORT. AND THEN WE WILL TALK ABOUT VISITATION WITH YOUR DAUGHTER.
YOU'RE HER *HERO,* SCOTT. JUST BE THE PERSON THAT SHE ALREADY *THINKS* YOU ARE.

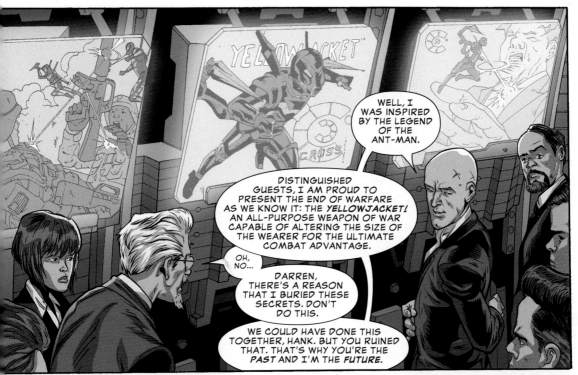

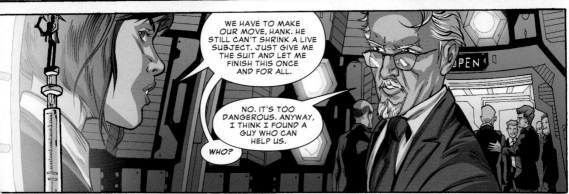

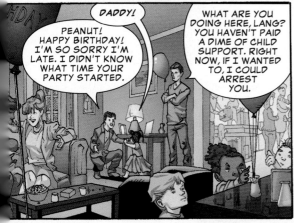

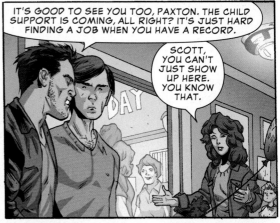

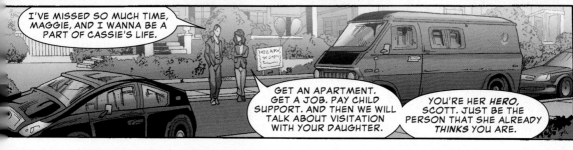

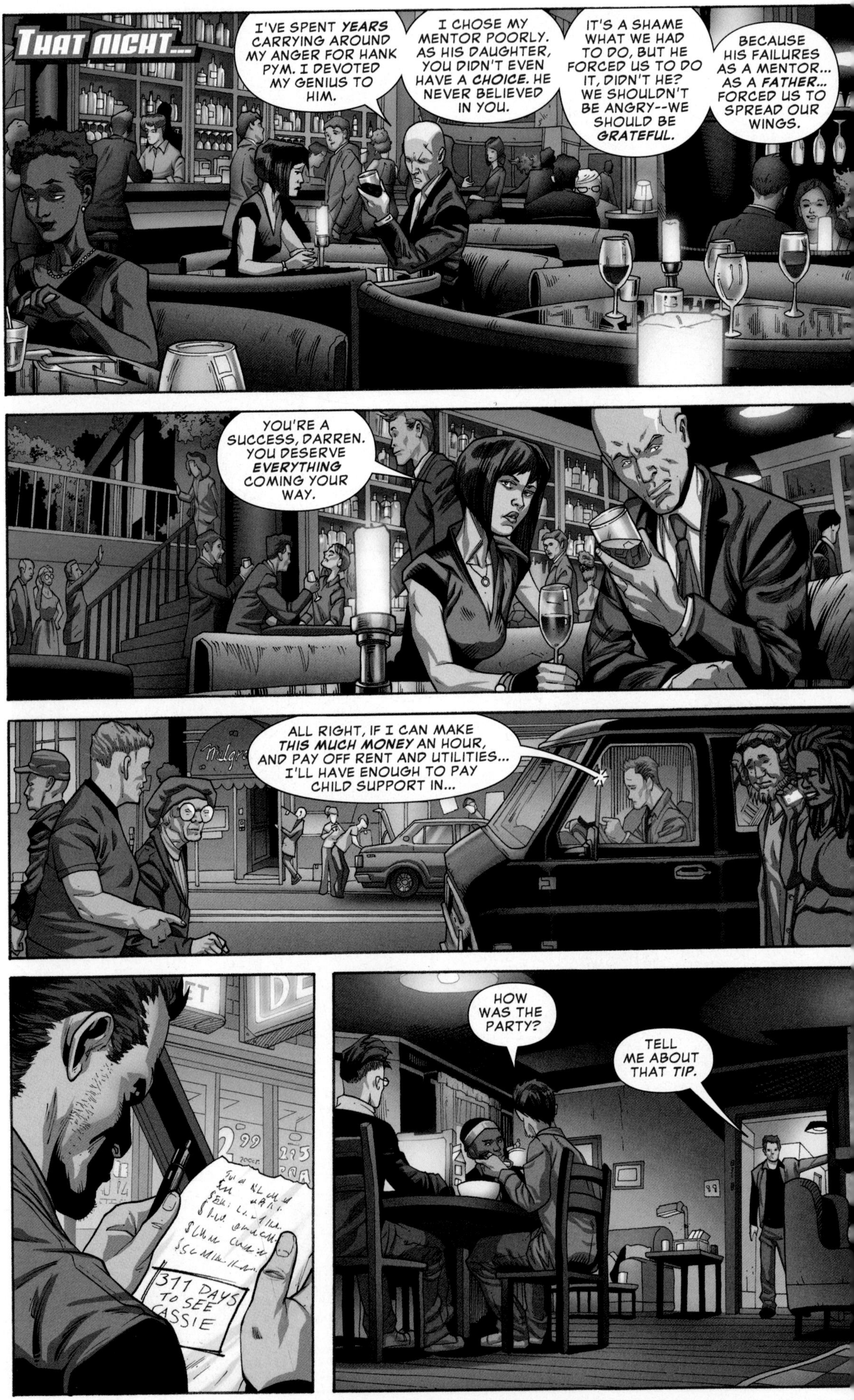
THAT NIGHT...
I'VE SPENT YEARS CARRYING AROUND MY ANGER FOR HANK PYM. I DEVOTED MY GENIUS TO HIM.
I CHOSE MY MENTOR POORLY. AS HIS DAUGHTER, YOU DIDN'T EVEN HAVE A CHOICE. HE NEVER BELIEVED IN YOU.
IT'S A SHAME WHAT WE HAD TO DO, BUT HE FORCED US TO DO IT, DIDN'T HE? WE SHOULDN'T BE ANGRY--WE SHOULD BE GRATEFUL.
BECAUSE HIS FAILURES AS A MENTOR... AS A FATHER... FORCED US TO SPREAD OUR WINGS.
YOU'RE A SUCCESS, DARREN. YOU DESERVE EVERYTHING COMING YOUR WAY.
ALL RIGHT, IF I CAN MAKE THIS MUCH MONEY AN HOUR, AND PAY OFF RENT AND UTILITIES... I'LL HAVE ENOUGH TO PAY CHILD SUPPORT IN...
311 DAYS TO SEE CASSIE
HOW WAS THE PARTY?
TELL ME ABOUT THAT TIP.

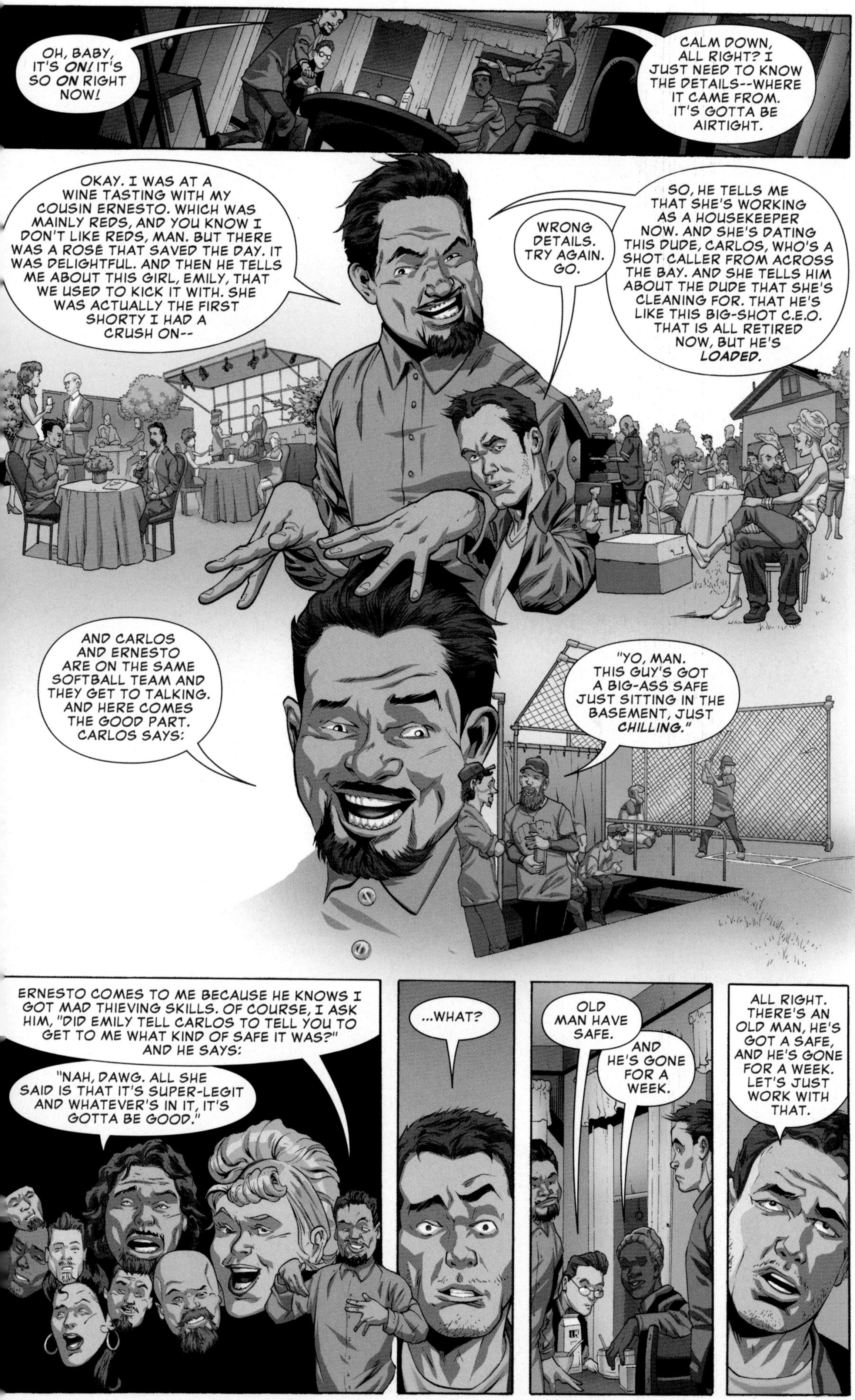
OH, BABY, IT'S ON! IT'S SO ON RIGHT NOW!
CALM DOWN, ALL RIGHT? I JUST NEED TO KNOW THE DETAILS--WHERE IT CAME FROM. IT'S GOTTA BE AIRTIGHT.
OKAY. I WAS AT A WINE TASTING WITH MY COUSIN ERNESTO. WHICH WAS MAINLY REDS, AND YOU KNOW I DON'T LIKE REDS, MAN. BUT THERE WAS A ROSÉ THAT SAVED THE DAY. IT WAS DELIGHTFUL. AND THEN HE TELLS ME ABOUT THIS GIRL, EMILY, THAT WE USED TO KICK IT WITH. SHE WAS ACTUALLY THE FIRST SHORTY I HAD A CRUSH ON--
WRONG DETAILS. TRY AGAIN. GO.
SO, HE TELLS ME THAT SHE'S WORKING AS A HOUSEKEEPER NOW. AND SHE'S DATING THIS DUDE, CARLOS, WHO'S A SHOT CALLER FROM ACROSS THE BAY. AND SHE TELLS HIM ABOUT THE DUDE THAT SHE'S CLEANING FOR. THAT HE'S LIKE THIS BIG-SHOT C.E.O. THAT IS ALL RETIRED NOW, BUT HE'S LOADED.
AND CARLOS AND ERNESTO ARE ON THE SAME SOFTBALL TEAM AND THEY GET TO TALKING. AND HERE COMES THE GOOD PART. CARLOS SAYS:
"YO, MAN. THIS GUY'S GOT A BIG-ASS SAFE JUST SITTING IN THE BASEMENT, JUST CHILLING."
ERNESTO COMES TO ME BECAUSE HE KNOWS I GOT MAD THIEVING SKILLS. OF COURSE, I ASK HIM, "DID EMILY TELL CARLOS TO TELL YOU TO GET TO ME WHAT KIND OF SAFE IT WAS?" AND HE SAYS:
"NAH, DAWG. ALL SHE SAID IS THAT IT'S SUPER-LEGIT AND WHATEVER'S IN IT, IT'S GOTTA BE GOOD."
...WHAT?
OLD MAN HAVE SAFE.
AND HE'S GONE FOR A WEEK.
ALL RIGHT. THERE'S AN OLD MAN, HE'S GOT A SAFE, AND HE'S GONE FOR A WEEK. LET'S JUST WORK WITH THAT.

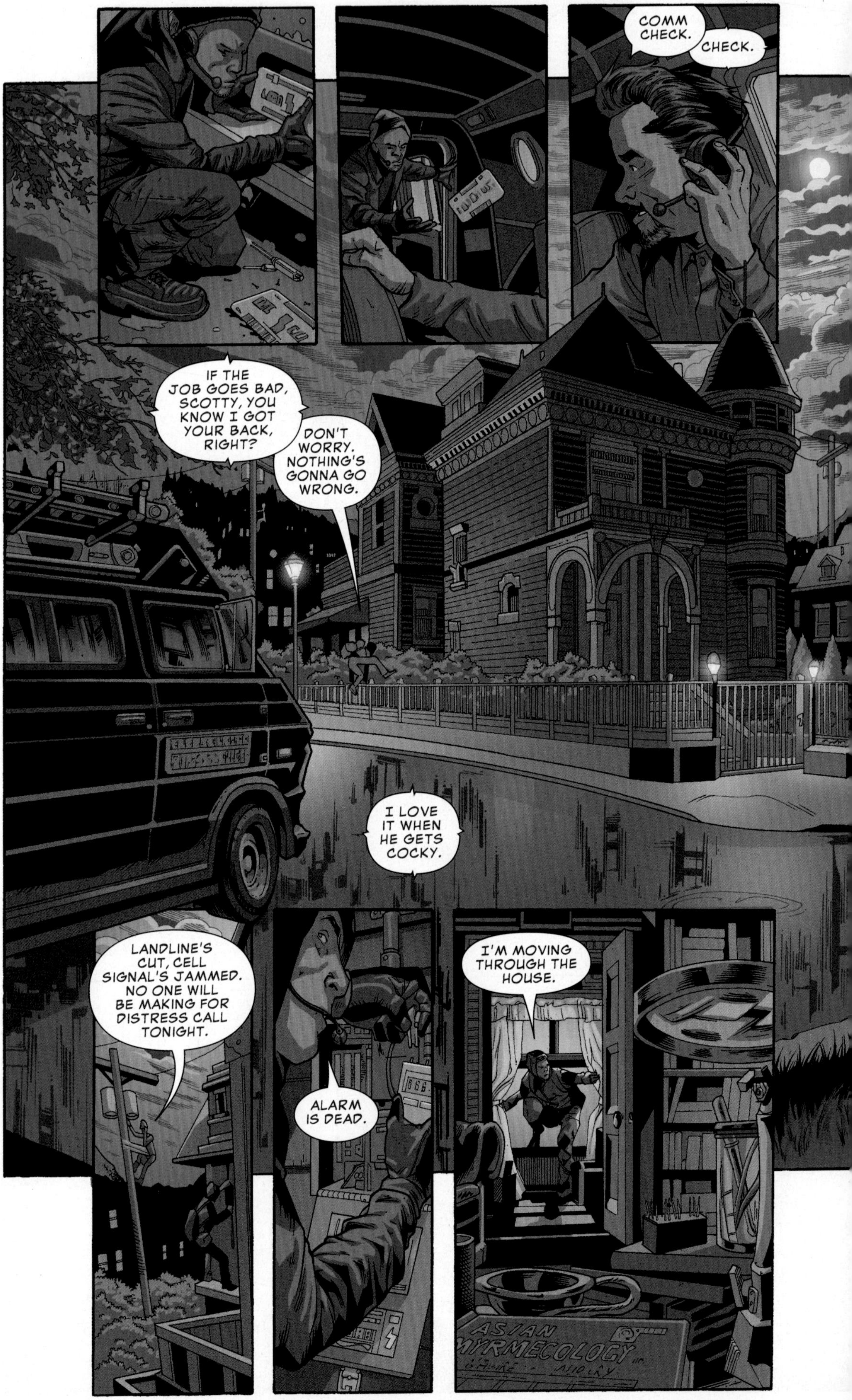
COMM CHECK.
CHECK.
IF THE JOB GOES BAD, SCOTTY, YOU KNOW I GOT YOUR BACK, RIGHT?
DON'T WORRY. NOTHING'S GONNA GO WRONG.
I LOVE IT WHEN HE GETS COCKY.
LANDLINE'S CUT, CELL SIGNAL'S JAMMED. NO ONE WILL BE MAKING FOR DISTRESS CALL TONIGHT.
ALARM IS DEAD.
I'M MOVING THROUGH THE HOUSE.
ASIAN MYRMECOLOGY

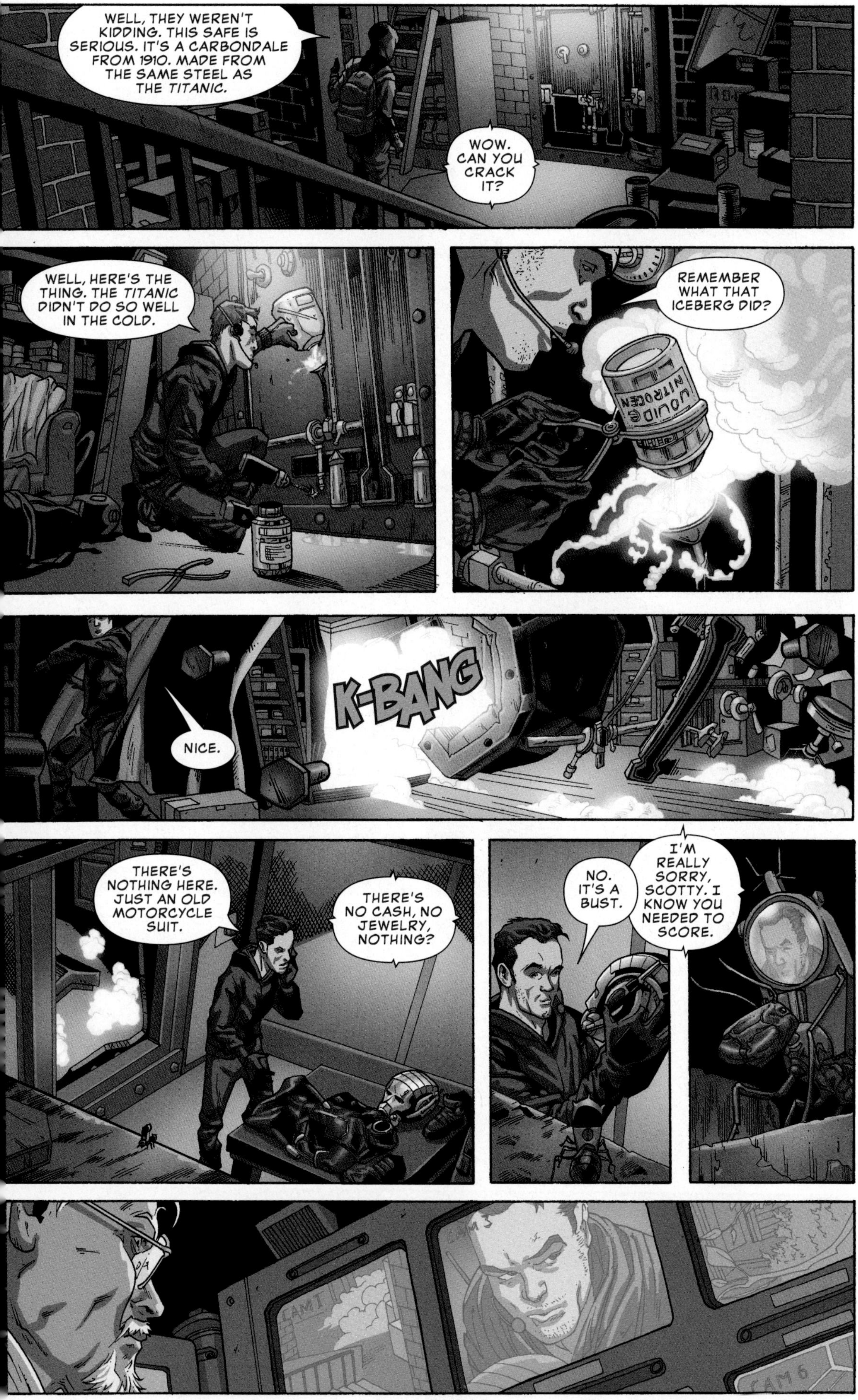
WELL, THEY WEREN'T KIDDING. THIS SAFE IS SERIOUS. IT'S A CARBONDALE FROM 1910. MADE FROM THE SAME STEEL AS THE *TITANIC*.
WOW. CAN YOU CRACK IT?
WELL, HERE'S THE THING. THE *TITANIC* DIDN'T DO SO WELL IN THE COLD.
REMEMBER WHAT THAT ICEBERG DID?
LIQUID NITROGEN
K-BANG
NICE.
THERE'S NOTHING HERE. JUST AN OLD MOTORCYCLE SUIT.
THERE'S NO CASH, NO JEWELRY, NOTHING?
NO. IT'S A BUST.
I'M REALLY SORRY, SCOTTY. I KNOW YOU NEEDED TO SCORE.
CAM 1
CAM 3
CAM 6

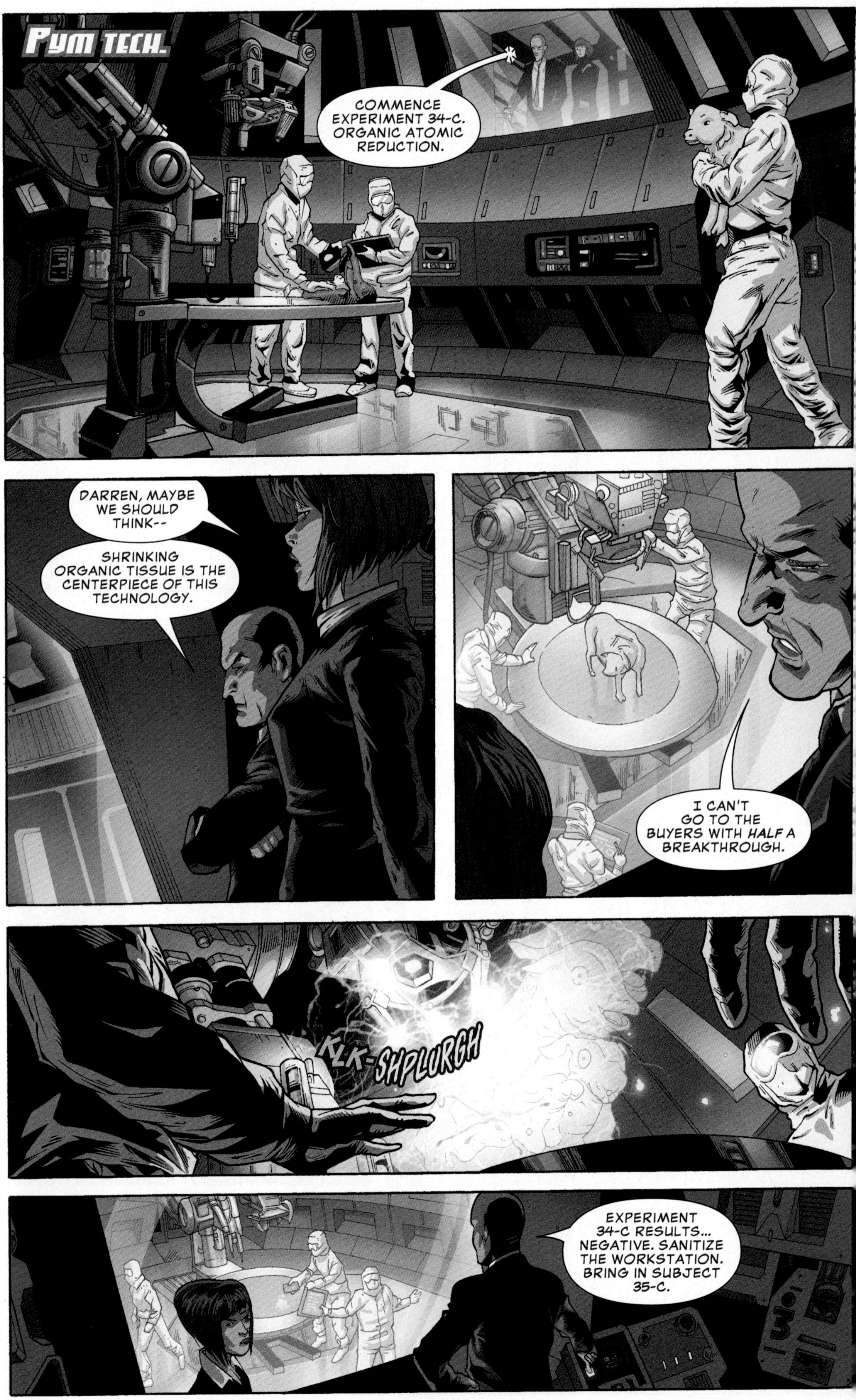
PYM TECH.
COMMENCE EXPERIMENT 34-C. ORGANIC ATOMIC REDUCTION.
DARREN, MAYBE WE SHOULD THINK--
SHRINKING ORGANIC TISSUE IS THE CENTERPIECE OF THIS TECHNOLOGY.
I CAN'T GO TO THE BUYERS WITH HALF A BREAKTHROUGH.
KLK-SHPLURGH
EXPERIMENT 34-C RESULTS... NEGATIVE. SANITIZE THE WORKSTATION. BRING IN SUBJECT 35-C.

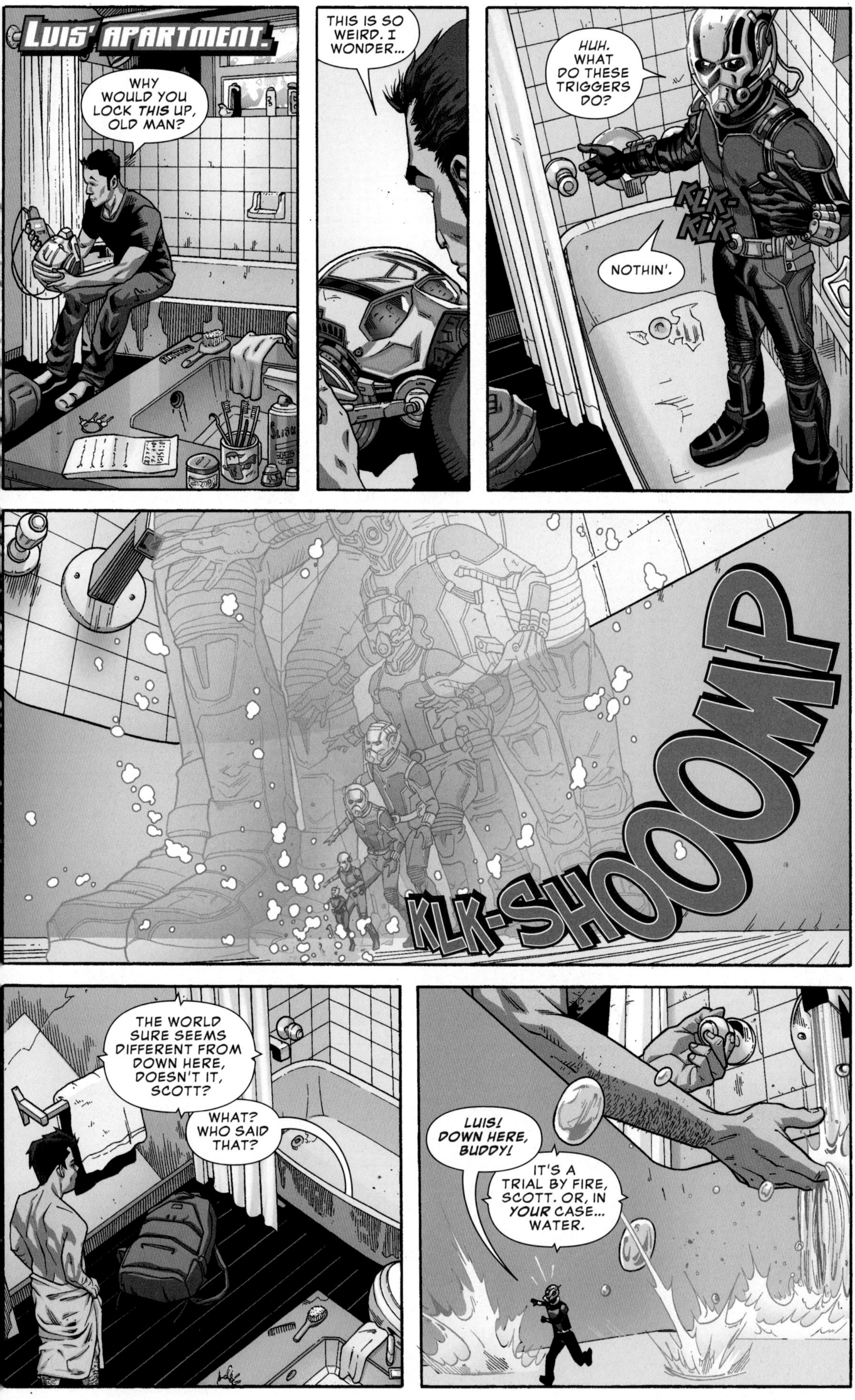
LUIS' APARTMENT.
WHY WOULD YOU LOCK THIS UP, OLD MAN?
THIS IS SO WEIRD. I WONDER...
HUH. WHAT DO THESE TRIGGERS DO?
KLK-KLK
NOTHIN'.
KLK-SHOOOOMP
THE WORLD SURE SEEMS DIFFERENT FROM DOWN HERE, DOESN'T IT, SCOTT?
WHAT? WHO SAID THAT?
LUIS! DOWN HERE, BUDDY!
IT'S A TRIAL BY FIRE, SCOTT. OR, IN YOUR CASE... WATER.

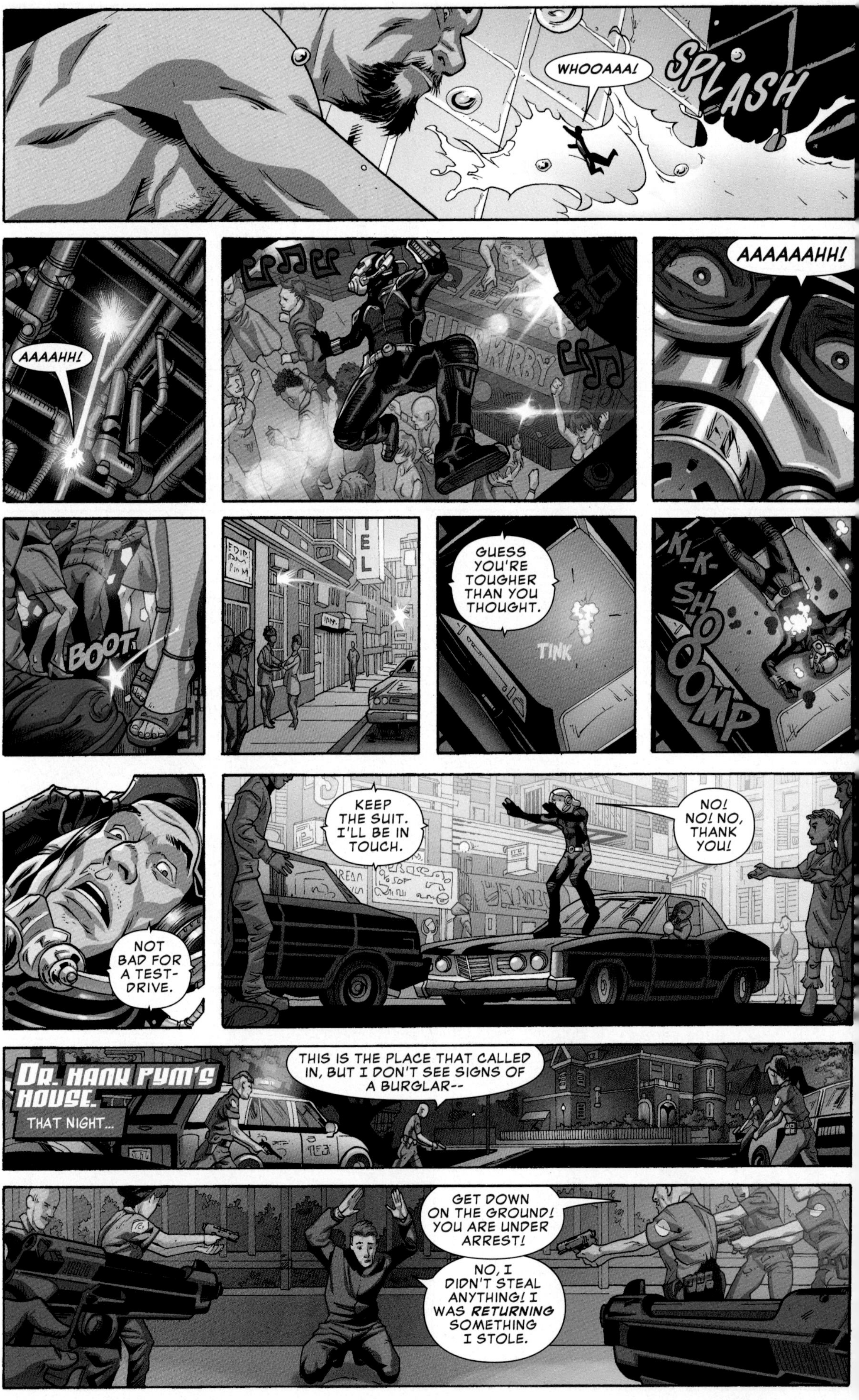
WHOOAAA!
SPLASH
AAAAHH!
AAAAAAHH!
BOOT
GUESS YOU'RE TOUGHER THAN YOU THOUGHT.
TINK
KLK-SHOOOMP
NOT BAD FOR A TEST-DRIVE.
KEEP THE SUIT. I'LL BE IN TOUCH.
NO! NO! NO, THANK YOU!
DR. HANK PYM'S HOUSE. THAT NIGHT...
THIS IS THE PLACE THAT CALLED IN, BUT I DON'T SEE SIGNS OF A BURGLAR--
GET DOWN ON THE GROUND! YOU ARE UNDER ARREST!
NO, I DIDN'T STEAL ANYTHING! I WAS RETURNING SOMETHING I STOLE.

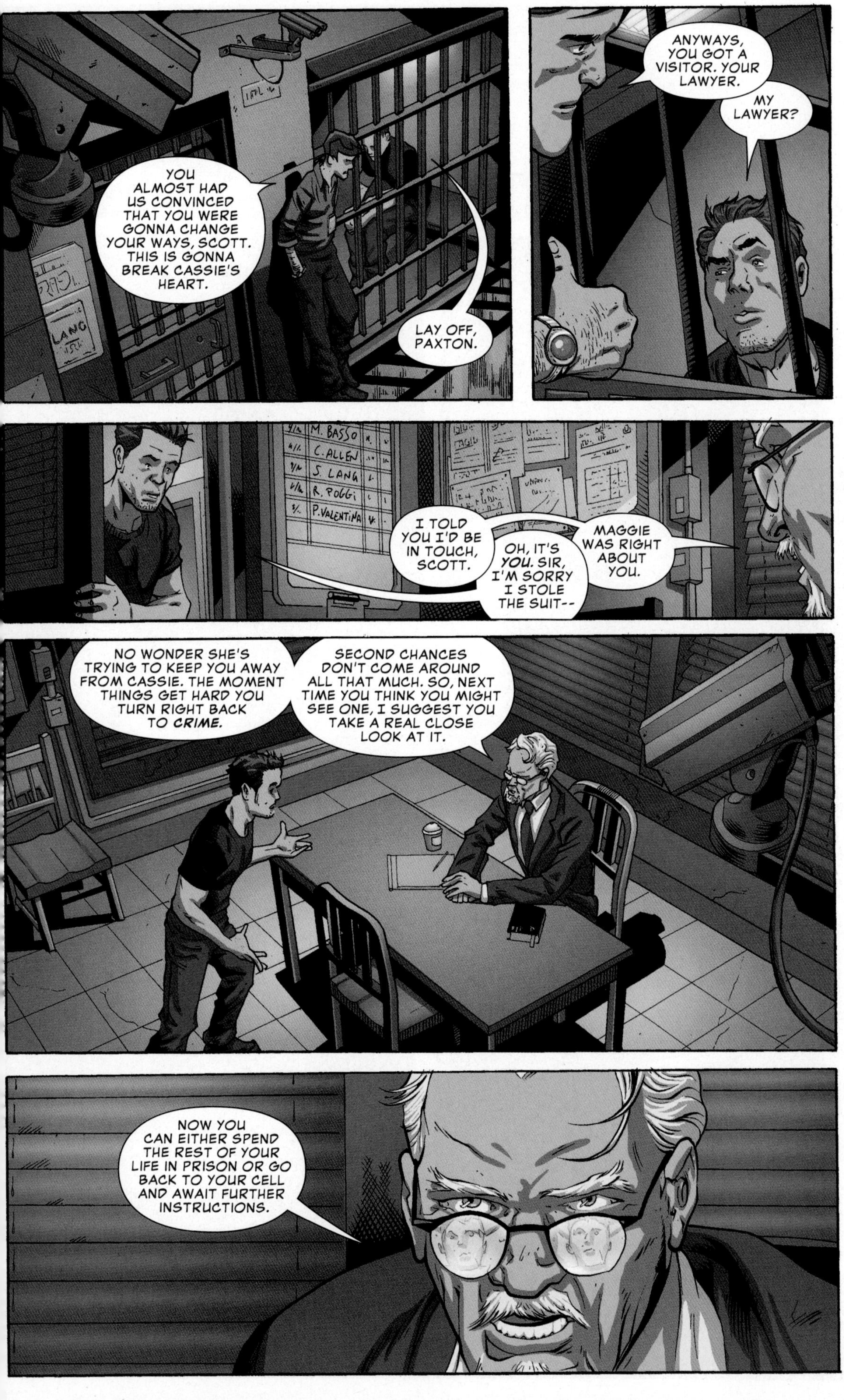

YOU ALMOST HAD US CONVINCED THAT YOU WERE GONNA CHANGE YOUR WAYS, SCOTT. THIS IS GONNA BREAK CASSIE'S HEART.
LANG
LAY OFF, PAXTON.
ANYWAYS, YOU GOT A VISITOR. YOUR LAWYER.
MY LAWYER?
M. BASSO
C. ALLEN
S. LANG
R. POGGI
P. VALENTINA
I TOLD YOU I'D BE IN TOUCH, SCOTT.
OH, IT'S *YOU.* SIR, I'M SORRY I STOLE THE SUIT--
MAGGIE WAS RIGHT ABOUT YOU.
NO WONDER SHE'S TRYING TO KEEP YOU AWAY FROM CASSIE. THE MOMENT THINGS GET HARD YOU TURN RIGHT BACK TO *CRIME.*
SECOND CHANCES DON'T COME AROUND ALL THAT MUCH. SO, NEXT TIME YOU THINK YOU MIGHT SEE ONE, I SUGGEST YOU TAKE A REAL CLOSE LOOK AT IT.
NOW YOU CAN EITHER SPEND THE REST OF YOUR LIFE IN PRISON OR GO BACK TO YOUR CELL AND AWAIT FURTHER INSTRUCTIONS.

UM...
KAY?

KLK-
SHOOMP

WHOOOOP
WHOOOOP

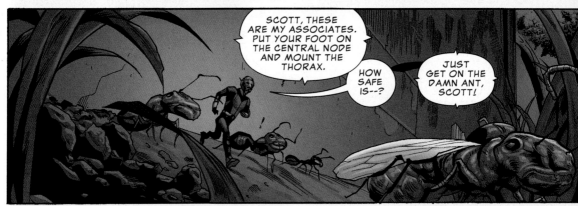

SCOTT, THESE ARE MY ASSOCIATES. PUT YOUR FOOT ON THE CENTRAL NODE AND MOUNT THE THORAX.

HOW SAFE IS--?

JUST GET ON THE DAMN ANT, SCOTT!

WAIT! WHOA! WHAT HAPPENS IF I THROW UP IN THIS HELMET?

IT'S MY HELMET, SCOTT. YOU DO NOT THROW UP.

I'M GETTING A LITTLE LIGHT-HEADED. I NEED A SNOOZE BUTTON.

HIT ME IN 5 MINUTES.

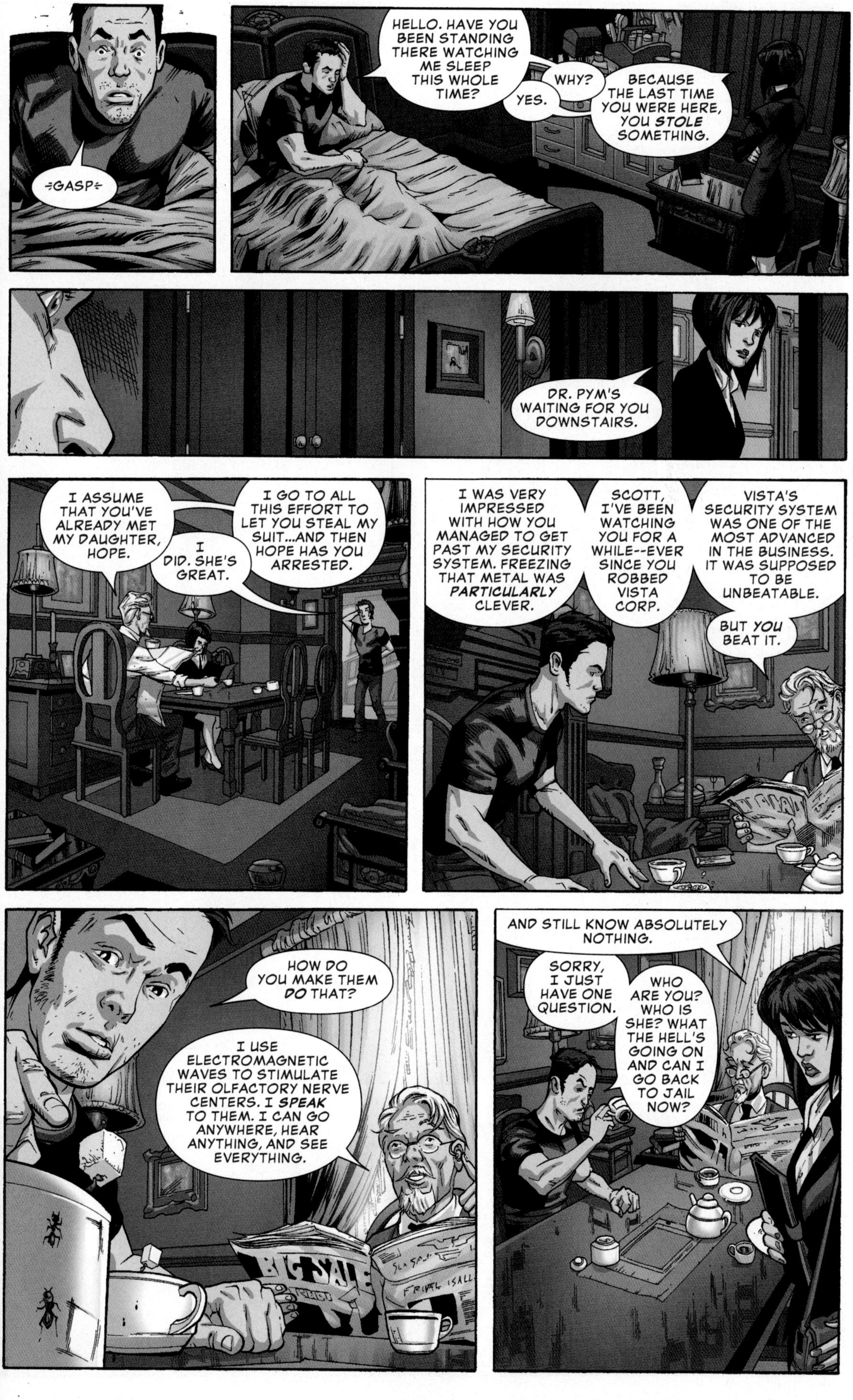

=GASP=
HELLO. HAVE YOU BEEN STANDING THERE WATCHING ME SLEEP THIS WHOLE TIME?
YES.
WHY?
BECAUSE THE LAST TIME YOU WERE HERE, YOU STOLE SOMETHING.
DR. PYM'S WAITING FOR YOU DOWNSTAIRS.
I ASSUME THAT YOU'VE ALREADY MET MY DAUGHTER, HOPE.
I DID. SHE'S GREAT.
I GO TO ALL THIS EFFORT TO LET YOU STEAL MY SUIT...AND THEN HOPE HAS YOU ARRESTED.
I WAS VERY IMPRESSED WITH HOW YOU MANAGED TO GET PAST MY SECURITY SYSTEM. FREEZING THAT METAL WAS PARTICULARLY CLEVER.
SCOTT, I'VE BEEN WATCHING YOU FOR A WHILE--EVER SINCE YOU ROBBED VISTA CORP.
VISTA'S SECURITY SYSTEM WAS ONE OF THE MOST ADVANCED IN THE BUSINESS. IT WAS SUPPOSED TO BE UNBEATABLE.
BUT YOU BEAT IT.
HOW DO YOU MAKE THEM DO THAT?
I USE ELECTROMAGNETIC WAVES TO STIMULATE THEIR OLFACTORY NERVE CENTERS. I SPEAK TO THEM. I CAN GO ANYWHERE, HEAR ANYTHING, AND SEE EVERYTHING.
AND STILL KNOW ABSOLUTELY NOTHING.
SORRY, I JUST HAVE ONE QUESTION.
WHO ARE YOU? WHO IS SHE? WHAT THE HELL'S GOING ON AND CAN I GO BACK TO JAIL NOW?

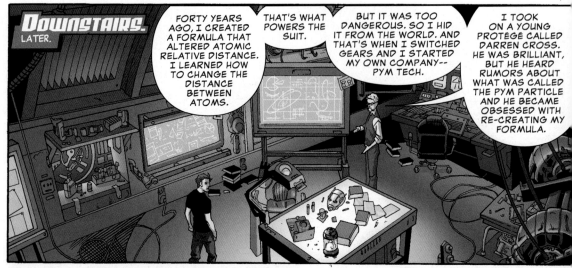

DOWNSTAIRS. LATER.

FORTY YEARS AGO, I CREATED A FORMULA THAT ALTERED ATOMIC RELATIVE DISTANCE. I LEARNED HOW TO CHANGE THE DISTANCE BETWEEN ATOMS.

THAT'S WHAT POWERS THE SUIT.

BUT IT WAS TOO DANGEROUS. SO I HID IT FROM THE WORLD. AND THAT'S WHEN I SWITCHED GEARS AND I STARTED MY OWN COMPANY-- PYM TECH.

I TOOK ON A YOUNG PROTÉGÉ CALLED DARREN CROSS. HE WAS BRILLIANT, BUT HE HEARD RUMORS ABOUT WHAT WAS CALLED THE PYM PARTICLE AND HE BECAME OBSESSED WITH RE-CREATING MY FORMULA.

"WITH THE HELP OF HOPE HE VOTED ME OUT OF MY OWN COMPANY. BUT HOPE RETURNED TO ME WHEN SHE SAW HOW CLOSE CROSS WAS TO CRACKING MY FORMULA."

I'M SORRY YOU HAVE SUCH DEEP CONCERNS ABOUT THE YELLOWJACKET, FRANK.

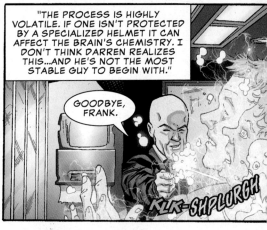

"THE PROCESS IS HIGHLY VOLATILE. IF ONE ISN'T PROTECTED BY A SPECIALIZED HELMET IT CAN AFFECT THE BRAIN'S CHEMISTRY. I DON'T THINK DARREN REALIZES THIS...AND HE'S NOT THE MOST STABLE GUY TO BEGIN WITH."

GOODBYE, FRANK.

KLK-SHPLURCH

THIS ISN'T THE FIRST TIME THESE GUYS HAVE TRIED TO GET THEIR HANDS ON GAME-CHANGING WEAPONRY. THAT'S MITCHELL CARSON, EX-HEAD OF DEFENSE AT S.H.I.E.L.D. PRESENTLY IN THE BUSINESS OF TOPPLING GOVERNMENTS.

"AND NOW, UNLESS WE BREAK IN, STEAL THE YELLOWJACKET AND DESTROY ALL THE DATA, DARREN CROSS IS GONNA UNLEASH CHAOS UPON THE WORLD."

I THINK OUR FIRST MOVE SHOULD BE CALLING THE AVENGERS.

THIS IS NOT SOME CUTE TECHNOLOGY LIKE THE IRON MAN SUIT. THIS COULD CHANGE THE TEXTURE OF REALITY.

I NEED SOMEBODY WHO CAN INFILTRATE A PLACE THAT'S DESIGNED TO PREVENT INFILTRATION.

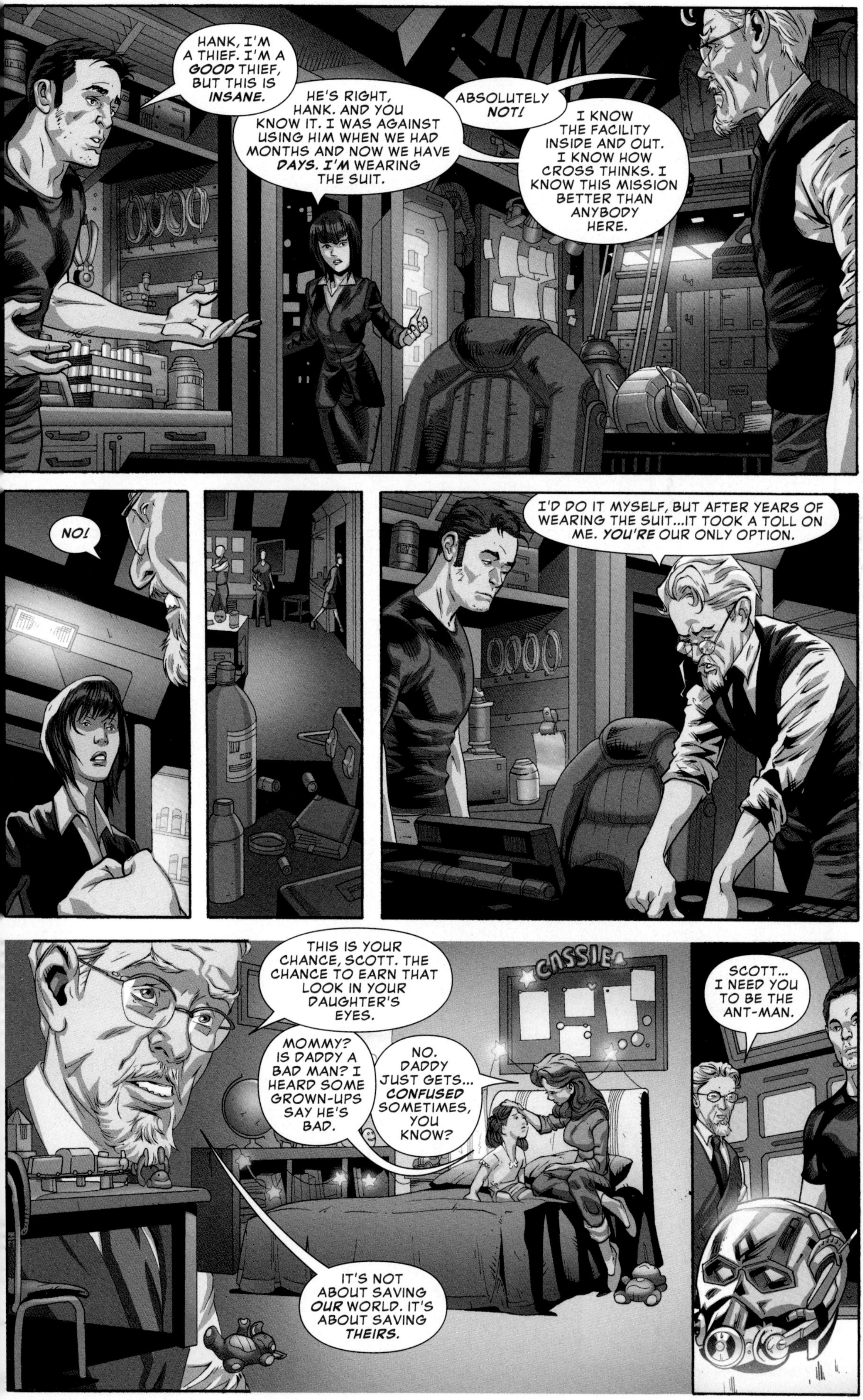
HANK, I'M A THIEF. I'M A GOOD THIEF, BUT THIS IS INSANE.
HE'S RIGHT, HANK. AND YOU KNOW IT. I WAS AGAINST USING HIM WHEN WE HAD MONTHS AND NOW WE HAVE DAYS. I'M WEARING THE SUIT.
ABSOLUTELY NOT!
I KNOW THE FACILITY INSIDE AND OUT. I KNOW HOW CROSS THINKS. I KNOW THIS MISSION BETTER THAN ANYBODY HERE.
NO!
I'D DO IT MYSELF, BUT AFTER YEARS OF WEARING THE SUIT...IT TOOK A TOLL ON ME. YOU'RE OUR ONLY OPTION.
THIS IS YOUR CHANCE, SCOTT. THE CHANCE TO EARN THAT LOOK IN YOUR DAUGHTER'S EYES.
CASSIE
MOMMY? IS DADDY A BAD MAN? I HEARD SOME GROWN-UPS SAY HE'S BAD.
NO. DADDY JUST GETS... CONFUSED SOMETIMES, YOU KNOW?
IT'S NOT ABOUT SAVING OUR WORLD. IT'S ABOUT SAVING THEIRS.
SCOTT... I NEED YOU TO BE THE ANT-MAN.

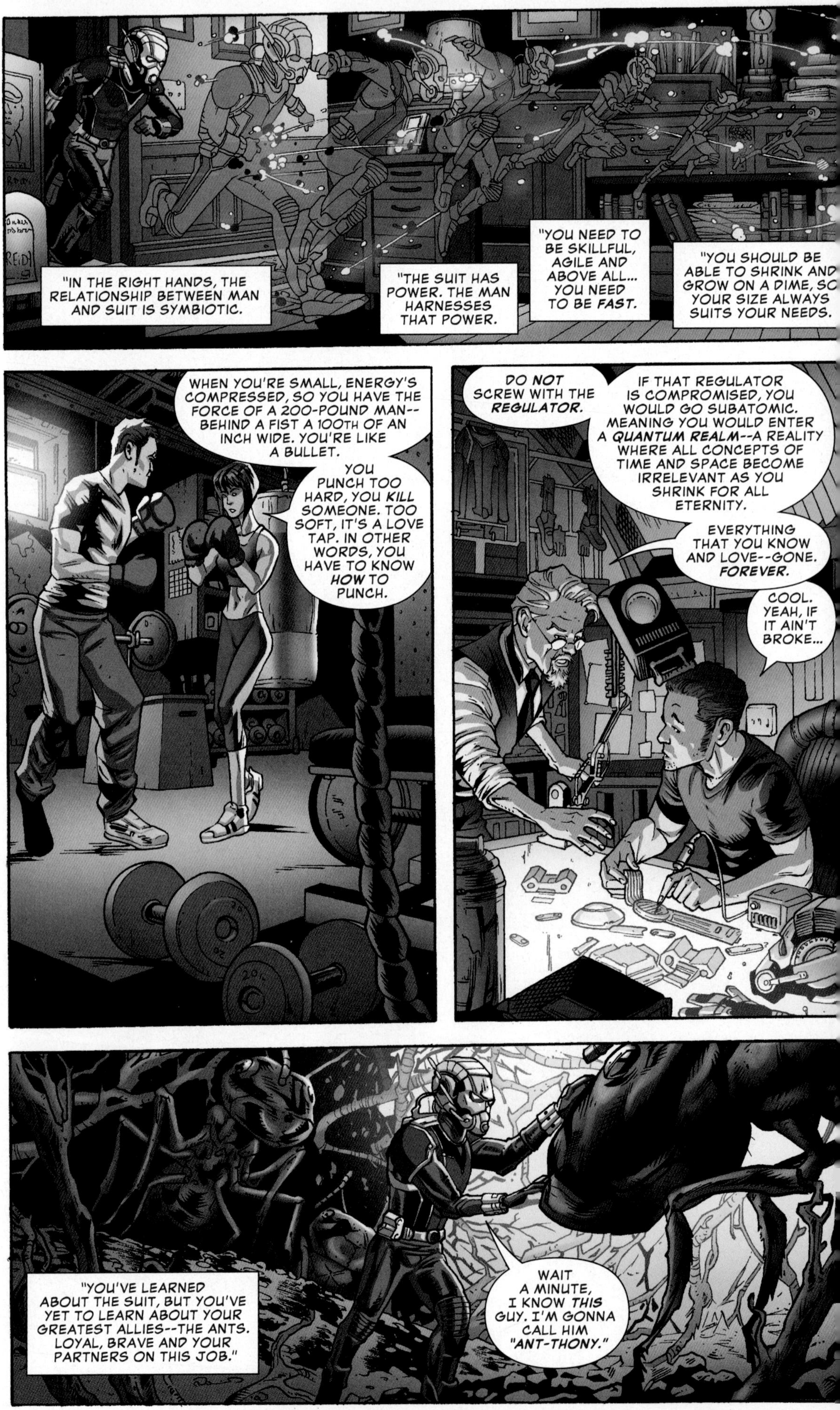
"IN THE RIGHT HANDS, THE RELATIONSHIP BETWEEN MAN AND SUIT IS SYMBIOTIC.
"THE SUIT HAS POWER. THE MAN HARNESSES THAT POWER.
"YOU NEED TO BE SKILLFUL, AGILE AND ABOVE ALL... YOU NEED TO BE *FAST.*
"YOU SHOULD BE ABLE TO SHRINK AND GROW ON A DIME, SO YOUR SIZE ALWAYS SUITS YOUR NEEDS.
WHEN YOU'RE SMALL, ENERGY'S COMPRESSED, SO YOU HAVE THE FORCE OF A 200-POUND MAN--BEHIND A FIST A 100TH OF AN INCH WIDE. YOU'RE LIKE A BULLET.
YOU PUNCH TOO HARD, YOU ***KILL*** SOMEONE. TOO SOFT, IT'S A LOVE TAP. IN OTHER WORDS, YOU HAVE TO KNOW ***HOW*** TO PUNCH.
*DO **NOT*** SCREW WITH THE ***REGULATOR.***
IF THAT REGULATOR IS COMPROMISED, YOU WOULD GO SUBATOMIC. MEANING YOU WOULD ENTER A ***QUANTUM REALM***--A REALITY WHERE ALL CONCEPTS OF TIME AND SPACE BECOME IRRELEVANT AS YOU SHRINK FOR ALL ETERNITY.
EVERYTHING THAT YOU KNOW AND LOVE--GONE. ***FOREVER.***
COOL. YEAH, IF IT AIN'T BROKE...
"YOU'VE LEARNED ABOUT THE SUIT, BUT YOU'VE YET TO LEARN ABOUT YOUR GREATEST ALLIES--THE ANTS. LOYAL, BRAVE AND YOUR PARTNERS ON THIS JOB."
WAIT A MINUTE, I KNOW ***THIS*** GUY. I'M GONNA CALL HIM ***"ANT-THONY."***

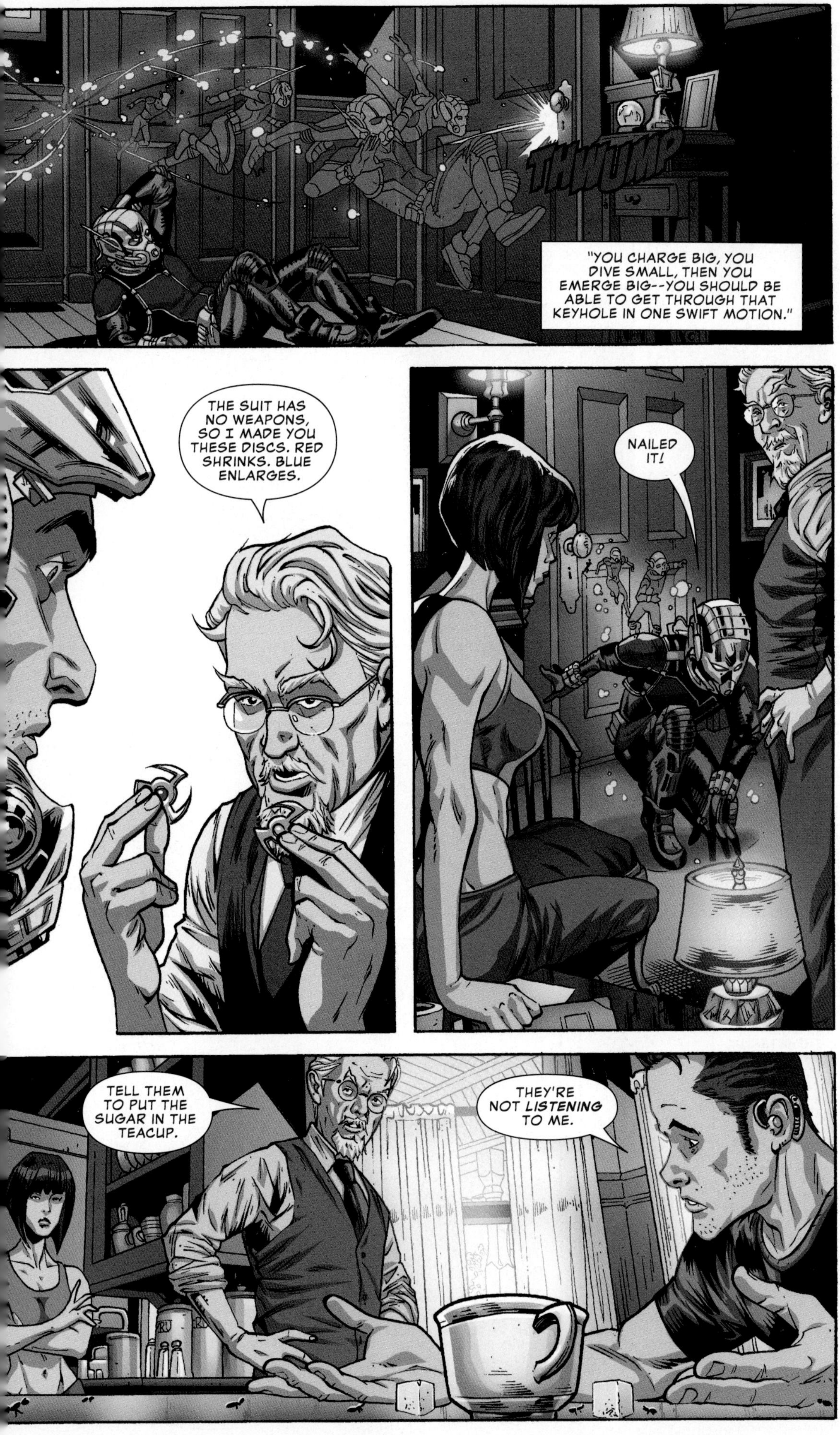
THWUMP
"YOU CHARGE BIG, YOU DIVE SMALL, THEN YOU EMERGE BIG--YOU SHOULD BE ABLE TO GET THROUGH THAT KEYHOLE IN ONE SWIFT MOTION."
THE SUIT HAS NO WEAPONS, SO I MADE YOU THESE DISCS. RED SHRINKS. BLUE ENLARGES.
NAILED IT!
TELL THEM TO PUT THE SUGAR IN THE TEACUP.
THEY'RE NOT *LISTENING* TO ME.

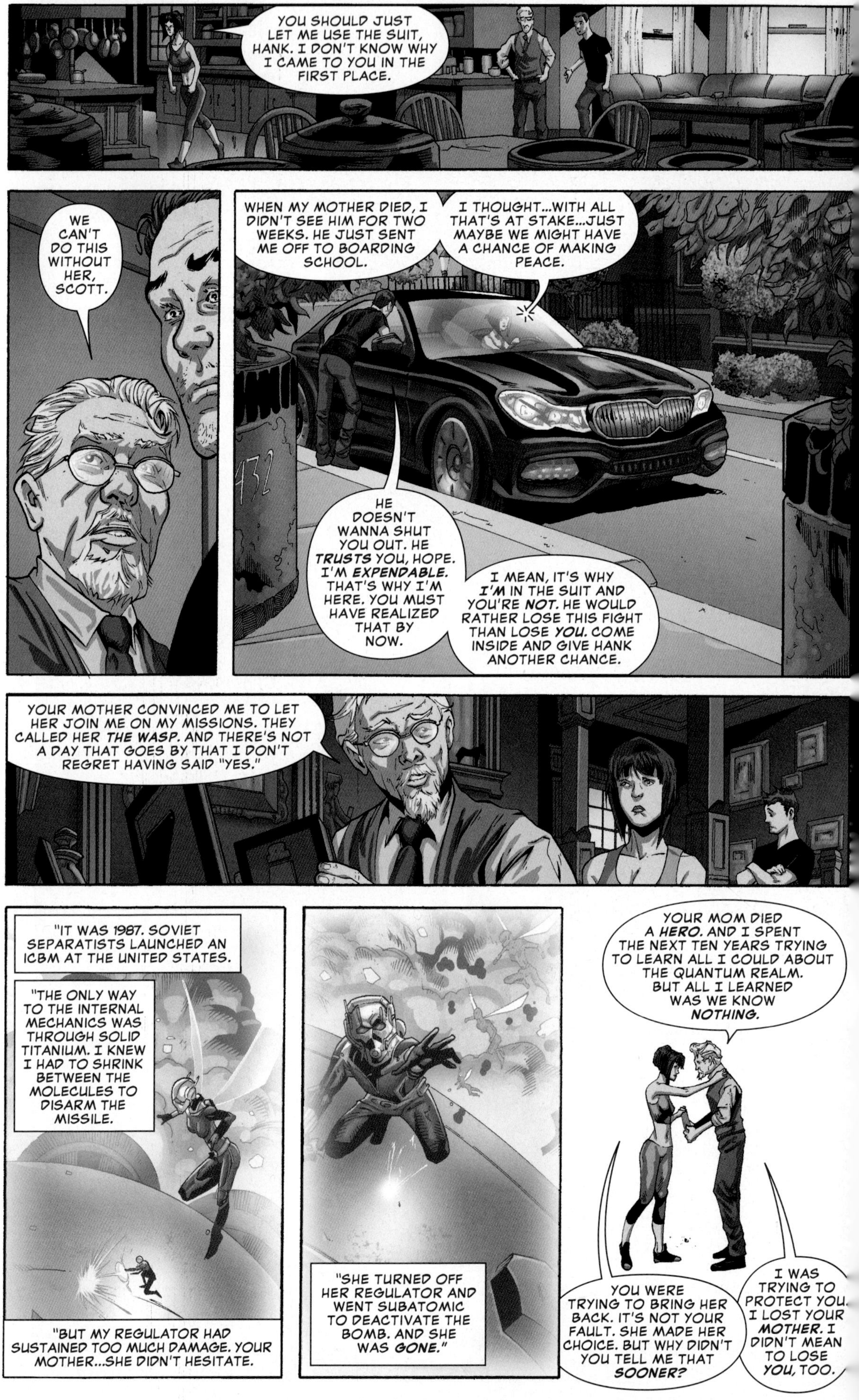
YOU SHOULD JUST LET ME USE THE SUIT, HANK. I DON'T KNOW WHY I CAME TO YOU IN THE FIRST PLACE.
WE CAN'T DO THIS WITHOUT HER, SCOTT.
WHEN MY MOTHER DIED, I DIDN'T SEE HIM FOR TWO WEEKS. HE JUST SENT ME OFF TO BOARDING SCHOOL.
I THOUGHT...WITH ALL THAT'S AT STAKE...JUST MAYBE WE MIGHT HAVE A CHANCE OF MAKING PEACE.
HE DOESN'T WANNA SHUT YOU OUT. HE TRUSTS YOU, HOPE. I'M EXPENDABLE. THAT'S WHY I'M HERE. YOU MUST HAVE REALIZED THAT BY NOW.
I MEAN, IT'S WHY I'M IN THE SUIT AND YOU'RE NOT. HE WOULD RATHER LOSE THIS FIGHT THAN LOSE YOU. COME INSIDE AND GIVE HANK ANOTHER CHANCE.
YOUR MOTHER CONVINCED ME TO LET HER JOIN ME ON MY MISSIONS. THEY CALLED HER THE WASP. AND THERE'S NOT A DAY THAT GOES BY THAT I DON'T REGRET HAVING SAID "YES."
"IT WAS 1987. SOVIET SEPARATISTS LAUNCHED AN ICBM AT THE UNITED STATES.
"THE ONLY WAY TO THE INTERNAL MECHANICS WAS THROUGH SOLID TITANIUM. I KNEW I HAD TO SHRINK BETWEEN THE MOLECULES TO DISARM THE MISSILE.
"BUT MY REGULATOR HAD SUSTAINED TOO MUCH DAMAGE. YOUR MOTHER...SHE DIDN'T HESITATE.
"SHE TURNED OFF HER REGULATOR AND WENT SUBATOMIC TO DEACTIVATE THE BOMB. AND SHE WAS GONE."
YOUR MOM DIED A HERO. AND I SPENT THE NEXT TEN YEARS TRYING TO LEARN ALL I COULD ABOUT THE QUANTUM REALM. BUT ALL I LEARNED WAS WE KNOW NOTHING.
YOU WERE TRYING TO BRING HER BACK. IT'S NOT YOUR FAULT. SHE MADE HER CHOICE. BUT WHY DIDN'T YOU TELL ME THAT SOONER?
I WAS TRYING TO PROTECT YOU. I LOST YOUR MOTHER. I DIDN'T MEAN TO LOSE YOU, TOO.

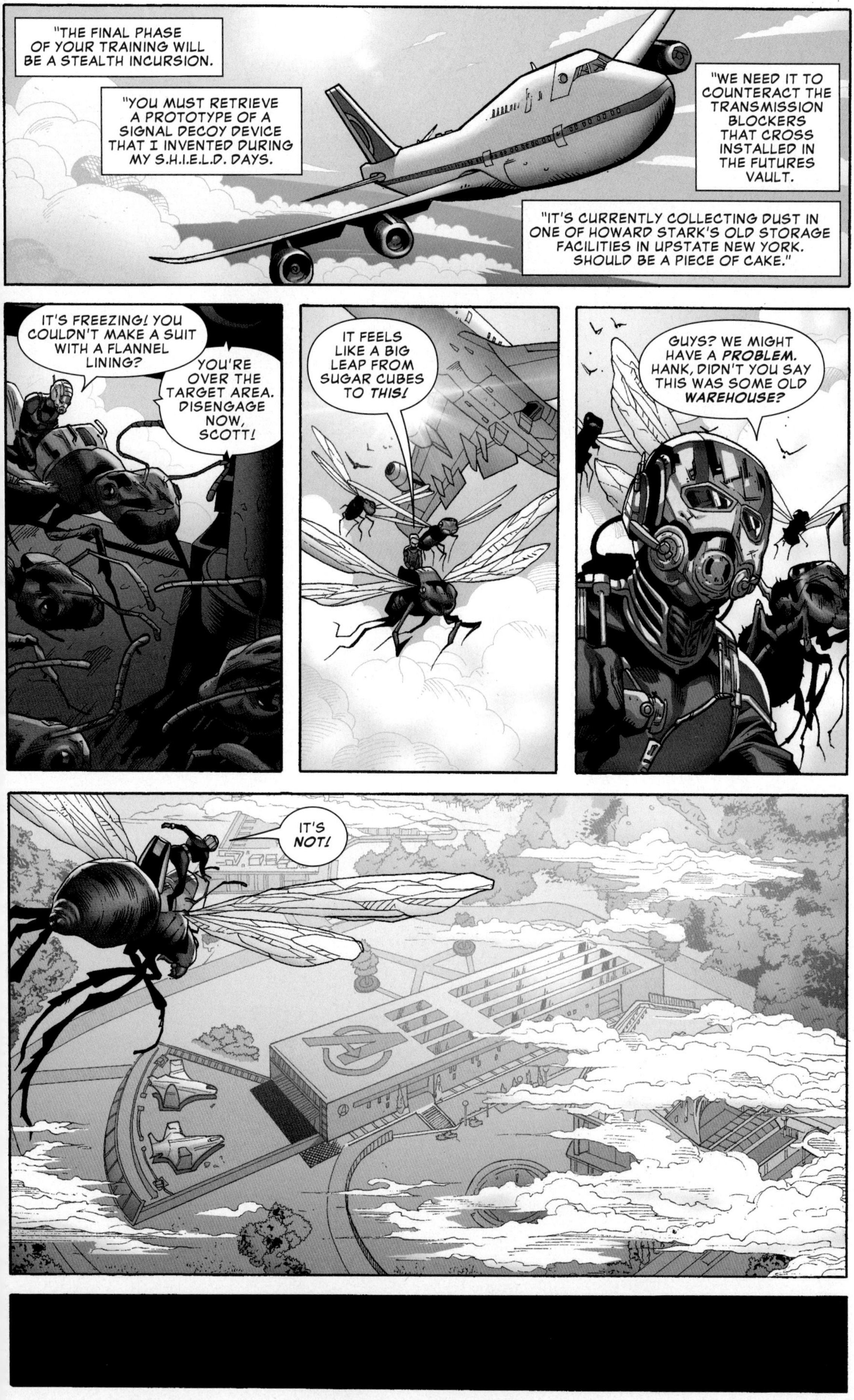
"THE FINAL PHASE OF YOUR TRAINING WILL BE A STEALTH INCURSION.
"YOU MUST RETRIEVE A PROTOTYPE OF A SIGNAL DECOY DEVICE THAT I INVENTED DURING MY S.H.I.E.L.D. DAYS.
"WE NEED IT TO COUNTERACT THE TRANSMISSION BLOCKERS THAT CROSS INSTALLED IN THE FUTURES VAULT.
"IT'S CURRENTLY COLLECTING DUST IN ONE OF HOWARD STARK'S OLD STORAGE FACILITIES IN UPSTATE NEW YORK. SHOULD BE A PIECE OF CAKE."
IT'S FREEZING! YOU COULDN'T MAKE A SUIT WITH A FLANNEL LINING?
YOU'RE OVER THE TARGET AREA. DISENGAGE NOW, SCOTT!
IT FEELS LIKE A BIG LEAP FROM SUGAR CUBES TO THIS!
GUYS? WE MIGHT HAVE A PROBLEM. HANK, DIDN'T YOU SAY THIS WAS SOME OLD WAREHOUSE?
IT'S NOT!

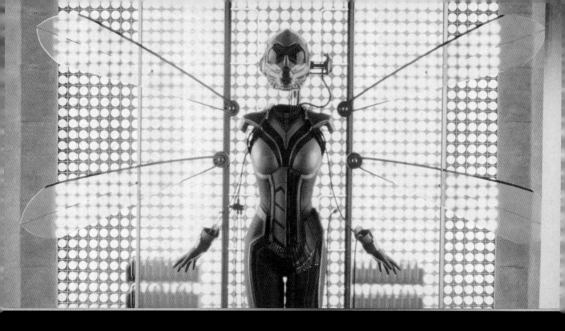

MARVEL'S ANT-MAN AND
THE WASP PRELUDE #2

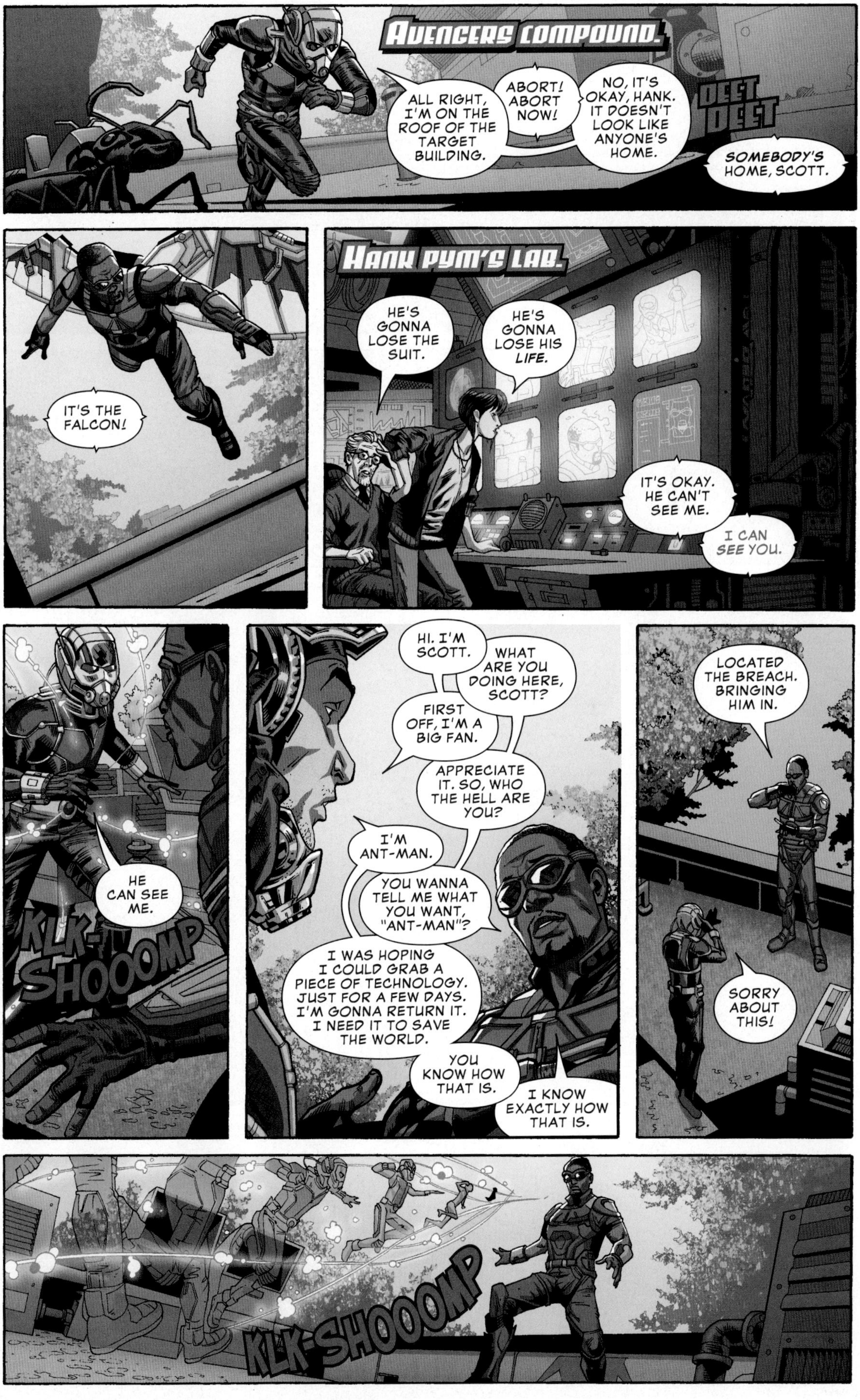
AVENGERS COMPOUND.
ALL RIGHT, I'M ON THE ROOF OF THE TARGET BUILDING.
ABORT! ABORT NOW!
NO, IT'S OKAY, HANK. IT DOESN'T LOOK LIKE ANYONE'S HOME.
DEET DEET
SOMEBODY'S HOME, SCOTT.
IT'S THE FALCON!
HANK PYM'S LAB.
HE'S GONNA LOSE THE SUIT.
HE'S GONNA LOSE HIS LIFE.
IT'S OKAY. HE CAN'T SEE ME.
I CAN SEE YOU.
HE CAN SEE ME.
KLK-SHOOOMP
HI. I'M SCOTT.
WHAT ARE YOU DOING HERE, SCOTT?
FIRST OFF, I'M A BIG FAN.
APPRECIATE IT. SO, WHO THE HELL ARE YOU?
I'M ANT-MAN.
YOU WANNA TELL ME WHAT YOU WANT, "ANT-MAN"?
I WAS HOPING I COULD GRAB A PIECE OF TECHNOLOGY. JUST FOR A FEW DAYS. I'M GONNA RETURN IT. I NEED IT TO SAVE THE WORLD.
YOU KNOW HOW THAT IS.
I KNOW EXACTLY HOW THAT IS.
LOCATED THE BREACH. BRINGING HIM IN.
SORRY ABOUT THIS!
KLK-SHOOOMP

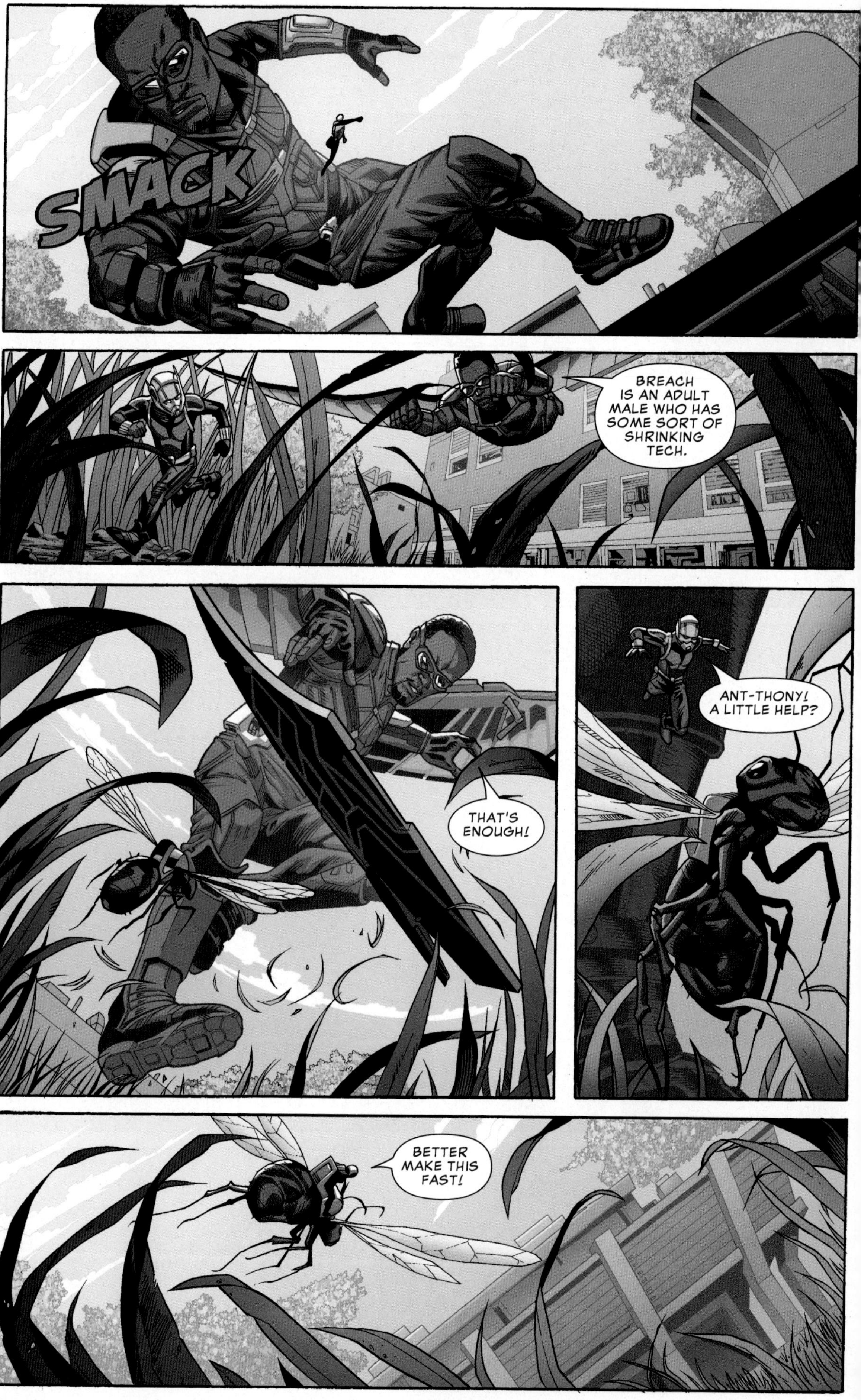
SMACK
BREACH IS AN ADULT MALE WHO HAS SOME SORT OF SHRINKING TECH.
THAT'S ENOUGH!
ANT-THONY! A LITTLE HELP?
BETTER MAKE THIS FAST!

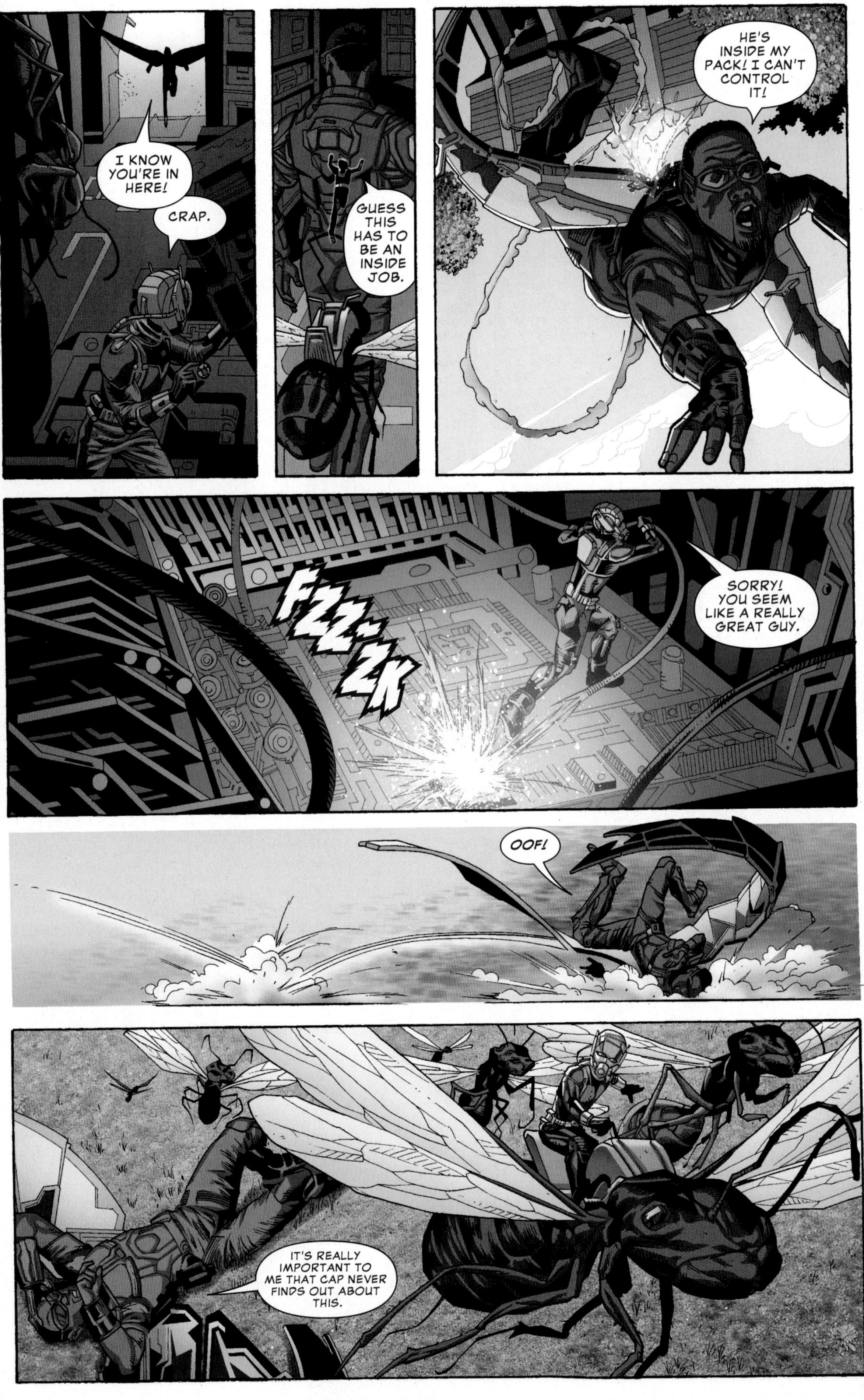
I KNOW YOU'RE IN HERE!
CRAP.
GUESS THIS HAS TO BE AN INSIDE JOB.
HE'S INSIDE MY PACK! I CAN'T CONTROL IT!
FZZ-ZK
SORRY! YOU SEEM LIKE A REALLY GREAT GUY.
OOF!
IT'S REALLY IMPORTANT TO ME THAT CAP NEVER FINDS OUT ABOUT THIS.

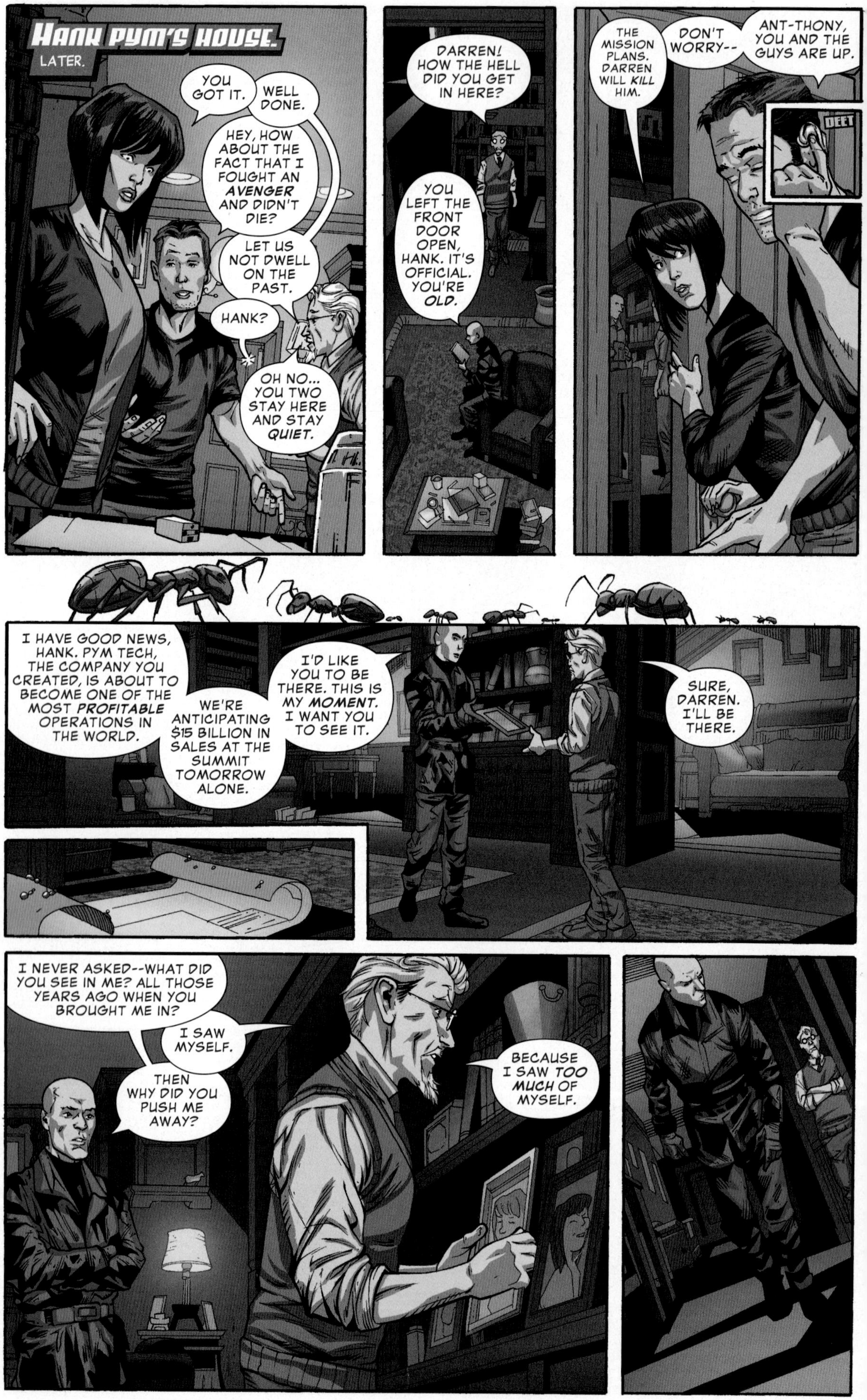
HANK PYM'S HOUSE.
LATER.
YOU GOT IT.
WELL DONE.
HEY, HOW ABOUT THE FACT THAT I FOUGHT AN AVENGER AND DIDN'T DIE?
LET US NOT DWELL ON THE PAST.
HANK?
OH NO... YOU TWO STAY HERE AND STAY QUIET.
DARREN! HOW THE HELL DID YOU GET IN HERE?
YOU LEFT THE FRONT DOOR OPEN, HANK. IT'S OFFICIAL. YOU'RE OLD.
THE MISSION PLANS. DARREN WILL KILL HIM.
DON'T WORRY--
ANT-THONY, YOU AND THE GUYS ARE UP.
DEET
I HAVE GOOD NEWS, HANK. PYM TECH, THE COMPANY YOU CREATED, IS ABOUT TO BECOME ONE OF THE MOST PROFITABLE OPERATIONS IN THE WORLD.
WE'RE ANTICIPATING $15 BILLION IN SALES AT THE SUMMIT TOMORROW ALONE.
I'D LIKE YOU TO BE THERE. THIS IS MY MOMENT. I WANT YOU TO SEE IT.
SURE, DARREN. I'LL BE THERE.
I NEVER ASKED--WHAT DID YOU SEE IN ME? ALL THOSE YEARS AGO WHEN YOU BROUGHT ME IN?
I SAW MYSELF.
THEN WHY DID YOU PUSH ME AWAY?
BECAUSE I SAW TOO MUCH OF MYSELF.

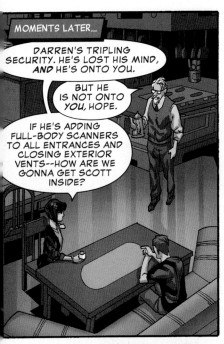

DARREN'S TRIPLING SECURITY. HE'S LOST HIS MIND, *AND* HE'S ONTO YOU.

BUT HE IS NOT ONTO YOU, HOPE.

IF HE'S ADDING FULL-BODY SCANNERS TO ALL ENTRANCES AND CLOSING EXTERIOR VENTS--HOW ARE WE GONNA GET SCOTT INSIDE?

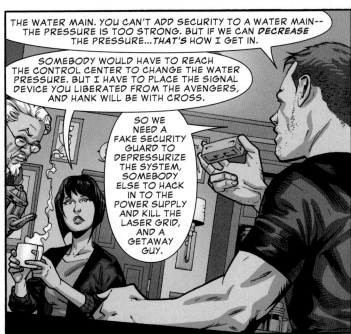

THE WATER MAIN. YOU CAN'T ADD SECURITY TO A WATER MAIN-- THE PRESSURE IS TOO STRONG. BUT IF WE CAN *DECREASE* THE PRESSURE...*THAT'S* HOW I GET IN.

SOMEBODY WOULD HAVE TO REACH THE CONTROL CENTER TO CHANGE THE WATER PRESSURE. BUT I HAVE TO PLACE THE SIGNAL DEVICE YOU LIBERATED FROM THE AVENGERS, AND HANK WILL BE WITH CROSS.

SO WE NEED A FAKE SECURITY GUARD TO DEPRESSURIZE THE SYSTEM, SOMEBODY ELSE TO HACK IN TO THE POWER SUPPLY AND KILL THE LASER GRID, AND A GETAWAY GUY.

NO, NO, NO. NOT THOSE THREE *WOMBATS.* NO WAY.

LATER.

IT'S NOT TOO OFTEN THAT YOU ROB A PLACE AND THEN GET WELCOMED BACK.

BECAUSE WE *JUST* ROBBED YOU.

ALL RIGHT, JUST SO WE'RE CLEAR, EVERYONE HERE KNOWS THEIR ROLE, RIGHT?

DAVE-- WHEELS ON THE GROUND.

KURT-- EYES IN THE SKY.

LUIS--

OH, MAN, YOU KNOW IT. YOU KNOW WHAT? I GET TO WEAR A UNIFORM. THAT'S WHAT'S UP.

LUIS.

I'M SORRY. I'M GOOD. I'M JUST EXCITED. PLUS, YOUR GIRLFRIEND'S REALLY HOT. THAT MAKES ME NERVOUS, TOO.

OH, MY LORD.

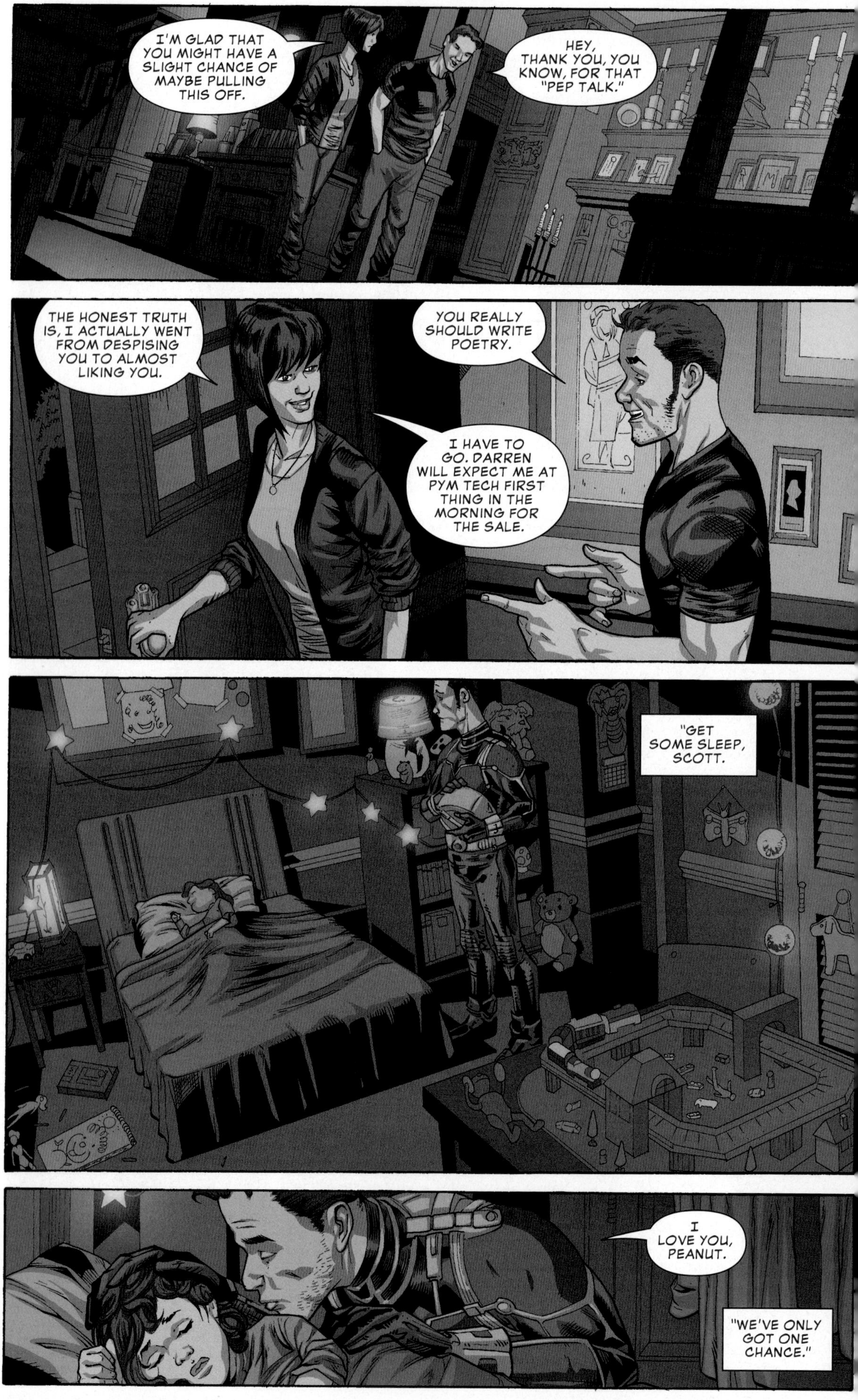
I'M GLAD THAT YOU MIGHT HAVE A SLIGHT CHANCE OF MAYBE PULLING THIS OFF.
HEY, THANK YOU, YOU KNOW, FOR THAT "PEP TALK."
THE HONEST TRUTH IS, I ACTUALLY WENT FROM DESPISING YOU TO ALMOST LIKING YOU.
YOU REALLY SHOULD WRITE POETRY.
I HAVE TO GO. DARREN WILL EXPECT ME AT PYM TECH FIRST THING IN THE MORNING FOR THE SALE.
"GET SOME SLEEP, SCOTT.
I LOVE YOU, PEANUT.
"WE'VE ONLY GOT ONE CHANCE."

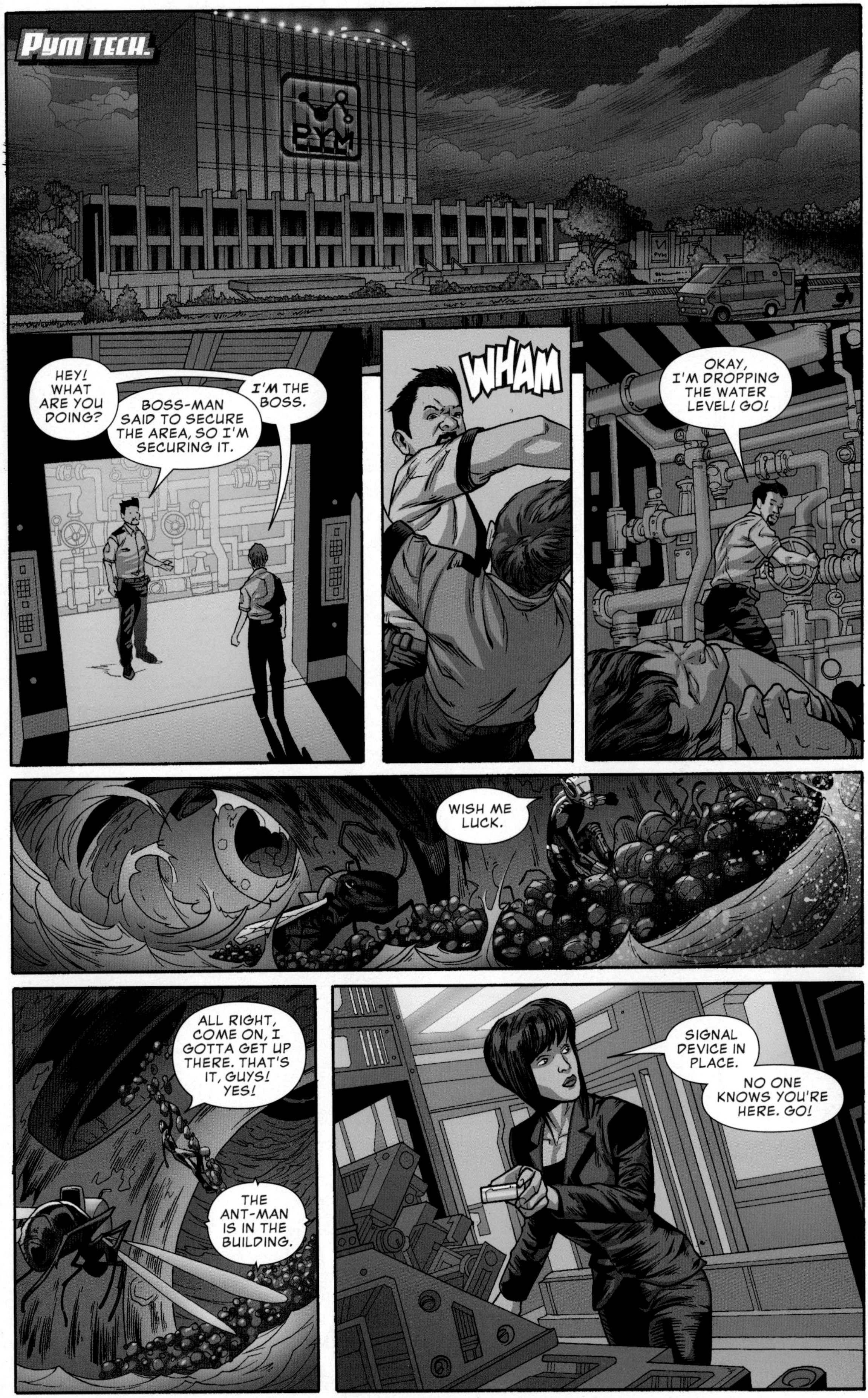
PYM TECH.
PYM
HEY! WHAT ARE YOU DOING?
BOSS-MAN SAID TO SECURE THE AREA, SO I'M SECURING IT.
I'M THE BOSS.
WHAM
OKAY, I'M DROPPING THE WATER LEVEL! GO!
WISH ME LUCK.
ALL RIGHT, COME ON, I GOTTA GET UP THERE. THAT'S IT, GUYS! YES!
THE ANT-MAN IS IN THE BUILDING.
SIGNAL DEVICE IN PLACE.
NO ONE KNOWS YOU'RE HERE. GO!

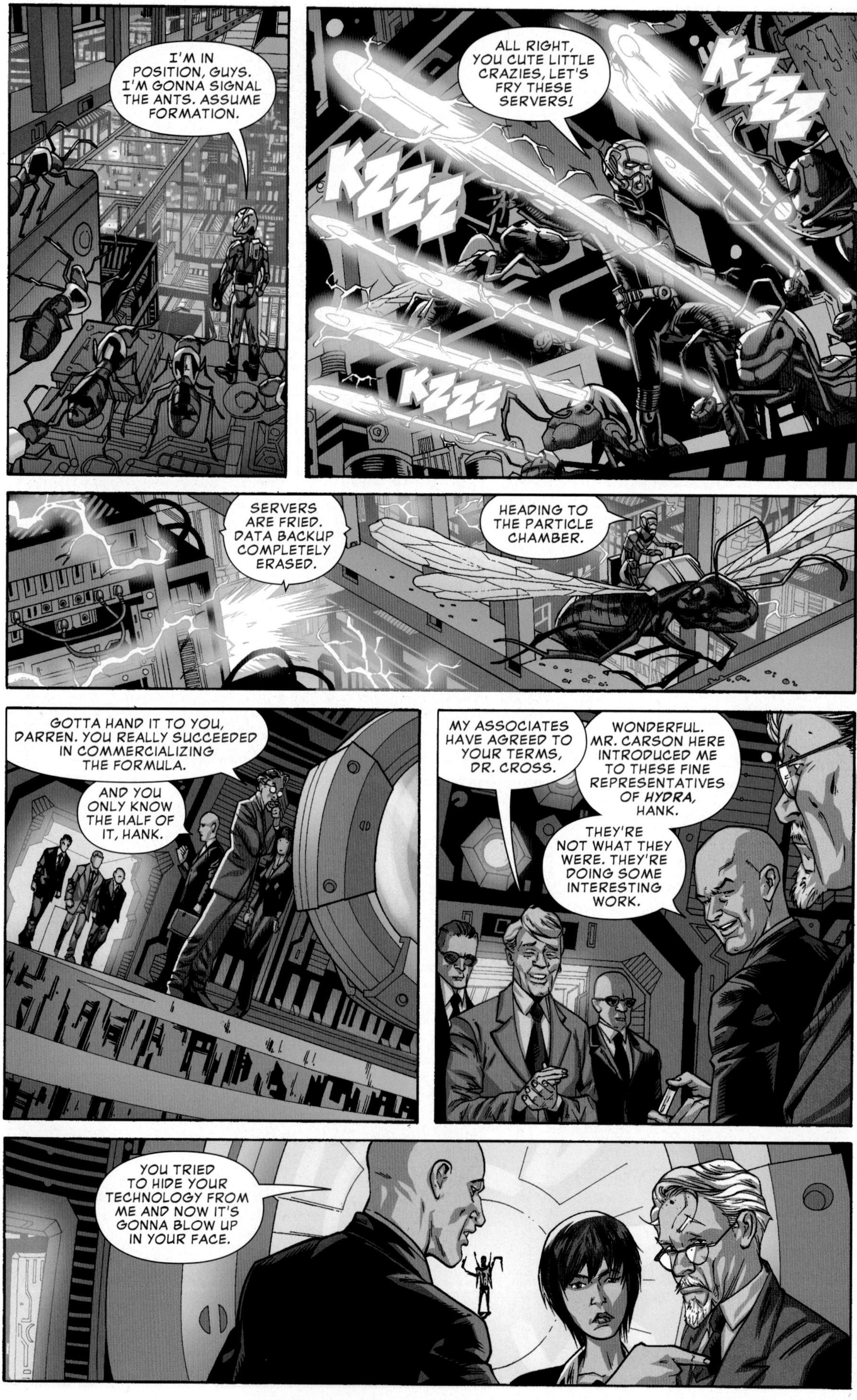

I'M IN POSITION, GUYS. I'M GONNA SIGNAL THE ANTS. ASSUME FORMATION.
ALL RIGHT, YOU CUTE LITTLE CRAZIES, LET'S FRY THESE SERVERS!
KZZZ
KZZZ
KZZZ
SERVERS ARE FRIED. DATA BACKUP COMPLETELY ERASED.
HEADING TO THE PARTICLE CHAMBER.
GOTTA HAND IT TO YOU, DARREN. YOU REALLY SUCCEEDED IN COMMERCIALIZING THE FORMULA.
AND YOU ONLY KNOW THE HALF OF IT, HANK.
MY ASSOCIATES HAVE AGREED TO YOUR TERMS, DR. CROSS.
WONDERFUL. MR. CARSON HERE INTRODUCED ME TO THESE FINE REPRESENTATIVES OF *HYDRA,* HANK.
THEY'RE NOT WHAT THEY WERE. THEY'RE DOING SOME INTERESTING WORK.
YOU TRIED TO HIDE YOUR TECHNOLOGY FROM ME AND NOW IT'S GONNA BLOW UP IN YOUR FACE.

ALL RIGHT, GUYS. I'M HERE. I'M SETTING THE CHARGES FOR 15 MINUTES TO BLOW THIS PLACE.

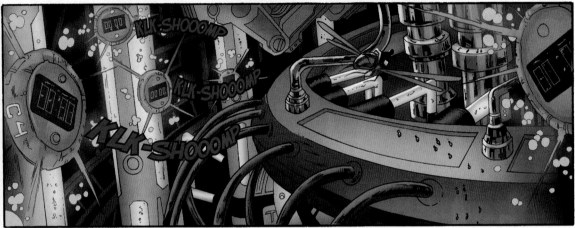

KLK-SHOOOMP

KLK-SHOOOMP

KLK-SHOOOMP

GUYS? HOW WE LOOKING ON THAT LASER GRID?

GO NOW!

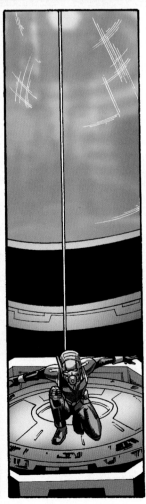

K-SHZZ

WHAT? WHERE'S THE YELLOW-JACKET SUIT?

AND WHY ARE THOSE LASERS BACK ON?

HEY, LITTLE GUY.

SCOTT LANG. A MARTYR WHO TOOK ON THE SYSTEM AND PAID THE PRICE, LOSING HIS FAMILY IN THE PROCESS.

HE ESCAPES HIS JAIL CELL WITHOUT LEAVING ANY CLUE AS TO HOW AND NOW HE BRINGS ME THE ANT-MAN SUIT--THE ONLY THING THAT CAN RIVAL MY CREATION.

DARREN, DON'T DO THIS. IF YOU SELL TO THESE MEN IT'S GONNA BE CHAOS.

I ALREADY HAVE.

AND FOR *TWICE THE PRICE*, THANKS TO YOU. IT'S NOT EASY TO SUCCESSFULLY INFILTRATE AN AVENGERS FACILITY.

THANKFULLY, WORD TRAVELS FAST. I'LL SELL THEM THE YELLOWJACKET, BUT I'M KEEPING THE PARTICLE TO MYSELF. IF THEY WANT THE *FUEL*, THEY'LL HAVE TO COME TO ME.

YOU CAN STOP THIS, DARREN. IT'S NOT TOO LATE.

IT'S BEEN TOO LATE FOR A LONG TIME NOW.

OOF!

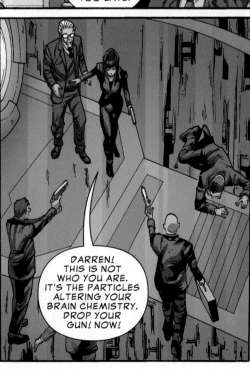

DARREN! THIS IS NOT WHO YOU ARE. IT'S THE PARTICLES ALTERING YOUR BRAIN CHEMISTRY. DROP YOUR GUN! NOW!

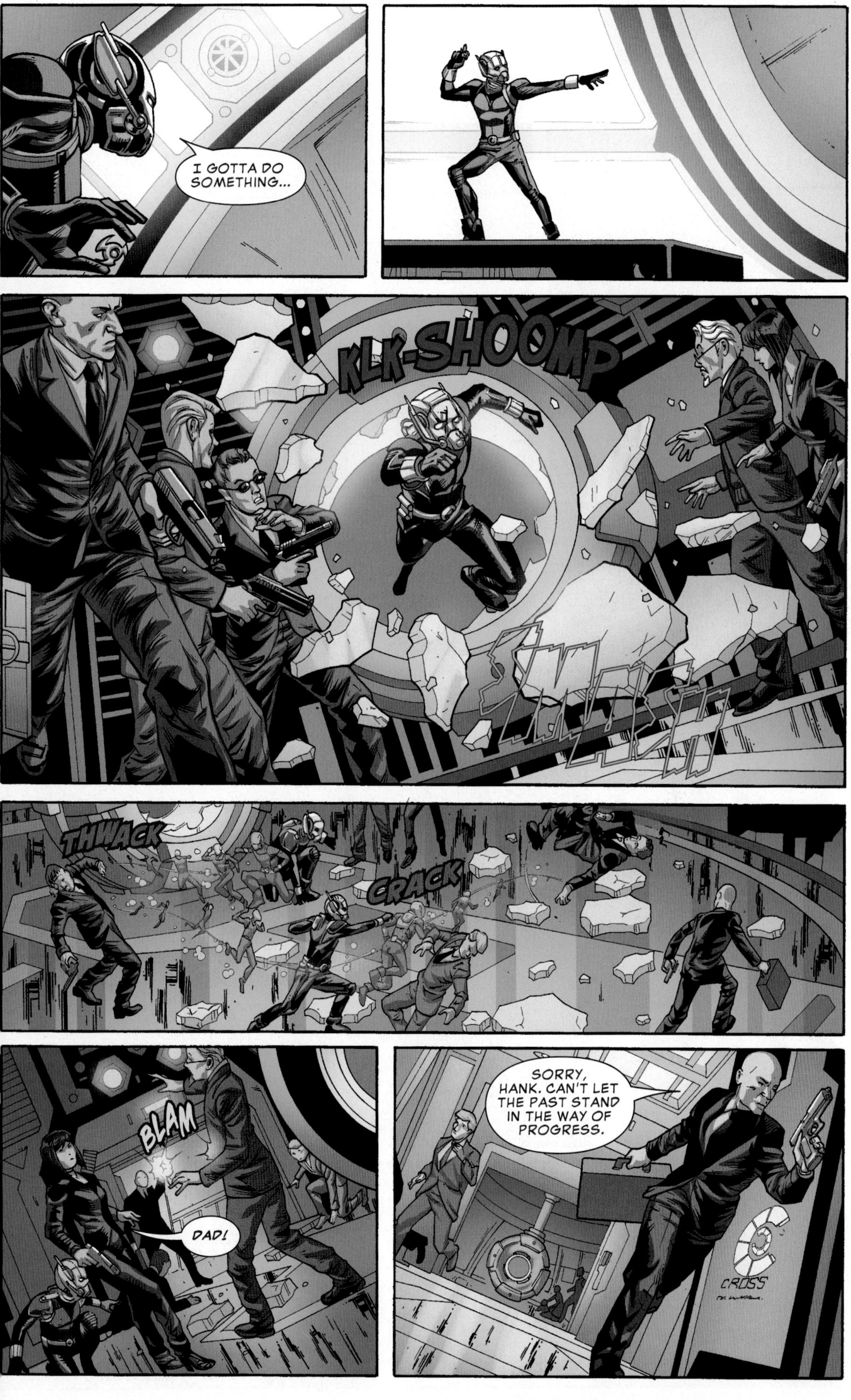
I GOTTA DO SOMETHING...
KLK-SHOOMP
SMASH
THWACK
CRACK
BLAM
DAD!
SORRY, HANK. CAN'T LET THE PAST STAND IN THE WAY OF PROGRESS.
CROSS

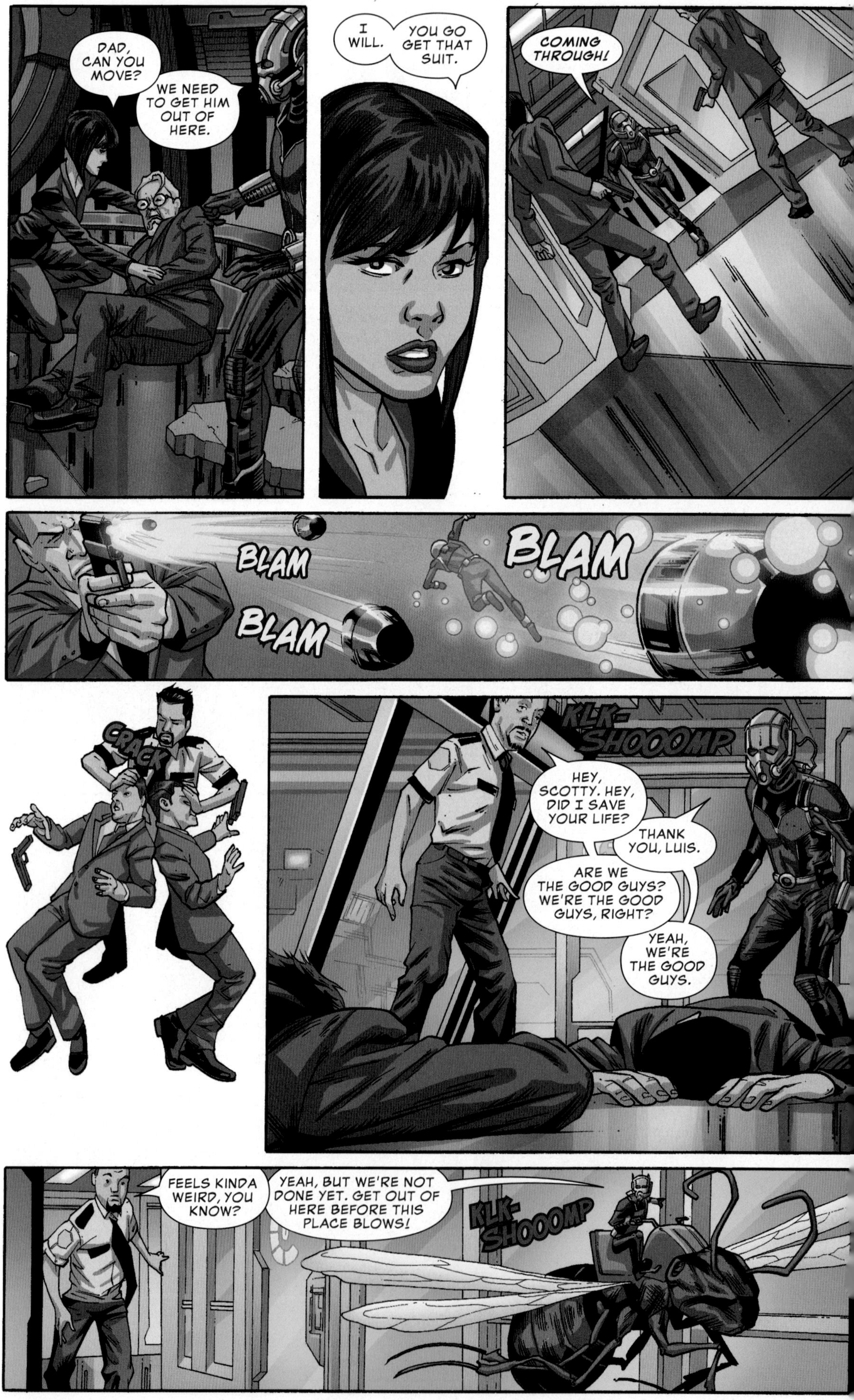
DAD, CAN YOU MOVE?
WE NEED TO GET HIM OUT OF HERE.
I WILL.
YOU GO GET THAT SUIT.
COMING THROUGH!
BLAM
BLAM
BLAM
CRACK
KLK-SHOOOMP
HEY, SCOTTY. HEY, DID I SAVE YOUR LIFE?
THANK YOU, LUIS.
ARE WE THE GOOD GUYS? WE'RE THE GOOD GUYS, RIGHT?
YEAH, WE'RE THE GOOD GUYS.
FEELS KINDA WEIRD, YOU KNOW?
YEAH, BUT WE'RE NOT DONE YET. GET OUT OF HERE BEFORE THIS PLACE BLOWS!
KLK-SHOOOMP

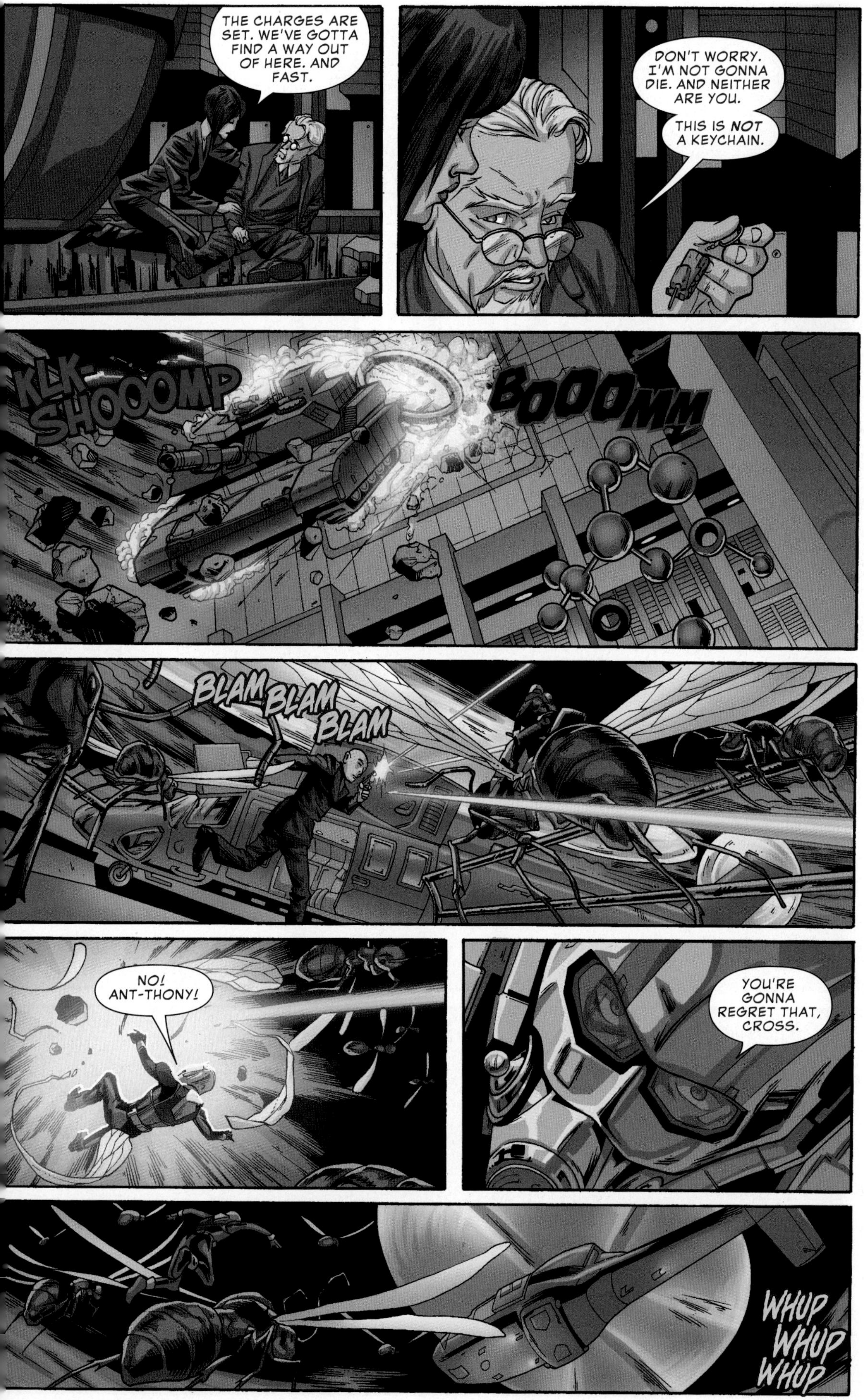
THE CHARGES ARE SET. WE'VE GOTTA FIND A WAY OUT OF HERE. AND FAST.
DON'T WORRY. I'M NOT GONNA DIE. AND NEITHER ARE YOU.
THIS IS NOT A KEYCHAIN.
KLK-SHOOOMP
BOOOMM
BLAM BLAM BLAM
NO! ANT-THONY!
YOU'RE GONNA REGRET THAT, CROSS.
WHUP WHUP WHUP

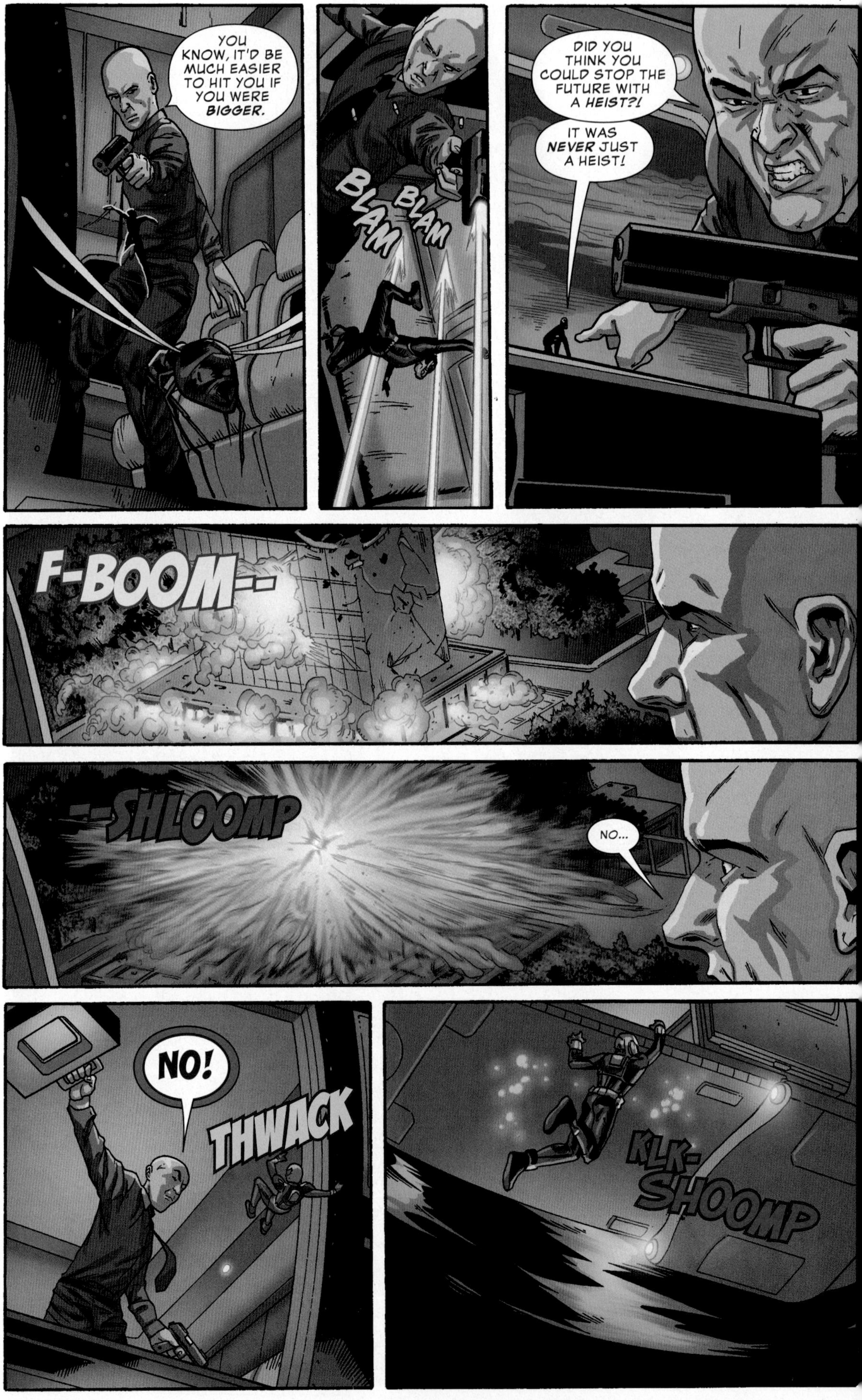
YOU KNOW, IT'D BE MUCH EASIER TO HIT YOU IF YOU WERE BIGGER.
BLAM BLAM
BLAM
DID YOU THINK YOU COULD STOP THE FUTURE WITH A HEIST?!
IT WAS NEVER JUST A HEIST!
F-BOOM--
--SHLOOMP
NO...
NO!
THWACK
KLK-SHOOMP

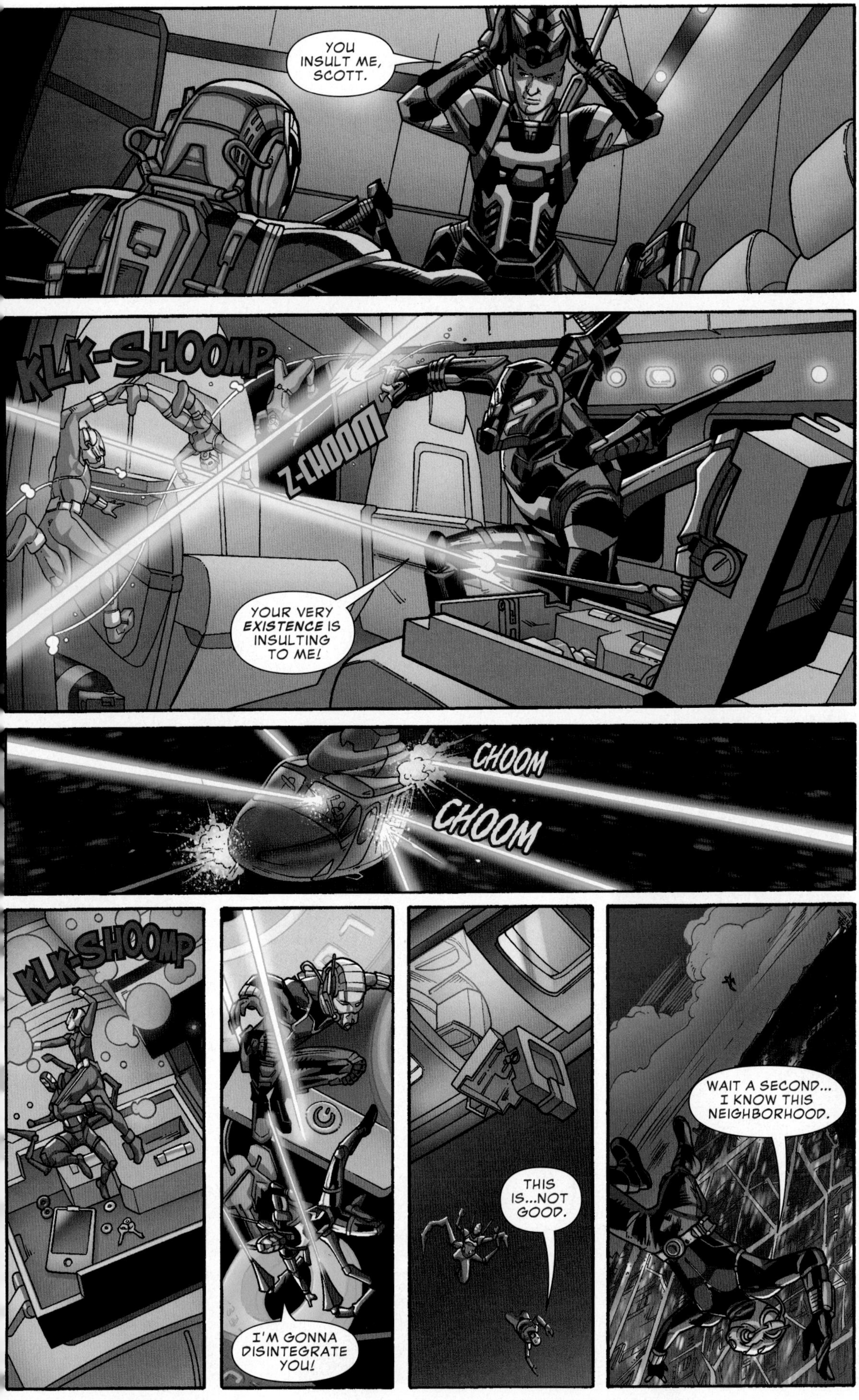
YOU INSULT ME, SCOTT.
KLK-SHOOMP
Z-CHOOM
YOUR VERY EXISTENCE IS INSULTING TO ME!
CHOOM
CHOOM
KLK-SHOOMP
I'M GONNA DISINTEGRATE YOU!
THIS IS...NOT GOOD.
WAIT A SECOND... I KNOW THIS NEIGHBORHOOD.

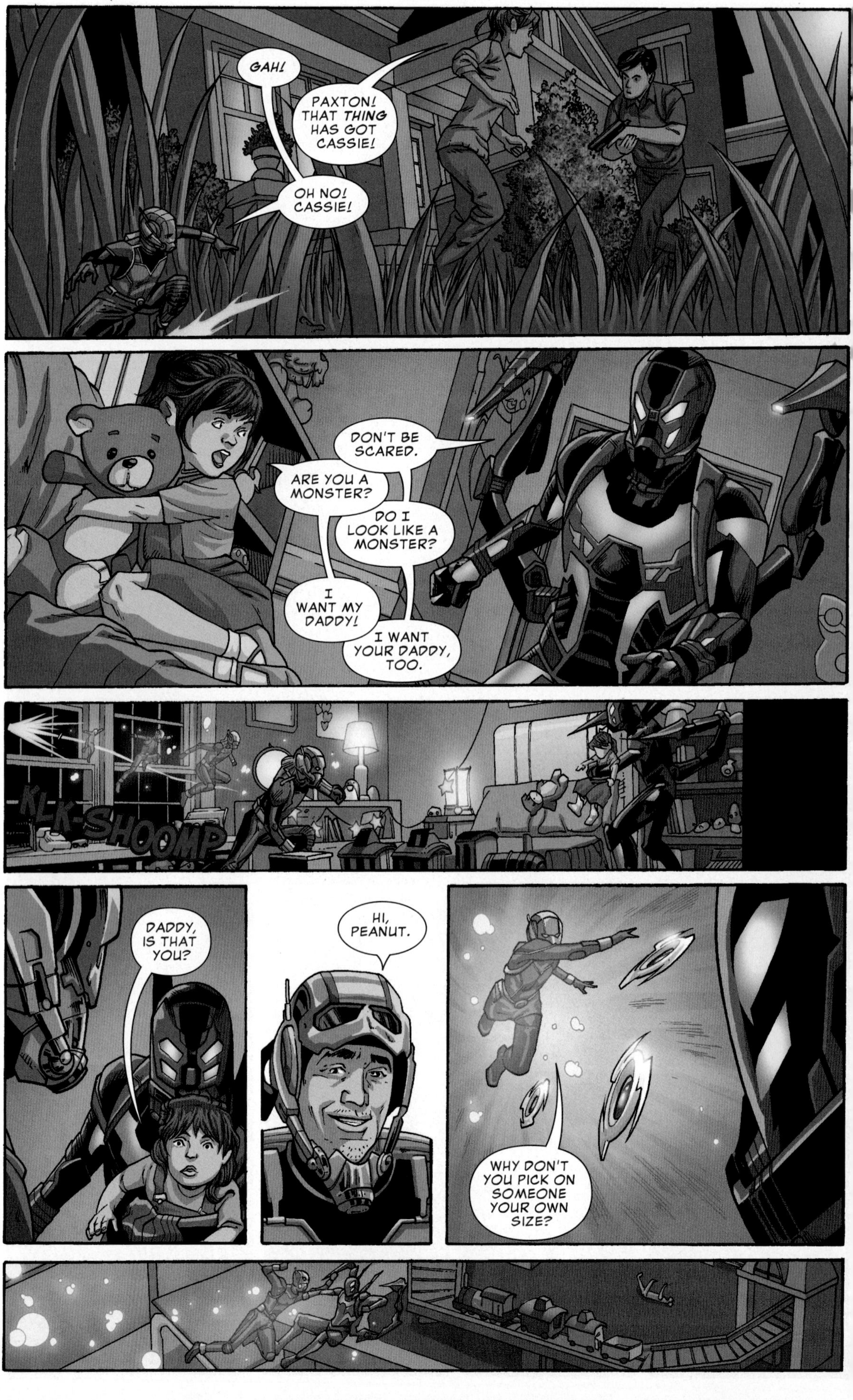
GAH!
PAXTON! THAT THING HAS GOT CASSIE!
OH NO! CASSIE!
DON'T BE SCARED.
ARE YOU A MONSTER?
DO I LOOK LIKE A MONSTER?
I WANT MY DADDY!
I WANT YOUR DADDY, TOO.
KLK-SHOOMP
DADDY, IS THAT YOU?
HI, PEANUT.
WHY DON'T YOU PICK ON SOMEONE YOUR OWN SIZE?

I'M GONNA SHOW YOU JUST HOW INSIGNIFICANT YOU ARE. I'M GONNA DESTROY EVERYTHING YOU LOVE.

CASSIE! GET BEHIND ME, SWEETHEART!

KLK-SHOOMP

SORRY, SWEETHEART. YOU HAVE TO HELP DADDY PAY FOR HIS MISTAKES.

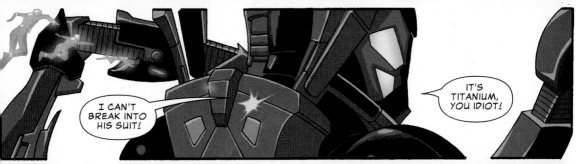

I CAN'T BREAK INTO HIS SUIT!

IT'S TITANIUM, YOU IDIOT!

KRNCH-

I'M GONNA HAVE TO TURN OFF THE REGULATOR AND SHRINK BETWEEN THE MOLECULES TO GET IN THERE.

SHOOOOMP

I LOVE YOU, CASSIE.

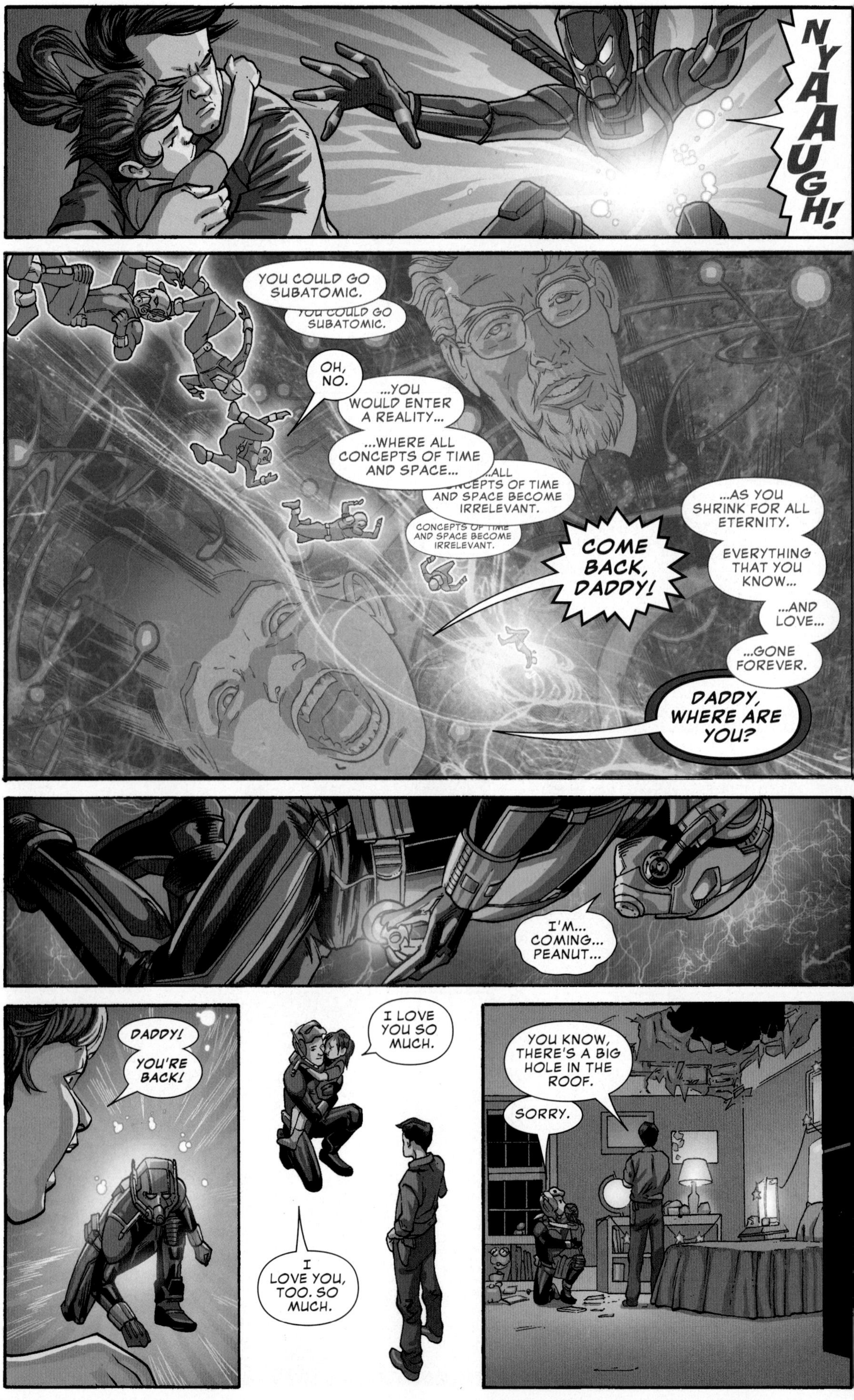
NYAAAUGH!
YOU COULD GO SUBATOMIC.
YOU COULD GO SUBATOMIC.
OH, NO.
...YOU WOULD ENTER A REALITY...
...WHERE ALL CONCEPTS OF TIME AND SPACE...
...ALL CONCEPTS OF TIME AND SPACE BECOME IRRELEVANT.
CONCEPTS OF TIME AND SPACE BECOME IRRELEVANT.
COME BACK, DADDY!
...AS YOU SHRINK FOR ALL ETERNITY.
EVERYTHING THAT YOU KNOW...
...AND LOVE...
...GONE FOREVER.
DADDY, WHERE ARE YOU?
I'M... COMING... PEANUT...
DADDY!
YOU'RE BACK!
I LOVE YOU SO MUCH.
I LOVE YOU, TOO. SO MUCH.
YOU KNOW, THERE'S A BIG HOLE IN THE ROOF.
SORRY.

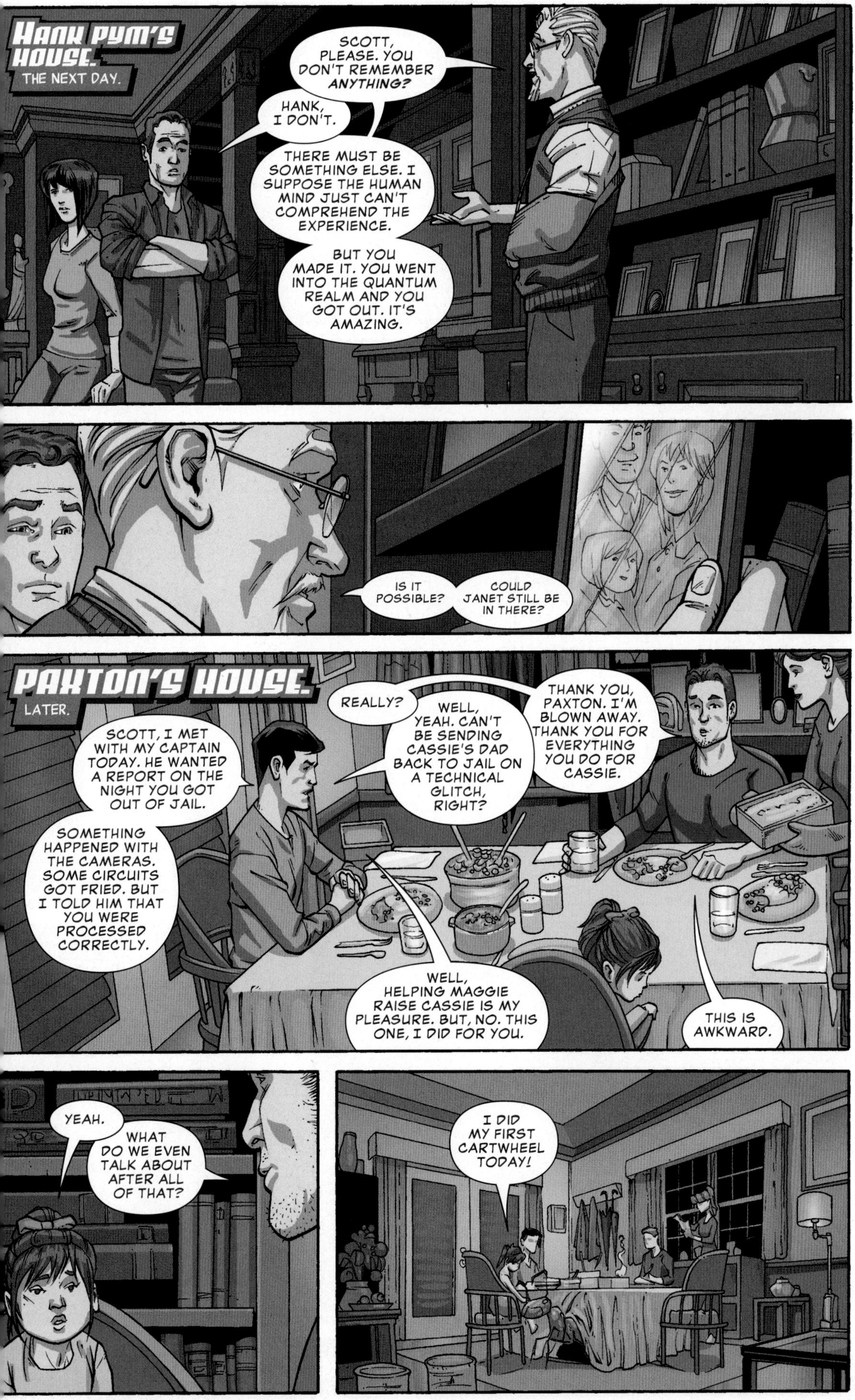
HANK PYM'S HOUSE.
THE NEXT DAY.
SCOTT, PLEASE. YOU DON'T REMEMBER *ANYTHING?*
HANK, I DON'T.
THERE MUST BE SOMETHING ELSE. I SUPPOSE THE HUMAN MIND JUST CAN'T COMPREHEND THE EXPERIENCE.
BUT YOU MADE IT. YOU WENT INTO THE QUANTUM REALM AND YOU GOT OUT. IT'S AMAZING.
IS IT POSSIBLE?
COULD JANET STILL BE IN THERE?
PAXTON'S HOUSE.
LATER.
SCOTT, I MET WITH MY CAPTAIN TODAY. HE WANTED A REPORT ON THE NIGHT YOU GOT OUT OF JAIL.
SOMETHING HAPPENED WITH THE CAMERAS. SOME CIRCUITS GOT FRIED. BUT I TOLD HIM THAT YOU WERE PROCESSED CORRECTLY.
REALLY?
WELL, YEAH. CAN'T BE SENDING CASSIE'S DAD BACK TO JAIL ON A TECHNICAL GLITCH, RIGHT?
THANK YOU, PAXTON. I'M BLOWN AWAY. THANK YOU FOR EVERYTHING YOU DO FOR CASSIE.
WELL, HELPING MAGGIE RAISE CASSIE IS MY PLEASURE. BUT, NO. THIS ONE, I DID FOR YOU.
THIS IS AWKWARD.
YEAH.
WHAT DO WE EVEN TALK ABOUT AFTER ALL OF THAT?
I DID MY FIRST CARTWHEEL TODAY!

THERE'S SOMETHING I WANT TO SHOW YOU, HOPE.

I REALIZED YOU CAN'T *DESTROY* POWER. ALL YOU CAN DO IS MAKE SURE THAT IT'S IN THE RIGHT HANDS.

DEET DEET DEET

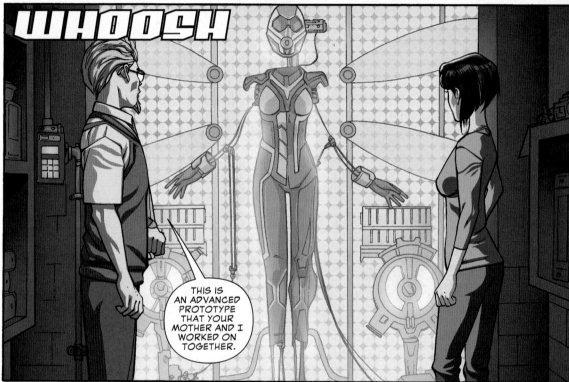

WHOOSH

THIS IS AN ADVANCED PROTOTYPE THAT YOUR MOTHER AND I WORKED ON TOGETHER.

BUT NOW I REALIZE THAT WE WERE WORKING ON IT FOR *YOU*.

MAYBE IT'S TIME WE FINISHED IT.

IT'S ABOUT DAMN TIME.

TO BE CONTINUED IN ANT-MAN AND THE WASP--*ONLY IN THEATERS!*

SCOTT LANG JOINS FORCES WITH THE ORIGINAL ANT-MAN AND THE WASP, HANK PYM AND JANET VAN DYNE, TO FIGHT THE TREACHEROUS TASKMASTER!

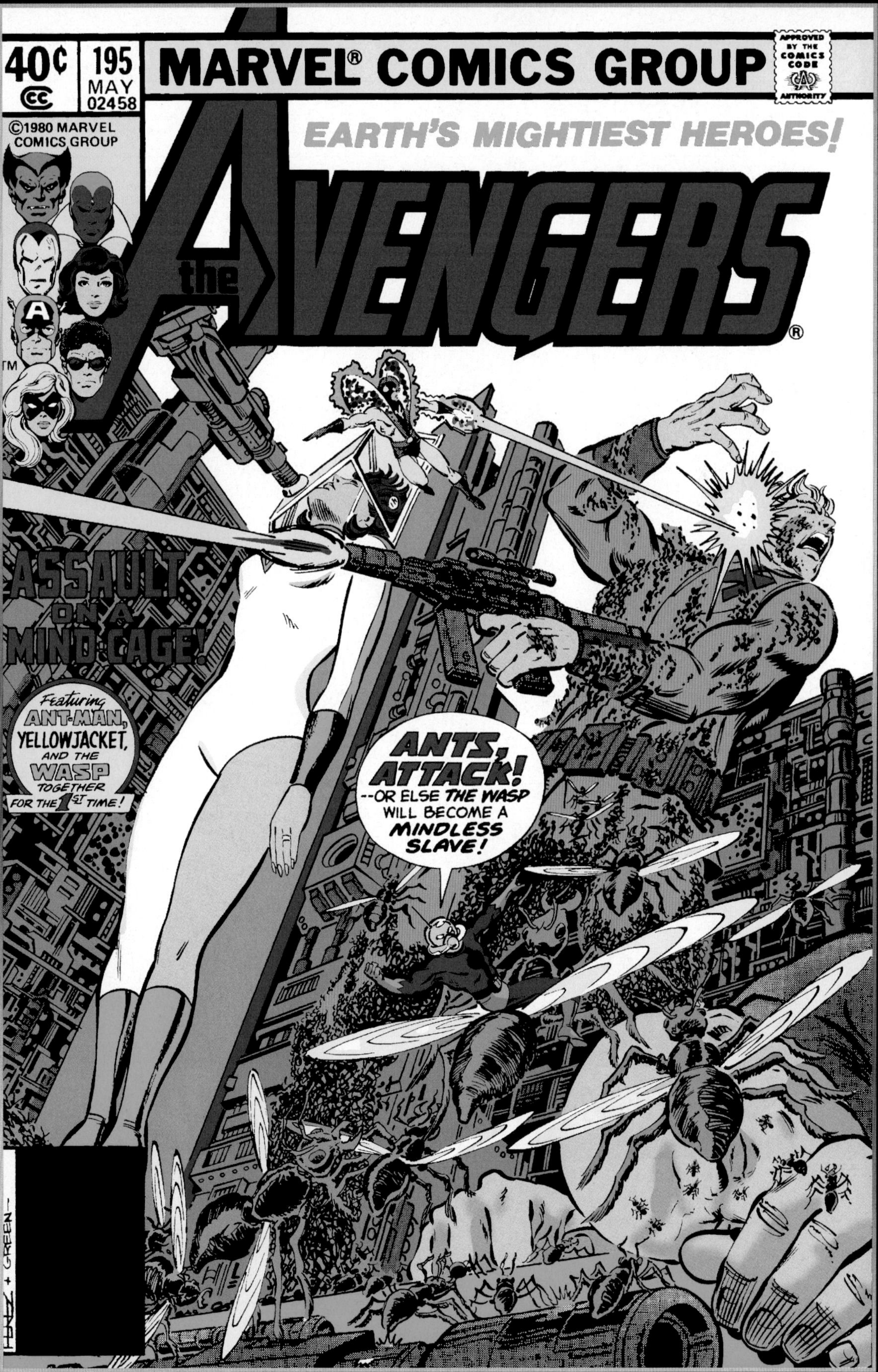

40¢
CC
195
MAY
02458
MARVEL® COMICS GROUP
APPROVED BY THE COMICS CODE AUTHORITY
©1980 MARVEL COMICS GROUP
TM
EARTH'S MIGHTIEST HEROES!
the AVENGERS®
ASSAULT ON A MIND CAGE!
Featuring ANT-MAN, YELLOWJACKET, AND THE WASP TOGETHER FOR THE 1ST TIME!
ANTS, ATTACK! --OR ELSE THE WASP WILL BECOME A MINDLESS SLAVE!

And there came a day when *Earth's mightiest heroes* found themselves *united* against a common threat. On that day, the *Avengers* were born—to fight the foes no *single* super-hero could withstand...

Stan Lee PRESENTS: THE MIGHTY AVENGERS!

DAVID MICHELINIE *Writer*	GEORGE PEREZ *Pencils*	ABEL & GREEN *Inks*	JOHN COSTANZA *Letters*	BEN SEAN *Colors*	JIM SALICRUP *Editor*	JIM SHOOTER *Editor-in-chief*

SOUTHAMPTON, LONG ISLAND, WHERE THE SOLOMON INSTITUTE FOR THE CRIMINALLY INSANE SQUATS ON THE FROZEN GROUND LIKE A SPRAWLING, GOTHIC TOAD.

AND WATCHING THAT STRUCTURE: THE VALIANT SUPER HERO TEAM CALLED THE AVENGERS, WHOSE OCCASIONAL SHUDDERS SPRING FROM A SOURCE FAR MORE SUBTLE THAN THE LATE WINTER COLD...

ARE YOU SURE THE WASP IS IN THERE, CAPTAIN AMERICA?

NOT COMPLETELY, YELLOWJACKET, BUT EVIDENCE DOES SEEM TO POINT THAT WAY.

THOUGH FOR THE WASP'S SAKE, I HOPE TO BLAZES THE EVIDENCE IS *WRONG!*

ASSAULT on a MIND CAGE!

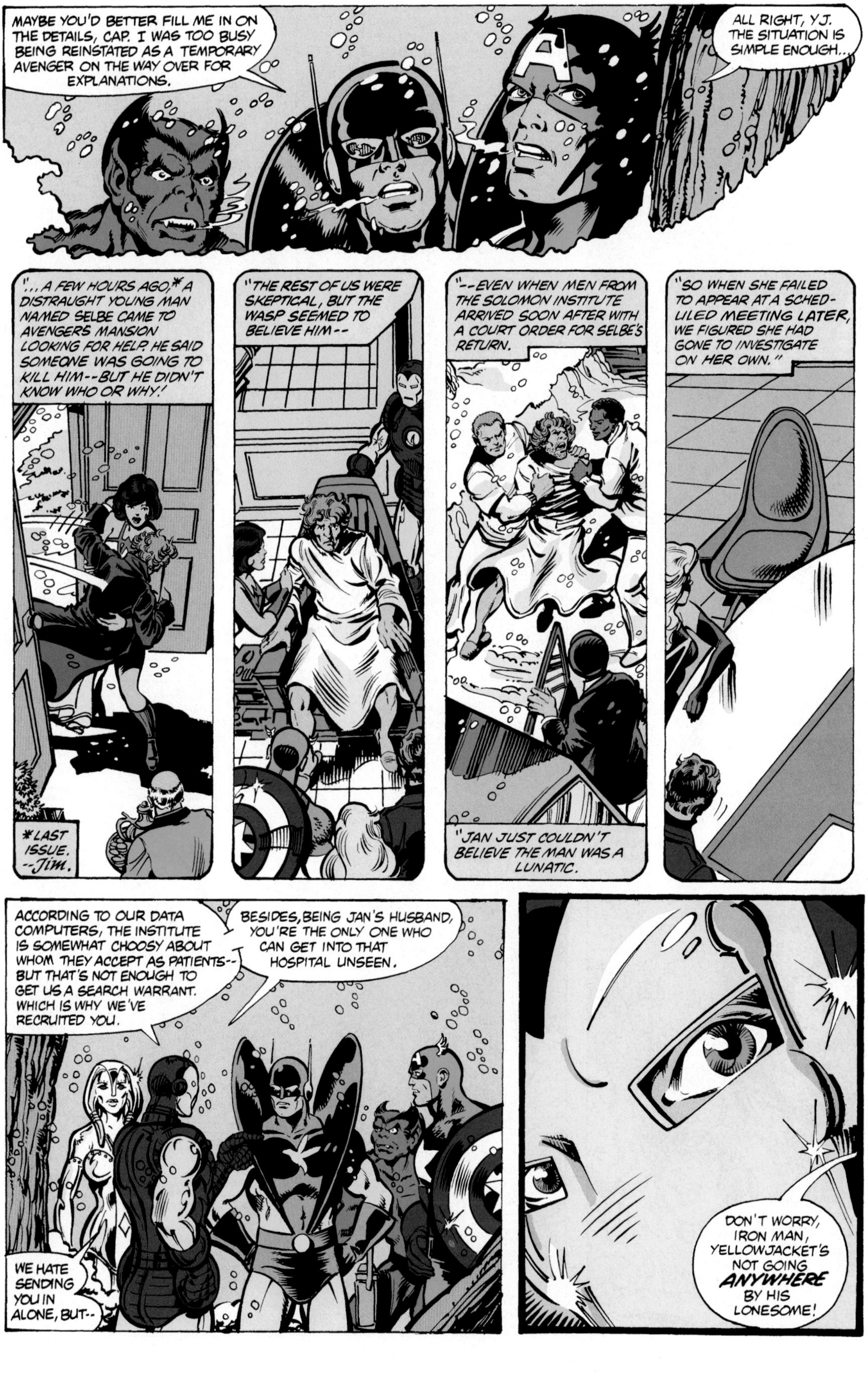
MAYBE YOU'D BETTER FILL ME IN ON THE DETAILS, CAP. I WAS TOO BUSY BEING REINSTATED AS A TEMPORARY AVENGER ON THE WAY OVER FOR EXPLANATIONS.
ALL RIGHT, YJ. THE SITUATION IS SIMPLE ENOUGH...
"...A FEW HOURS AGO,* A DISTRAUGHT YOUNG MAN NAMED SELBE CAME TO AVENGERS MANSION LOOKING FOR HELP. HE SAID SOMEONE WAS GOING TO KILL HIM--BUT HE DIDN'T KNOW WHO OR WHY!
*LAST ISSUE. --Jim.
"THE REST OF US WERE SKEPTICAL, BUT THE WASP SEEMED TO BELIEVE HIM--
"--EVEN WHEN MEN FROM THE SOLOMON INSTITUTE ARRIVED SOON AFTER WITH A COURT ORDER FOR SELBE'S RETURN.
"JAN JUST COULDN'T BELIEVE THE MAN WAS A LUNATIC.
"SO WHEN SHE FAILED TO APPEAR AT A SCHED-ULED MEETING LATER, WE FIGURED SHE HAD GONE TO INVESTIGATE ON HER OWN."
ACCORDING TO OUR DATA COMPUTERS, THE INSTITUTE IS SOMEWHAT CHOOSY ABOUT WHOM THEY ACCEPT AS PATIENTS--BUT THAT'S NOT ENOUGH TO GET US A SEARCH WARRANT. WHICH IS WHY WE'VE RECRUITED YOU.
BESIDES, BEING JAN'S HUSBAND, YOU'RE THE ONLY ONE WHO CAN GET INTO THAT HOSPITAL UNSEEN.
WE HATE SENDING YOU IN ALONE, BUT--
DON'T WORRY, IRON MAN, YELLOWJACKET'S NOT GOING ANYWHERE BY HIS LONESOME!

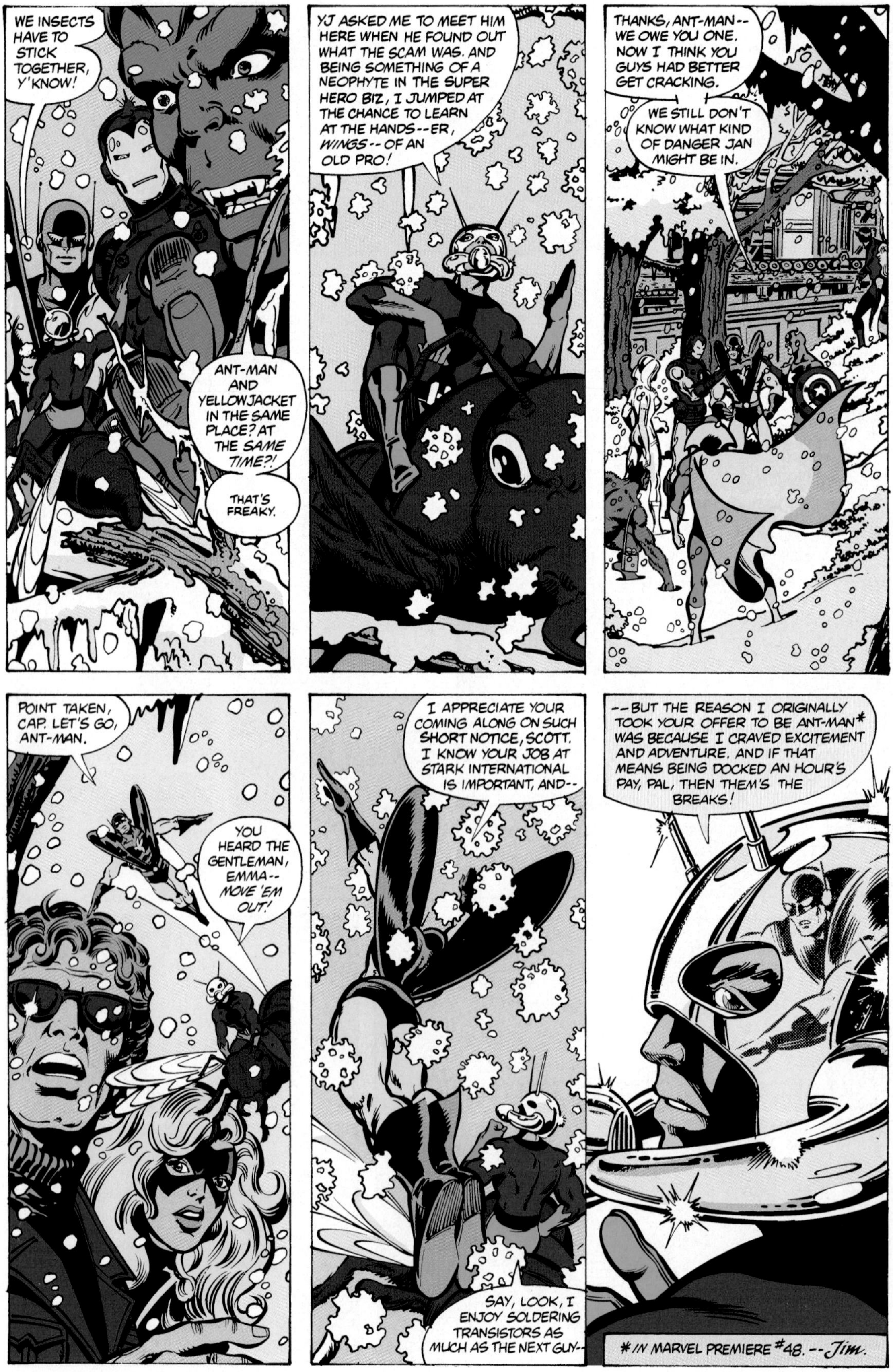
WE INSECTS HAVE TO STICK TOGETHER, Y'KNOW!
ANT-MAN AND YELLOWJACKET IN THE SAME PLACE? AT THE SAME TIME?!
THAT'S FREAKY.
YJ ASKED ME TO MEET HIM HERE WHEN HE FOUND OUT WHAT THE SCAM WAS. AND BEING SOMETHING OF A NEOPHYTE IN THE SUPER HERO BIZ, I JUMPED AT THE CHANCE TO LEARN AT THE HANDS--ER, WINGS--OF AN OLD PRO!
THANKS, ANT-MAN--WE OWE YOU ONE. NOW I THINK YOU GUYS HAD BETTER GET CRACKING.
WE STILL DON'T KNOW WHAT KIND OF DANGER JAN MIGHT BE IN.
POINT TAKEN, CAP. LET'S GO, ANT-MAN.
YOU HEARD THE GENTLEMAN, EMMA--MOVE 'EM OUT!
I APPRECIATE YOUR COMING ALONG ON SUCH SHORT NOTICE, SCOTT. I KNOW YOUR JOB AT STARK INTERNATIONAL IS IMPORTANT, AND--
SAY, LOOK, I ENJOY SOLDERING TRANSISTORS AS MUCH AS THE NEXT GUY--
--BUT THE REASON I ORIGINALLY TOOK YOUR OFFER TO BE ANT-MAN* WAS BECAUSE I CRAVED EXCITEMENT AND ADVENTURE. AND IF THAT MEANS BEING DOCKED AN HOUR'S PAY, PAL, THEN THEM'S THE BREAKS!
*IN MARVEL PREMIERE #48. --Jim.

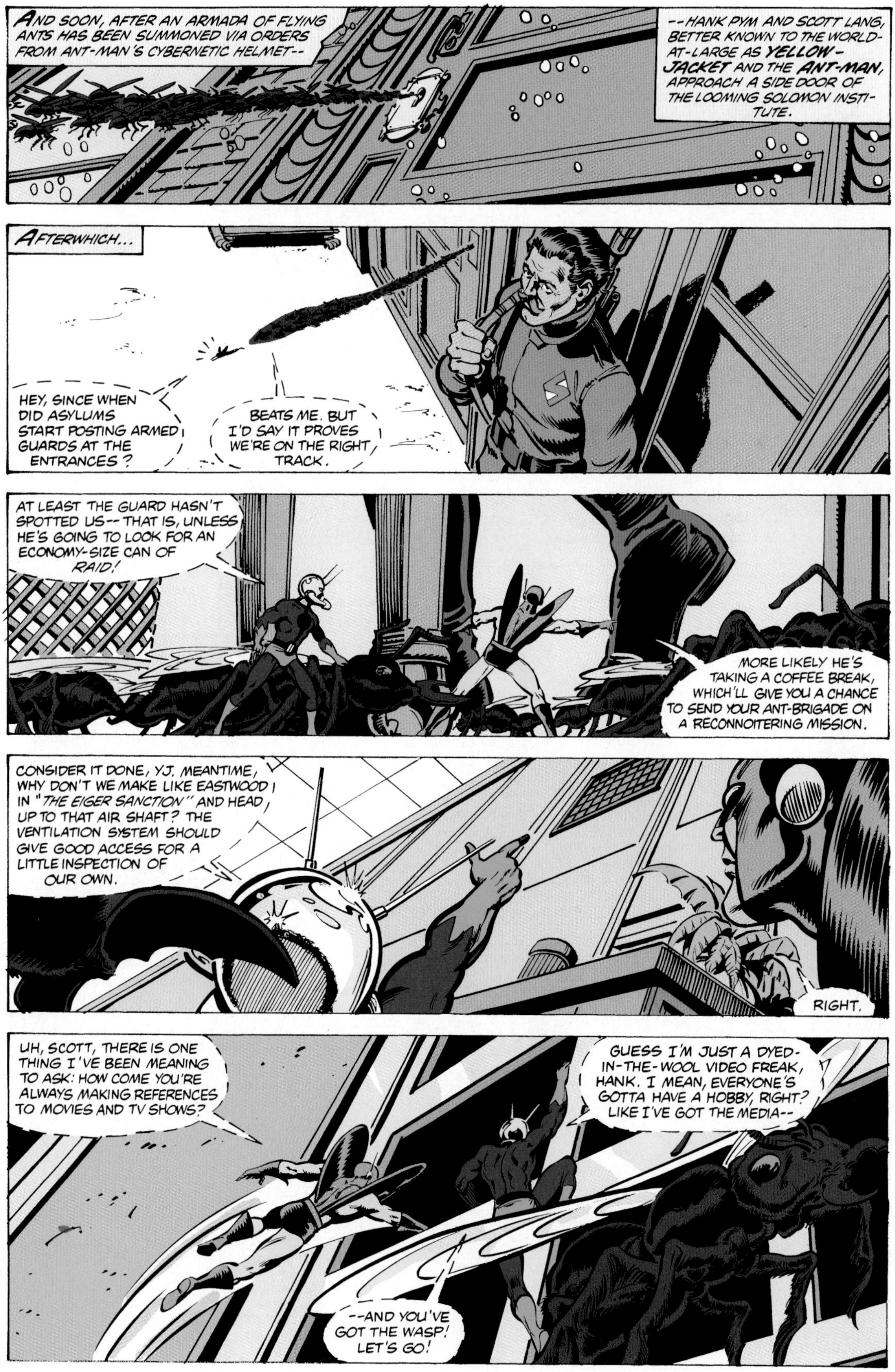
AND SOON, AFTER AN ARMADA OF FLYING ANTS HAS BEEN SUMMONED VIA ORDERS FROM ANT-MAN'S CYBERNETIC HELMET--
--HANK PYM AND SCOTT LANG, BETTER KNOWN TO THE WORLD-AT-LARGE AS YELLOW-JACKET AND THE ANT-MAN, APPROACH A SIDE DOOR OF THE LOOMING SOLOMON INSTI-TUTE.
AFTERWHICH...
HEY, SINCE WHEN DID ASYLUMS START POSTING ARMED GUARDS AT THE ENTRANCES?
BEATS ME. BUT I'D SAY IT PROVES WE'RE ON THE RIGHT TRACK.
AT LEAST THE GUARD HASN'T SPOTTED US--THAT IS, UNLESS HE'S GOING TO LOOK FOR AN ECONOMY-SIZE CAN OF RAID!
MORE LIKELY HE'S TAKING A COFFEE BREAK, WHICH'LL GIVE YOU A CHANCE TO SEND YOUR ANT-BRIGADE ON A RECONNOITERING MISSION.
CONSIDER IT DONE, YJ. MEANTIME, WHY DON'T WE MAKE LIKE EASTWOOD IN "THE EIGER SANCTION" AND HEAD UP TO THAT AIR SHAFT? THE VENTILATION SYSTEM SHOULD GIVE GOOD ACCESS FOR A LITTLE INSPECTION OF OUR OWN.
RIGHT.
UH, SCOTT, THERE IS ONE THING I'VE BEEN MEANING TO ASK: HOW COME YOU'RE ALWAYS MAKING REFERENCES TO MOVIES AND TV SHOWS?
GUESS I'M JUST A DYED-IN-THE-WOOL VIDEO FREAK, HANK. I MEAN, EVERYONE'S GOTTA HAVE A HOBBY, RIGHT? LIKE I'VE GOT THE MEDIA--
--AND YOU'VE GOT THE WASP! LET'S GO!

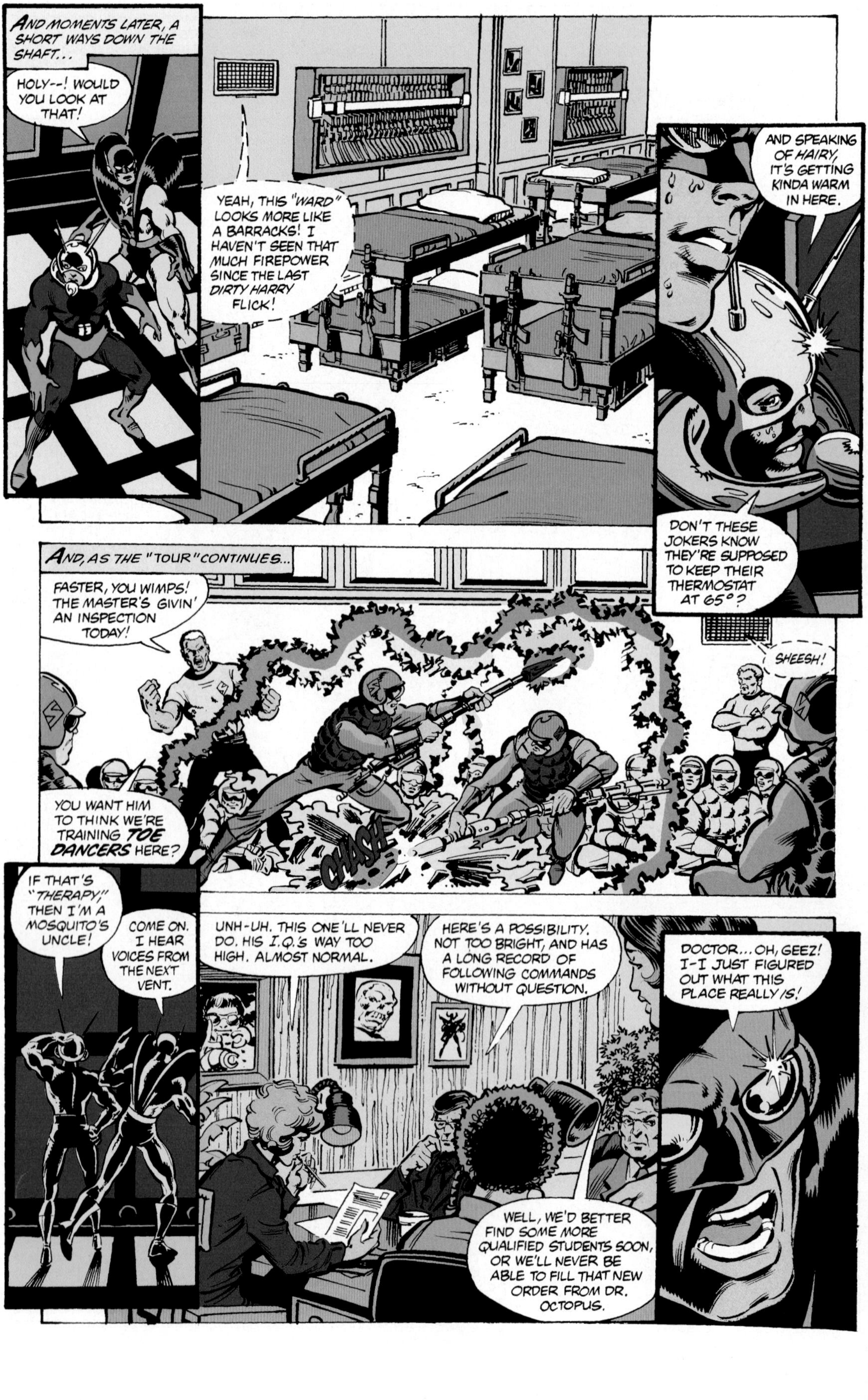
AND MOMENTS LATER, A SHORT WAYS DOWN THE SHAFT...
HOLY--! WOULD YOU LOOK AT THAT!
YEAH, THIS "WARD" LOOKS MORE LIKE A BARRACKS! I HAVEN'T SEEN THAT MUCH FIREPOWER SINCE THE LAST DIRTY HARRY FLICK!
AND SPEAKING OF HAIRY, IT'S GETTING KINDA WARM IN HERE.
DON'T THESE JOKERS KNOW THEY'RE SUPPOSED TO KEEP THEIR THERMOSTAT AT 65°?
AND, AS THE "TOUR" CONTINUES...
FASTER, YOU WIMPS! THE MASTER'S GIVIN' AN INSPECTION TODAY!
SHEESH!
YOU WANT HIM TO THINK WE'RE TRAINING TOE DANCERS HERE?
CRASH
IF THAT'S "THERAPY," THEN I'M A MOSQUITO'S UNCLE!
COME ON. I HEAR VOICES FROM THE NEXT VENT.
UNH-UH. THIS ONE'LL NEVER DO. HIS I.Q.'S WAY TOO HIGH. ALMOST NORMAL.
HERE'S A POSSIBILITY. NOT TOO BRIGHT, AND HAS A LONG RECORD OF FOLLOWING COMMANDS WITHOUT QUESTION.
WELL, WE'D BETTER FIND SOME MORE QUALIFIED STUDENTS SOON, OR WE'LL NEVER BE ABLE TO FILL THAT NEW ORDER FROM DR. OCTOPUS.
DOCTOR... OH, GEEZ! I-I JUST FIGURED OUT WHAT THIS PLACE REALLY IS!

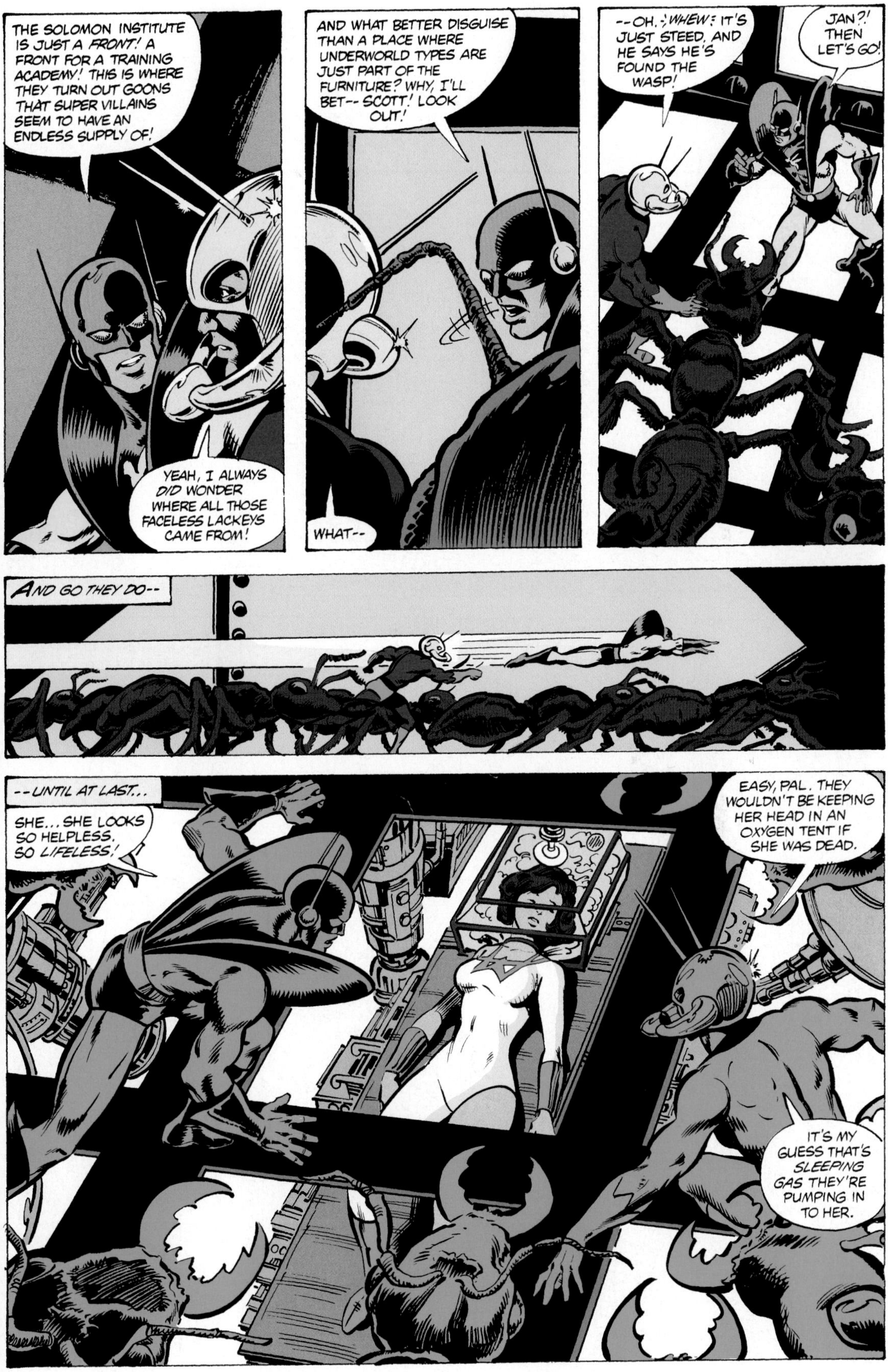
THE SOLOMON INSTITUTE IS JUST A FRONT! A FRONT FOR A TRAINING ACADEMY! THIS IS WHERE THEY TURN OUT GOONS THAT SUPER VILLAINS SEEM TO HAVE AN ENDLESS SUPPLY OF!
YEAH, I ALWAYS DID WONDER WHERE ALL THOSE FACELESS LACKEYS CAME FROM!
AND WHAT BETTER DISGUISE THAN A PLACE WHERE UNDERWORLD TYPES ARE JUST PART OF THE FURNITURE? WHY, I'LL BET-- SCOTT! LOOK OUT!
WHAT--
--OH. WHEW! IT'S JUST STEED, AND HE SAYS HE'S FOUND THE WASP!
JAN?! THEN LET'S GO!
AND GO THEY DO--
--UNTIL AT LAST...
SHE... SHE LOOKS SO HELPLESS. SO LIFELESS!
EASY, PAL. THEY WOULDN'T BE KEEPING HER HEAD IN AN OXYGEN TENT IF SHE WAS DEAD.
IT'S MY GUESS THAT'S SLEEPING GAS THEY'RE PUMPING IN TO HER.

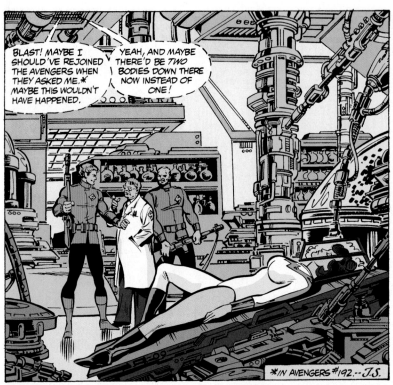

BLAST! MAYBE I SHOULD'VE REJOINED THE AVENGERS WHEN THEY ASKED ME.* MAYBE THIS WOULDN'T HAVE HAPPENED.

YEAH, AND MAYBE THERE'D BE *TWO* BODIES DOWN THERE NOW INSTEAD OF ONE!

*IN AVENGERS #192.--J.S.

I...I GUESS YOU'RE RIGHT, SCOTT.

BUT HOW DO WE GET JAN OUT OF THERE?

THAT'S NO PROBLEM, YJ.

NOT WHEN WE'VE GOT MORE ANTS AT OUR COMMAND THAN YOU CAN SHAKE A *FLY SWATTER* AT!

AND IN MINUTES...

I TELL YA, THIS BIMBO WAS BUILT LIKE A CONCRETE-- HEY!

YOU GUYS HEAR SOMETHIN'? LIKE A BIG BUZZ?

WOULD YOU BELIEVE...A BUZZ BOMB?

EEYYAGH! ANTS! TH-TH-THOUSANDS OF 'EM!

:GAGK:

M-MY EYES--!

I WOULDN'T WORRY ABOUT MY EYES IF I WERE YOU, FRIEND. THANKS TO ONE OF MY DISRUPTER BLASTS--

--YOU AREN'T GOING TO BE *USING* THEM FOR AWHILE!

SKZATT!

AND COURTESY OF MY GROWTH MOMENTUM COMBINED WITH MY STRIKING POWER, IT'S BEDTIME FOR THESE BONZOS, TOO!

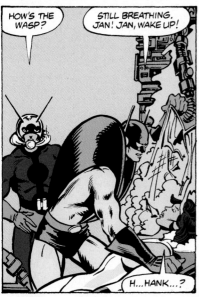

HOW'S THE WASP?

STILL BREATHING, JAN! JAN, WAKE UP!

H...HANK...?

ARE YOU OKAY, HON?

JUST... SLIGHTLY EMBARRASSED. I-IT ONLY HURTS ...WHEN I THINK.

"I'M SURE THE OTHERS TOLD YOU... ABOUT SELBE? WELL, I JUST HAD TO KNOW THE TRUTH...SO I FOLLOWED THE MEN WHO TOOK HIM AWAY.

"IT WAS SO COLD...I WAS ALMOST AS BLUE AS MY BOOTS BY THE TIME WE REACHED THE SOLOMON INSTITUTE..."

"...BUT THAT WAS NOTHING COMPARED TO THE CHILL I FELT WHEN I SAW THOSE STORMTROOPER GUARDS...AND HEARD THE ORDERLIES TOLD TO PREPARE SELBE FOR SOME SORT OF OPERATION!

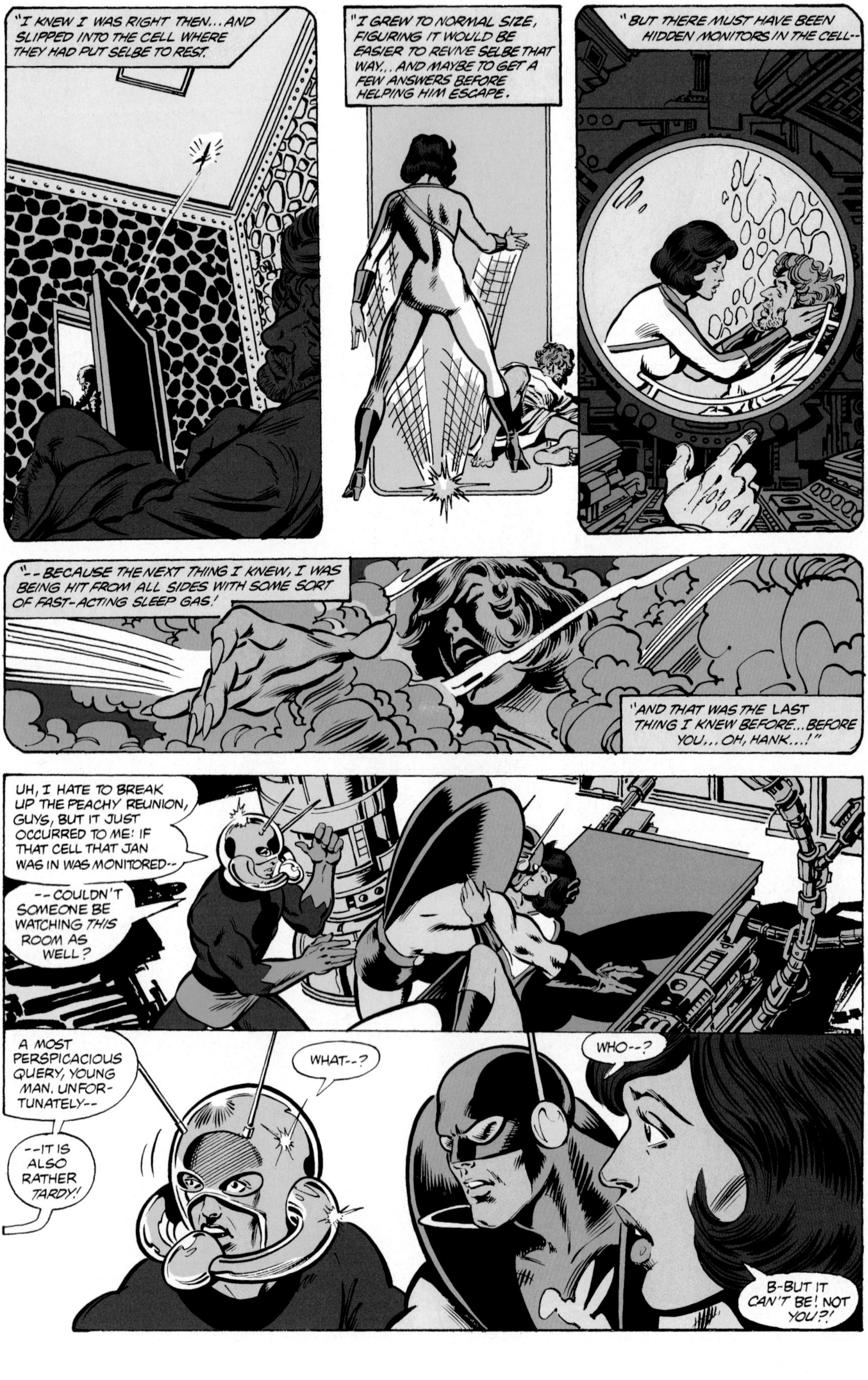
"I KNEW I WAS RIGHT THEN... AND SLIPPED INTO THE CELL WHERE THEY HAD PUT SELBE TO REST.
"I GREW TO NORMAL SIZE, FIGURING IT WOULD BE EASIER TO REVIVE SELBE THAT WAY... AND MAYBE TO GET A FEW ANSWERS BEFORE HELPING HIM ESCAPE.
"BUT THERE MUST HAVE BEEN HIDDEN MONITORS IN THE CELL--
"--BECAUSE THE NEXT THING I KNEW, I WAS BEING HIT FROM ALL SIDES WITH SOME SORT OF FAST-ACTING SLEEP GAS!
"AND THAT WAS THE LAST THING I KNEW BEFORE... BEFORE YOU... OH, HANK...!"
UH, I HATE TO BREAK UP THE PEACHY REUNION, GUYS, BUT IT JUST OCCURRED TO ME: IF THAT CELL THAT JAN WAS IN WAS MONITORED--
--COULDN'T SOMEONE BE WATCHING THIS ROOM AS WELL?
A MOST PERSPICACIOUS QUERY, YOUNG MAN. UNFORTUNATELY--
--IT IS ALSO RATHER TARDY!
WHAT--?
WHO--?
B-BUT IT CAN'T BE! NOT YOU?!

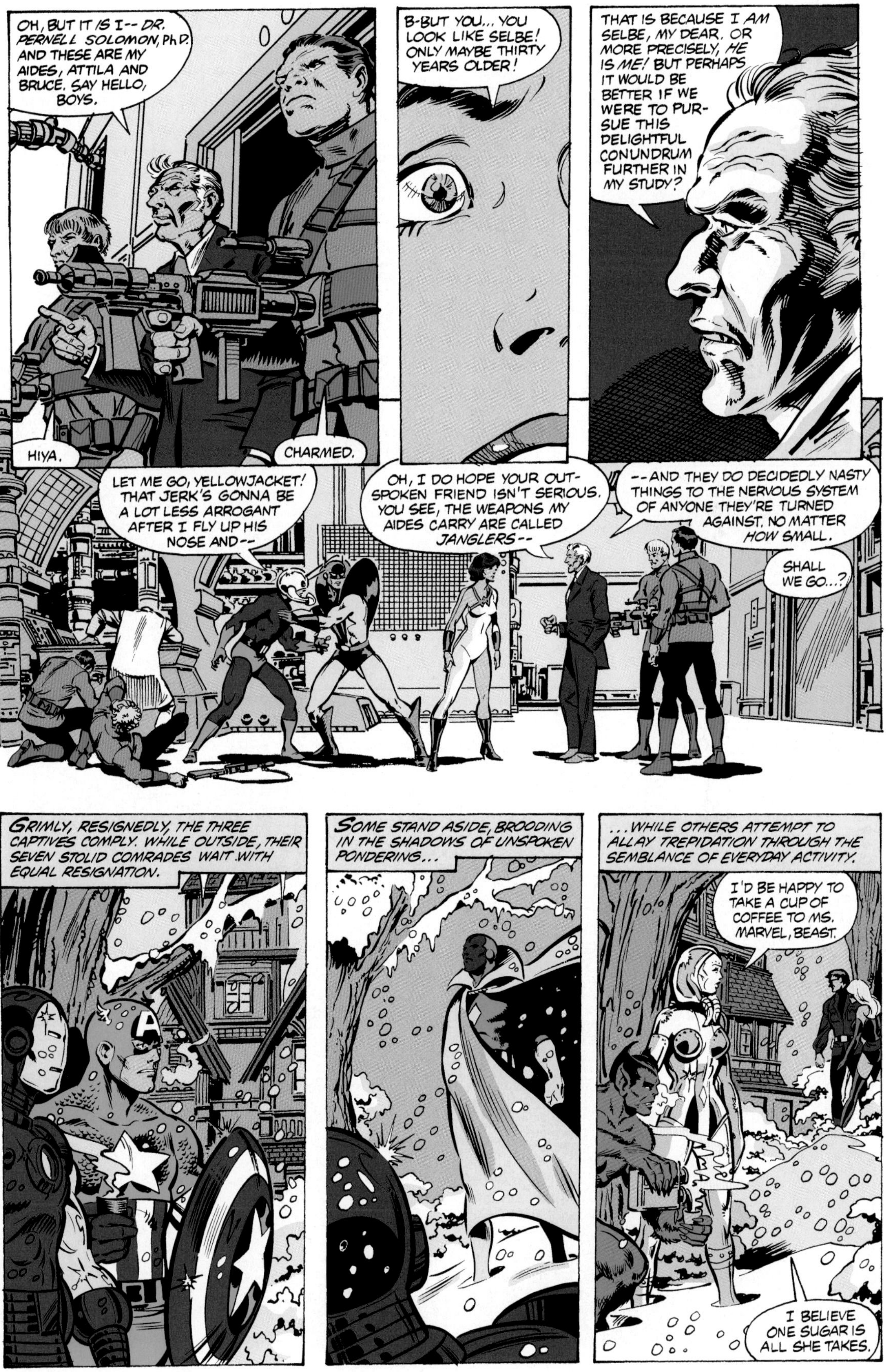
OH, BUT IT IS I-- DR. PERNELL SOLOMON, Ph.D. AND THESE ARE MY AIDES, ATTILA AND BRUCE. SAY HELLO, BOYS.
HIYA.
CHARMED.
B-BUT YOU... YOU LOOK LIKE SELBE! ONLY MAYBE THIRTY YEARS OLDER!
THAT IS BECAUSE I AM SELBE, MY DEAR, OR MORE PRECISELY, HE IS ME! BUT PERHAPS IT WOULD BE BETTER IF WE WERE TO PURSUE THIS DELIGHTFUL CONUNDRUM FURTHER IN MY STUDY?
LET ME GO, YELLOWJACKET! THAT JERK'S GONNA BE A LOT LESS ARROGANT AFTER I FLY UP HIS NOSE AND--
OH, I DO HOPE YOUR OUTSPOKEN FRIEND ISN'T SERIOUS. YOU SEE, THE WEAPONS MY AIDES CARRY ARE CALLED JANGLERS--
--AND THEY DO DECIDEDLY NASTY THINGS TO THE NERVOUS SYSTEM OF ANYONE THEY'RE TURNED AGAINST, NO MATTER HOW SMALL.
SHALL WE GO...?
GRIMLY, RESIGNEDLY, THE THREE CAPTIVES COMPLY. WHILE OUTSIDE, THEIR SEVEN STOLID COMRADES WAIT WITH EQUAL RESIGNATION.
SOME STAND ASIDE, BROODING IN THE SHADOWS OF UNSPOKEN PONDERING...
...WHILE OTHERS ATTEMPT TO ALLAY TREPIDATION THROUGH THE SEMBLANCE OF EVERYDAY ACTIVITY.
I'D BE HAPPY TO TAKE A CUP OF COFFEE TO MS. MARVEL, BEAST.
I BELIEVE ONE SUGAR IS ALL SHE TAKES.

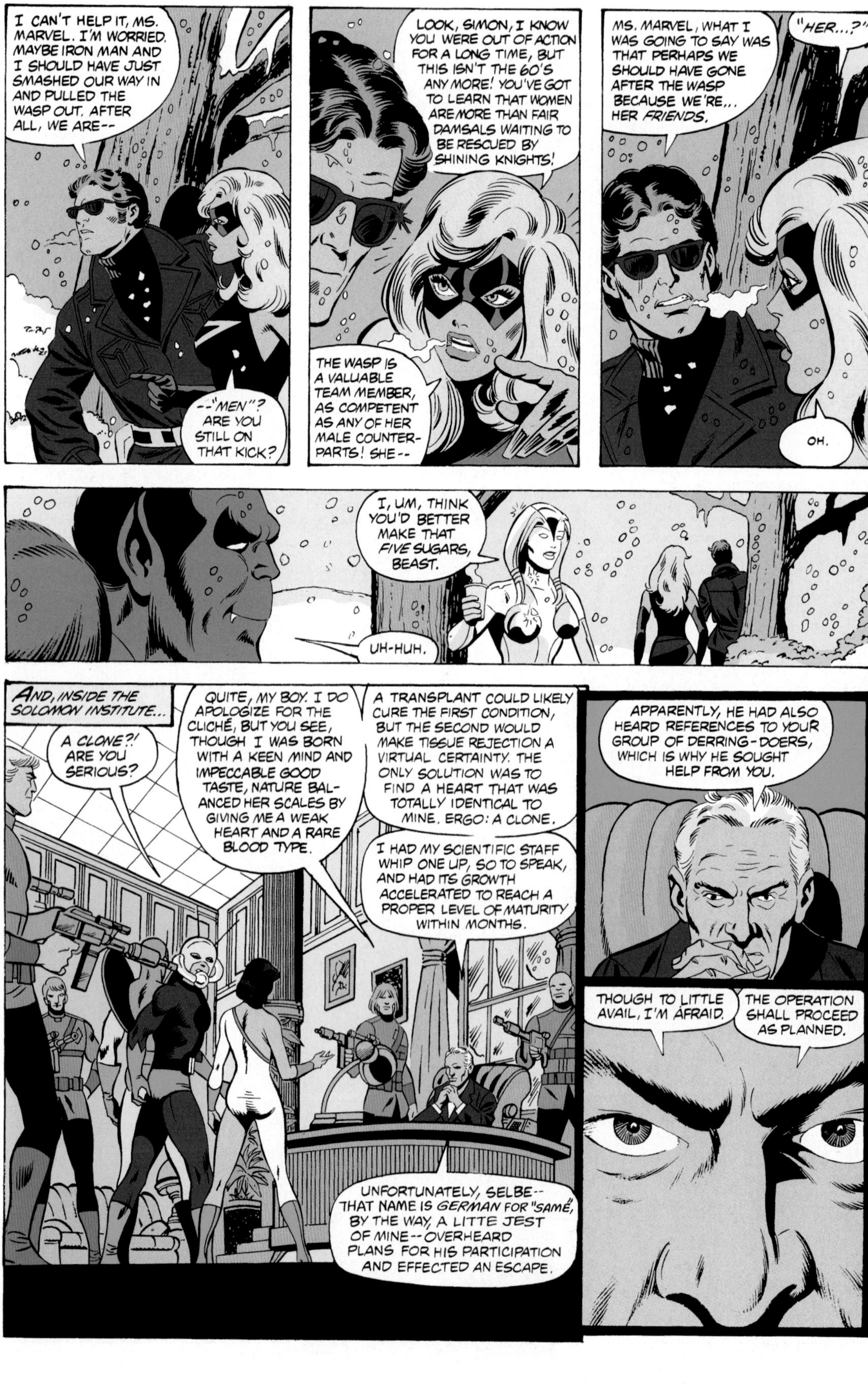
I CAN'T HELP IT, MS. MARVEL. I'M WORRIED. MAYBE IRON MAN AND I SHOULD HAVE JUST SMASHED OUR WAY IN AND PULLED THE WASP OUT. AFTER ALL, WE ARE--
--"MEN"? ARE YOU STILL ON THAT KICK?
LOOK, SIMON, I KNOW YOU WERE OUT OF ACTION FOR A LONG TIME, BUT THIS ISN'T THE 60'S ANY MORE! YOU'VE GOT TO LEARN THAT WOMEN ARE MORE THAN FAIR DAMSALS WAITING TO BE RESCUED BY SHINING KNIGHTS!
THE WASP IS A VALUABLE TEAM MEMBER, AS COMPETENT AS ANY OF HER MALE COUNTER-PARTS! SHE--
MS. MARVEL, WHAT I WAS GOING TO SAY WAS THAT PERHAPS WE SHOULD HAVE GONE AFTER THE WASP BECAUSE WE'RE... HER FRIENDS.
"HER...?"
OH.
I, UM, THINK YOU'D BETTER MAKE THAT FIVE SUGARS, BEAST.
UH-HUH.
AND, INSIDE THE SOLOMON INSTITUTE...
A CLONE?! ARE YOU SERIOUS?
QUITE, MY BOY. I DO APOLOGIZE FOR THE CLICHÉ, BUT YOU SEE, THOUGH I WAS BORN WITH A KEEN MIND AND IMPECCABLE GOOD TASTE, NATURE BALANCED HER SCALES BY GIVING ME A WEAK HEART AND A RARE BLOOD TYPE.
A TRANSPLANT COULD LIKELY CURE THE FIRST CONDITION, BUT THE SECOND WOULD MAKE TISSUE REJECTION A VIRTUAL CERTAINTY. THE ONLY SOLUTION WAS TO FIND A HEART THAT WAS TOTALLY IDENTICAL TO MINE. ERGO: A CLONE.
I HAD MY SCIENTIFIC STAFF WHIP ONE UP, SO TO SPEAK, AND HAD ITS GROWTH ACCELERATED TO REACH A PROPER LEVEL OF MATURITY WITHIN MONTHS.
UNFORTUNATELY, SELBE-- THAT NAME IS GERMAN FOR "SAME", BY THE WAY, A LITTE JEST OF MINE--OVERHEARD PLANS FOR HIS PARTICIPATION AND EFFECTED AN ESCAPE.
APPARENTLY, HE HAD ALSO HEARD REFERENCES TO YOUR GROUP OF DERRING-DOERS, WHICH IS WHY HE SOUGHT HELP FROM YOU.
THOUGH TO LITTLE AVAIL, I'M AFRAID.
THE OPERATION SHALL PROCEED AS PLANNED.

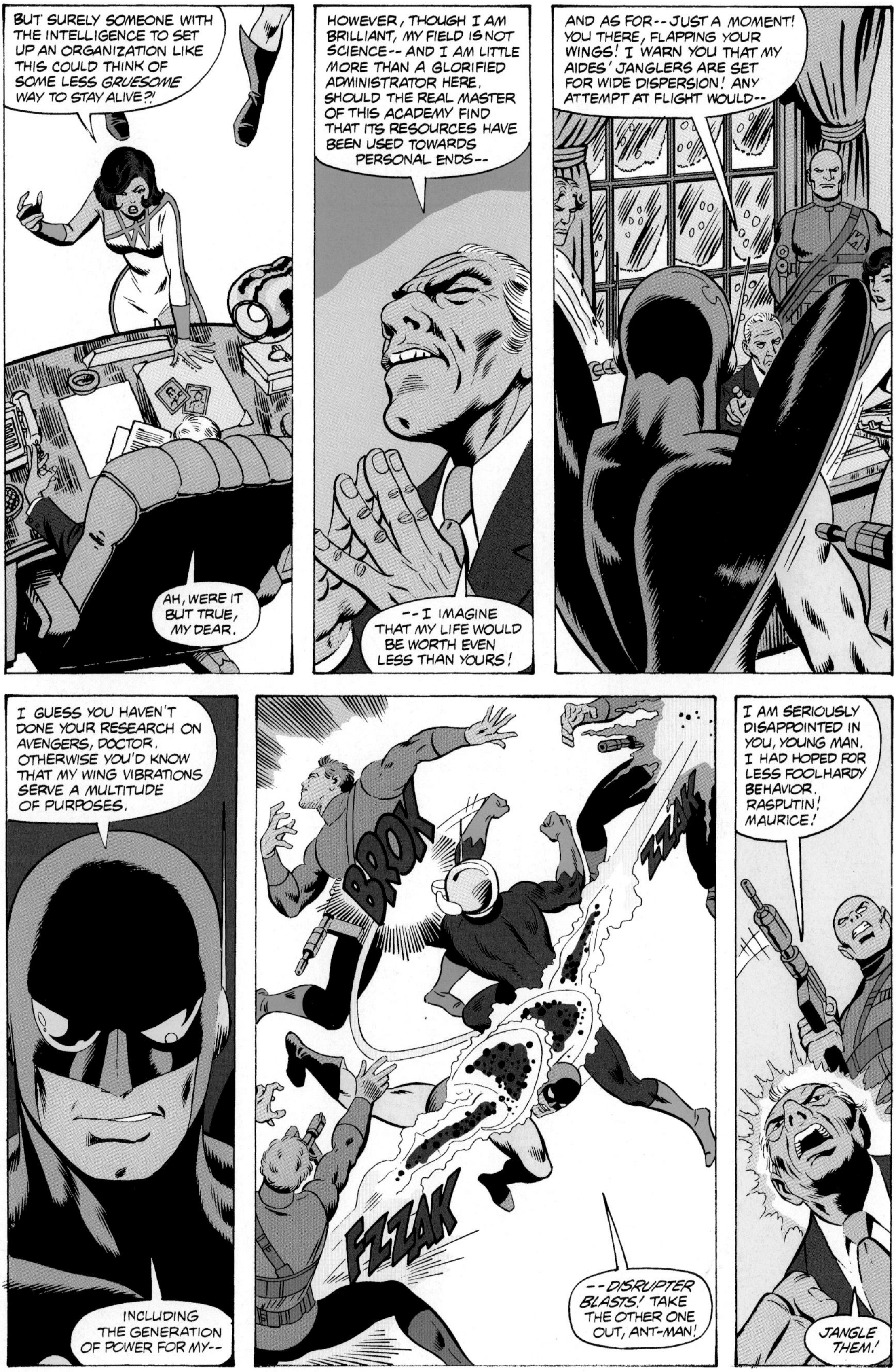
BUT SURELY SOMEONE WITH THE INTELLIGENCE TO SET UP AN ORGANIZATION LIKE THIS COULD THINK OF SOME LESS GRUESOME WAY TO STAY ALIVE?!
AH, WERE IT BUT TRUE, MY DEAR.
HOWEVER, THOUGH I AM BRILLIANT, MY FIELD IS NOT SCIENCE-- AND I AM LITTLE MORE THAN A GLORIFIED ADMINISTRATOR HERE. SHOULD THE REAL MASTER OF THIS ACADEMY FIND THAT ITS RESOURCES HAVE BEEN USED TOWARDS PERSONAL ENDS--
--I IMAGINE THAT MY LIFE WOULD BE WORTH EVEN LESS THAN YOURS!
AND AS FOR-- JUST A MOMENT! YOU THERE, FLAPPING YOUR WINGS! I WARN YOU THAT MY AIDES' JANGLERS ARE SET FOR WIDE DISPERSION! ANY ATTEMPT AT FLIGHT WOULD--
I GUESS YOU HAVEN'T DONE YOUR RESEARCH ON AVENGERS, DOCTOR. OTHERWISE YOU'D KNOW THAT MY WING VIBRATIONS SERVE A MULTITUDE OF PURPOSES.
INCLUDING THE GENERATION OF POWER FOR MY--
BROK
ZZZAK
FZZAK
--DISRUPTER BLASTS! TAKE THE OTHER ONE OUT, ANT-MAN!
I AM SERIOUSLY DISAPPOINTED IN YOU, YOUNG MAN. I HAD HOPED FOR LESS FOOLHARDY BEHAVIOR. RASPUTIN! MAURICE!
JANGLE THEM!

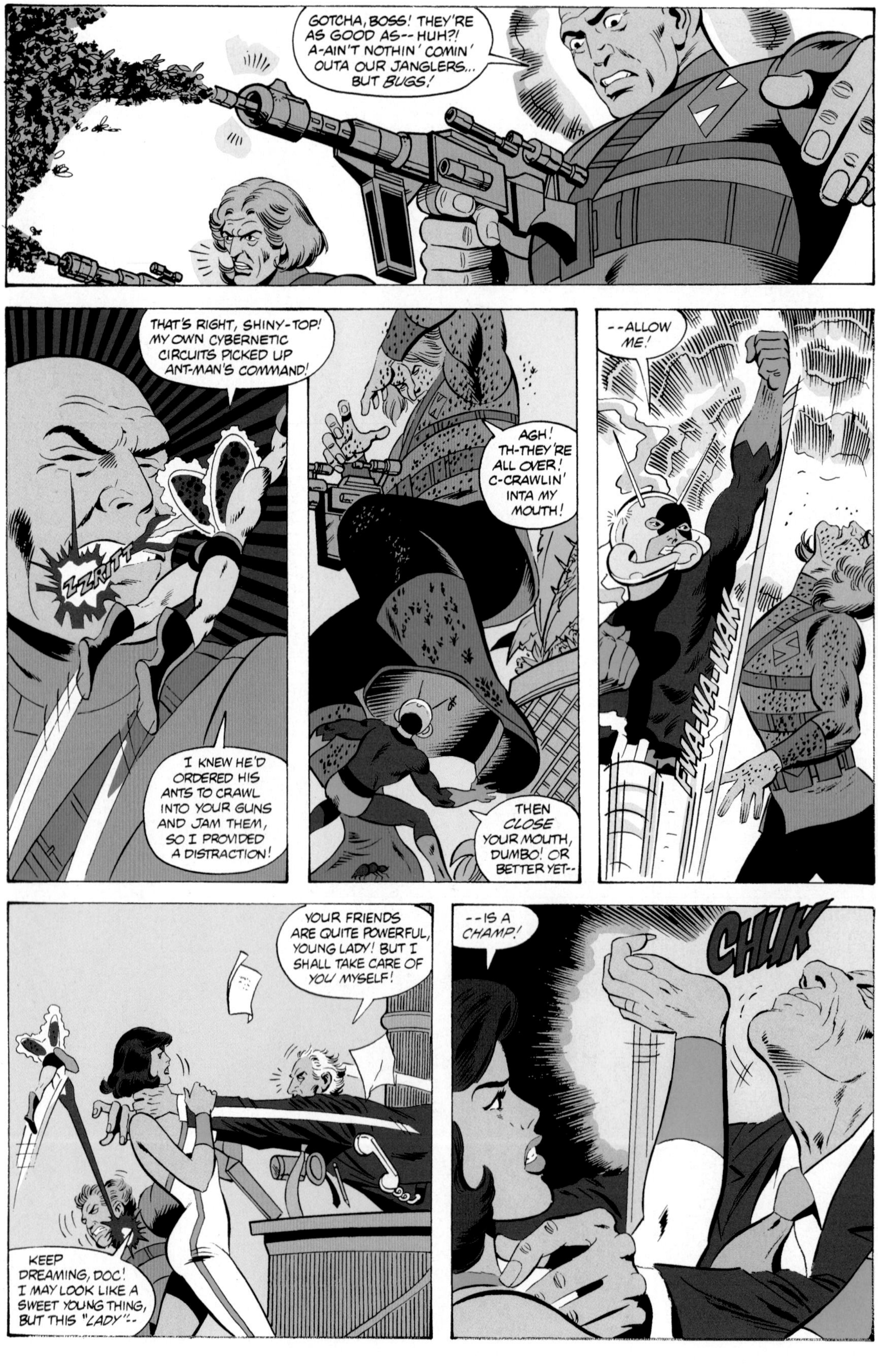
GOTCHA, BOSS! THEY'RE AS GOOD AS-- HUH?! A-AIN'T NOTHIN' COMIN' OUTA OUR JANGLERS... BUT BUGS!
THAT'S RIGHT, SHINY-TOP! MY OWN CYBERNETIC CIRCUITS PICKED UP ANT-MAN'S COMMAND!
ZZRITT
I KNEW HE'D ORDERED HIS ANTS TO CRAWL INTO YOUR GUNS AND JAM THEM, SO I PROVIDED A DISTRACTION!
AGH! TH-THEY'RE ALL OVER! C-CRAWLIN' INTA MY MOUTH!
THEN CLOSE YOUR MOUTH, DUMBO! OR BETTER YET--
--ALLOW ME!
FWA-WA-WAK
YOUR FRIENDS ARE QUITE POWERFUL, YOUNG LADY! BUT I SHALL TAKE CARE OF YOU MYSELF!
KEEP DREAMING, DOC! I MAY LOOK LIKE A SWEET YOUNG THING, BUT THIS "LADY"--
--IS A CHAMP!
CHUK

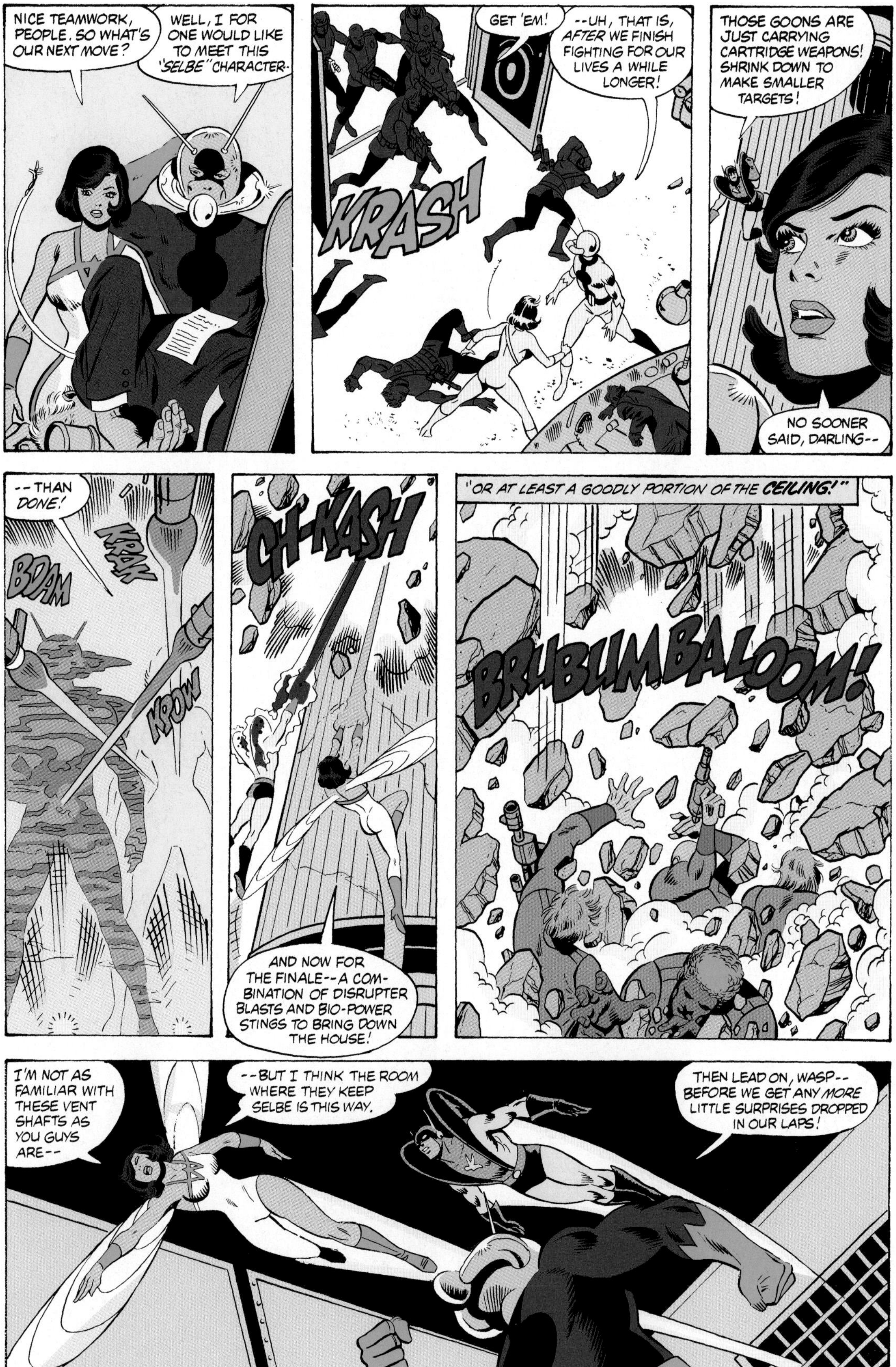
NICE TEAMWORK, PEOPLE. SO WHAT'S OUR NEXT MOVE?
WELL, I FOR ONE WOULD LIKE TO MEET THIS "SELBE" CHARACTER--
GET 'EM!
--UH, THAT IS, AFTER WE FINISH FIGHTING FOR OUR LIVES A WHILE LONGER!
KRASH
THOSE GOONS ARE JUST CARRYING CARTRIDGE WEAPONS! SHRINK DOWN TO MAKE SMALLER TARGETS!
NO SOONER SAID, DARLING--
--THAN DONE!
KRAK
BDAM
KPOW
CH-KASH
AND NOW FOR THE FINALE--A COMBINATION OF DISRUPTER BLASTS AND BIO-POWER STINGS TO BRING DOWN THE HOUSE!
"OR AT LEAST A GOODLY PORTION OF THE CEILING!"
BRUBUMBALOOM!
I'M NOT AS FAMILIAR WITH THESE VENT SHAFTS AS YOU GUYS ARE--
--BUT I THINK THE ROOM WHERE THEY KEEP SELBE IS THIS WAY.
THEN LEAD ON, WASP--BEFORE WE GET ANY MORE LITTLE SURPRISES DROPPED IN OUR LAPS!

HOWEVER, THE NEXT "SURPRISE" IS ABOUT TO DROP ELSEWHERE!

VEHICLE APPROACHING FROM THE WEST, IRON MAN.

CAN YOU IDENTIFY?

NEGATIVE, CAP. THE CONFIGURATION IS UNFAMILIAR.

MY SENSORS DETECT GREAT POWER.

YES, AND MOBILITY.

THAT'S SWELL, BUT WHAT THE HECK *IS* IT?

THE SINISTER CRAFT GLIDES SLOWLY DOWN FROM A GUN-GRAY SKY... HOVERS FOR A MOMENT... AND THEN SETTLES WITH A METALLIC WHISPER.

THE MASTER HAS ARRIVED!

I THINK, AVENGERS, THAT WE'D BETTER GET READY FOR ANYTHING!

AND, INSIDE...

THAT'S IT! SELBE'S CHAMBER! AND THERE'S JUST ONE GUARD! YOU WANT HIM, HANK?

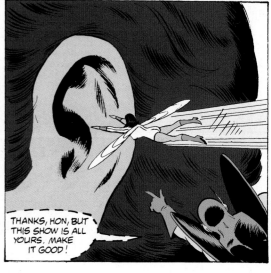

THANKS, HON, BUT THIS SHOW IS ALL YOURS. MAKE IT GOOD!

HMM, THE BEAST WOULD PROBABLY MAKE SOME CRACK ABOUT MY BEING IN THE *EARY* CANAL, BUT I'M NOT HERE TO GET LAUGHS.

I'M HERE TO GET THIS GENTLEMAN'S--

--ATTENTION!

PHWEEEEET

AAAGG!

YOU KNOW SOMETHING, FRIEND? YOU REALLY OUGHT TO CLEAN YOUR EARS MORE OFTEN.

CHOK

I DON'T THINK I'LL *EVER* GET ALL THAT WAX OFF MY BOOTS!

GOOD WORK, JAN. LET'S JUST PRAY THAT ONE OF THE GUARD'S KEYS FIT THAT CELL DOOR!

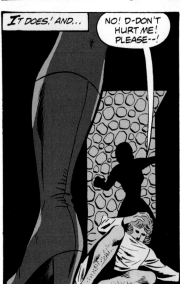

IT DOES! AND...

NO! D-DON'T HURT ME! PLEASE--!

TAKE IT EASY, SELBE. IT'S ME--THE WASP. I DON'T HAVE TIME TO EXPLAIN--

--BUT WE'RE GETTING YOU OUT OF HERE! THEN MY FRIENDS ARE GOING TO FIND THE MAN BEHIND ALL THIS MADNESS AND--

SORRY, SWEETS, BUT IT LOOKS LIKE YOU'VE ALREADY *FOUND* HIM!

WHO--?

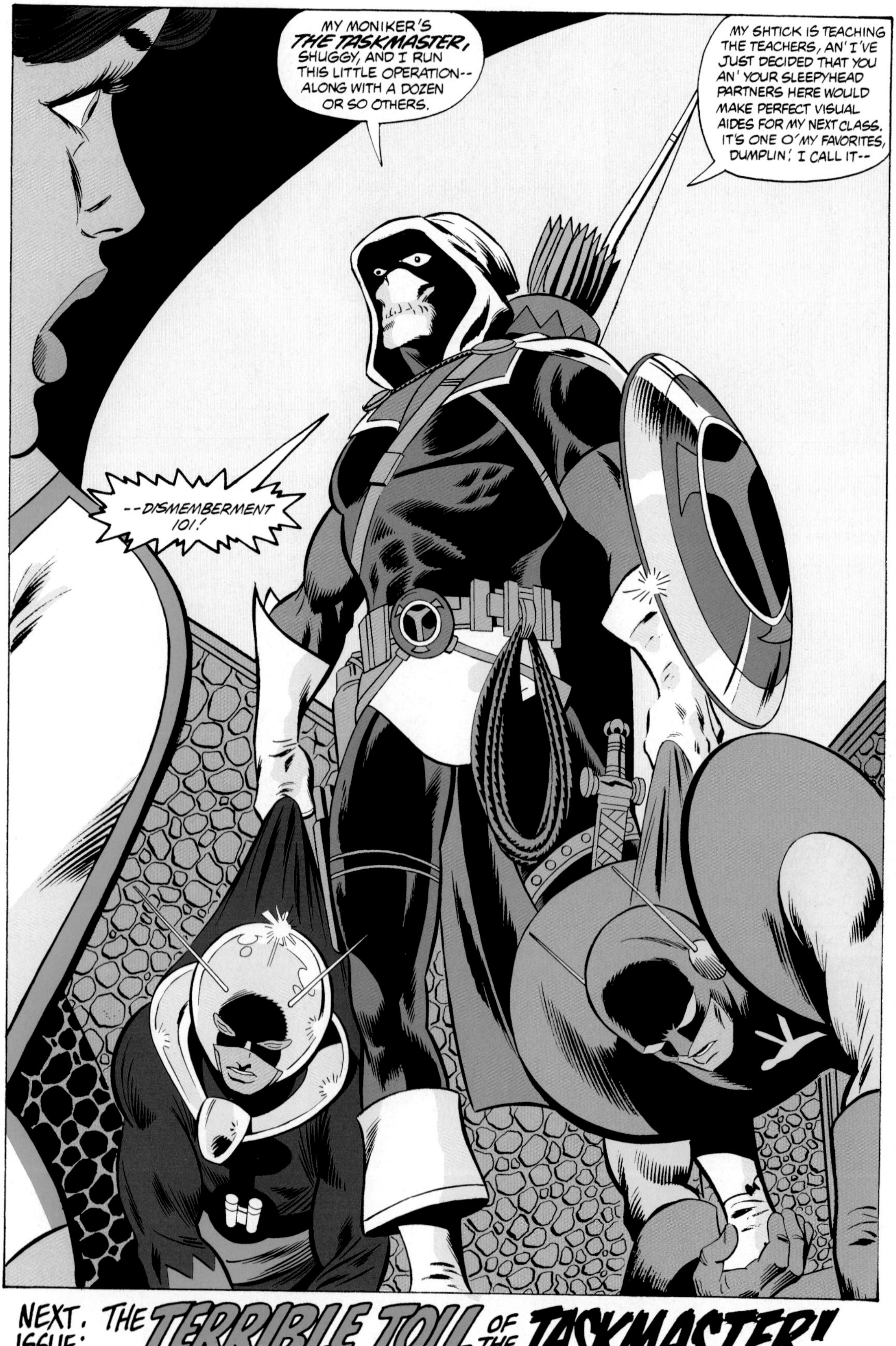
MY MONIKER'S THE TASKMASTER, SHUGGY, AND I RUN THIS LITTLE OPERATION-- ALONG WITH A DOZEN OR SO OTHERS.
MY SHTICK IS TEACHING THE TEACHERS, AN' I'VE JUST DECIDED THAT YOU AN' YOUR SLEEPYHEAD PARTNERS HERE WOULD MAKE PERFECT VISUAL AIDES FOR MY NEXT CLASS. IT'S ONE O' MY FAVORITES, DUMPLIN'. I CALL IT--
--DISMEMBERMENT 101!

NEXT ISSUE: THE TERRIBLE TOLL OF THE TASKMASTER!

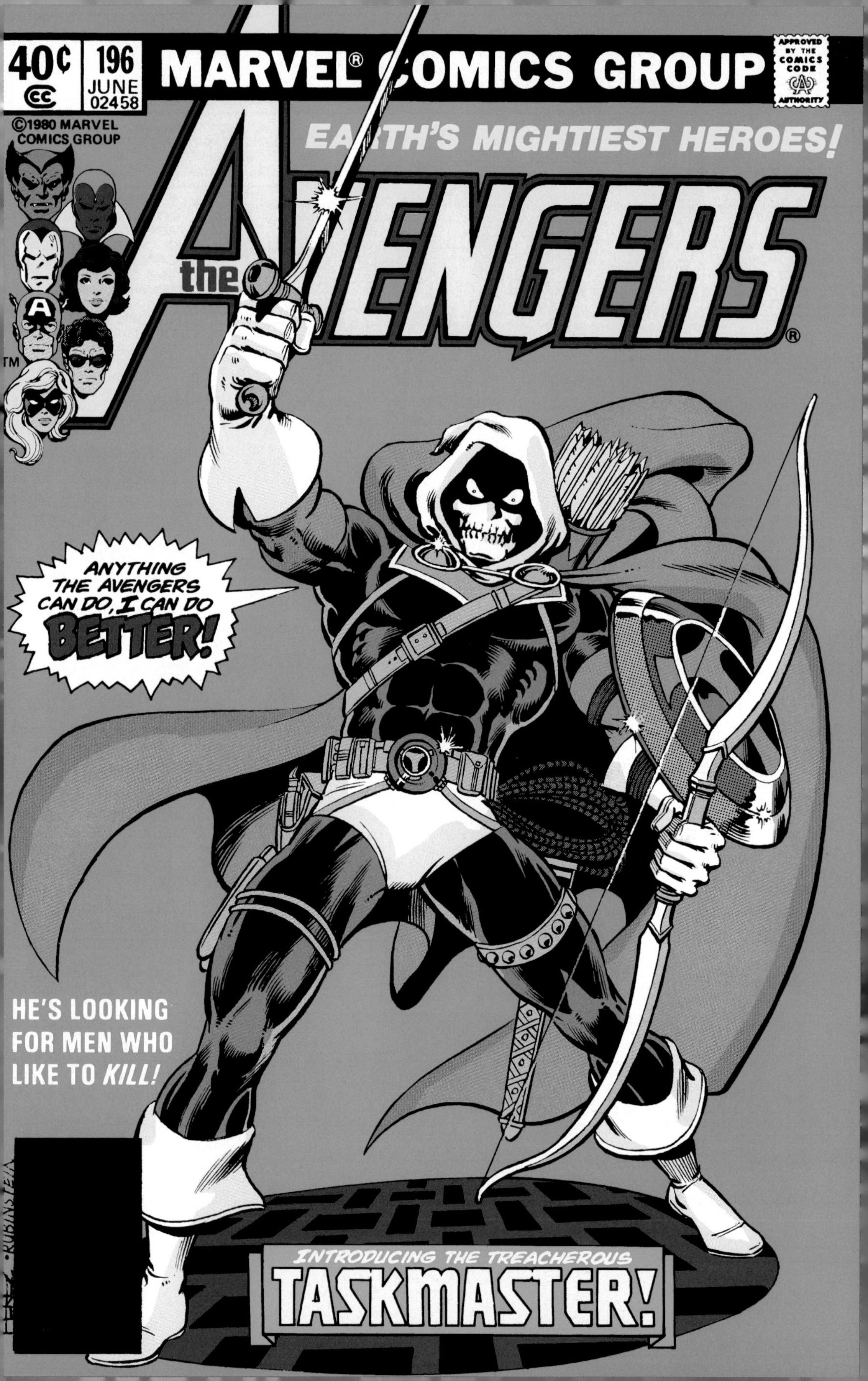
40¢
196
JUNE
02458
MARVEL® COMICS GROUP
APPROVED BY THE COMICS CODE AUTHORITY
©1980 MARVEL COMICS GROUP
EARTH'S MIGHTIEST HEROES!
the AVENGERS®
ANYTHING THE AVENGERS CAN DO, I CAN DO BETTER!
HE'S LOOKING FOR MEN WHO LIKE TO KILL!
INTRODUCING THE TREACHEROUS
TASKMASTER!

And there came a day when *Earth's mightiest heroes* found themselves *united* against a common threat. On that day, the *Avengers* were born—to fight the foes no *single* super-hero could withstand!

Stan Lee PRESENTS: THE MIGHTY AVENGERS! ®

THE FRENCH HAVE A SAYING: CHERCHEZ LA FEMME-- "LOOK FOR THE WOMAN" AND THAT'S EXACTLY WHAT ANT-MAN AND YELLOWJACKET HAVE DONE, JOURNEYING TO LONG ISLAND, TO THE SOLOMON INSTITUTE FOR THE CRIMINALLY INSANE, IN SEARCH OF THE MISSING WASP.

A SHORT TIME AGO, THEY HAD FOUND HER. UNFORTUNATELY, AN EVEN SHORTER TIME AGO, THE TASKMASTER HAD FOUND THEM!

I SURE HOPE YOU "GET SMALL" TYPES AREN'T PLANNIN' ON USIN' YOUR POWERS TO ESCAPE. 'CAUSE THOSE STASIS CLAMPS MY SCIENCE BOYS COOKED UP BIND DIRECTLY TO THE ATOMIC STRUCTURE OF YOUR WRISTS AN' ANKLES, AN' WHILE THEY CAN'T KEEP YA FROM SHRINKIN' OUTA SIGHT--

--THEY DO MAKE SURE THAT YOUR HANDS AN' FEET DON'T GO WITH YA!

THE TERRIBLE TOLL OF THE TASKMASTER

| DAVID MICHELINIE writer | GEORGE PÉREZ penciler | JACK ABEL inker | JOHN COSTANZA letterer | CARL GAFFORD colorist | JIM SALICRUP editor | JIM SHOOTER editor-in-chief |

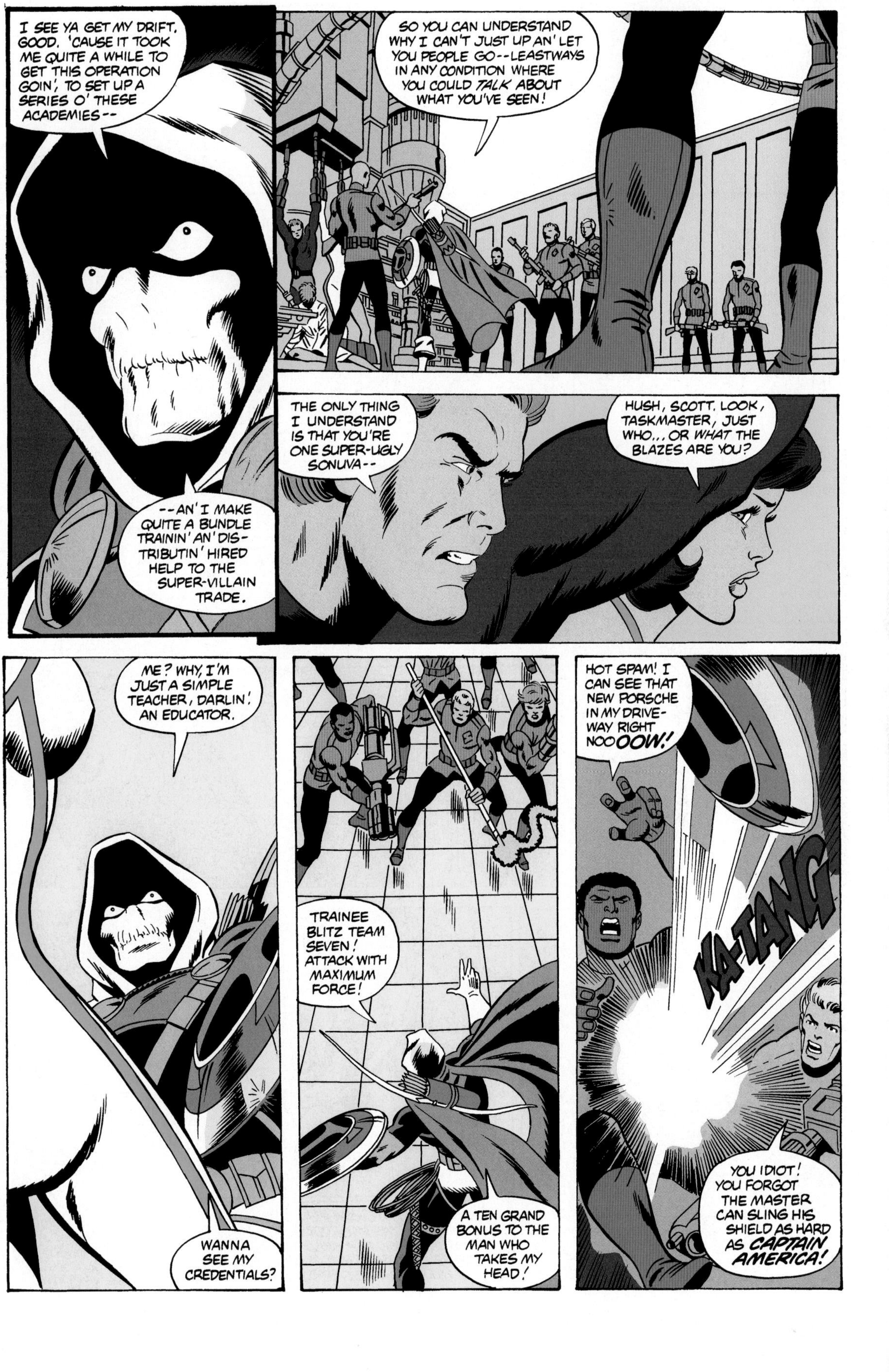
I SEE YA GET MY DRIFT. GOOD. 'CAUSE IT TOOK ME QUITE A WHILE TO GET THIS OPERATION GOIN', TO SET UP A SERIES O' THESE ACADEMIES--
--AN' I MAKE QUITE A BUNDLE TRAININ' AN' DISTRIBUTIN' HIRED HELP TO THE SUPER-VILLAIN TRADE.
SO YOU CAN UNDERSTAND WHY I CAN'T JUST UP AN' LET YOU PEOPLE GO--LEASTWAYS IN ANY CONDITION WHERE YOU COULD TALK ABOUT WHAT YOU'VE SEEN!
THE ONLY THING I UNDERSTAND IS THAT YOU'RE ONE SUPER-UGLY SONUVA--
HUSH, SCOTT. LOOK, TASKMASTER, JUST WHO... OR WHAT THE BLAZES ARE YOU?
ME? WHY, I'M JUST A SIMPLE TEACHER, DARLIN'. AN EDUCATOR.
WANNA SEE MY CREDENTIALS?
TRAINEE BLITZ TEAM SEVEN! ATTACK WITH MAXIMUM FORCE!
A TEN GRAND BONUS TO THE MAN WHO TAKES MY HEAD!
HOT SPAM! I CAN SEE THAT NEW PORSCHE IN MY DRIVEWAY RIGHT NOOOOW!
KA-TANG
YOU IDIOT! YOU FORGOT THE MASTER CAN SLING HIS SHIELD AS HARD AS CAPTAIN AMERICA!

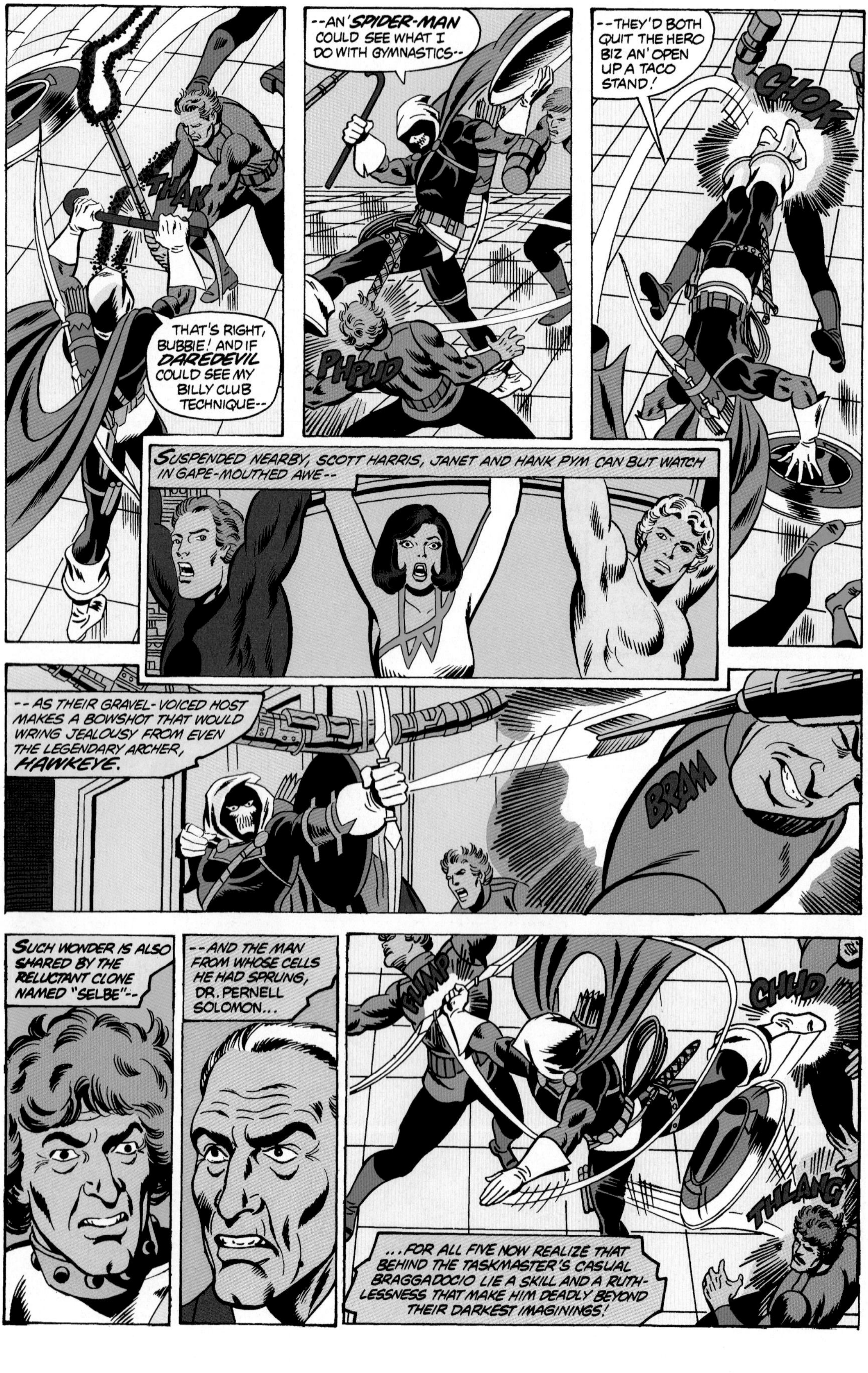

THAK
THAT'S RIGHT, BUBBIE! AND IF DAREDEVIL COULD SEE MY BILLY CLUB TECHNIQUE--
--AN' SPIDER-MAN COULD SEE WHAT I DO WITH GYMNASTICS--
PHPUD
--THEY'D BOTH QUIT THE HERO BIZ AN' OPEN UP A TACO STAND!
CHOK
SUSPENDED NEARBY, SCOTT HARRIS, JANET AND HANK PYM CAN BUT WATCH IN GAPE-MOUTHED AWE--
--AS THEIR GRAVEL-VOICED HOST MAKES A BOWSHOT THAT WOULD WRING JEALOUSY FROM EVEN THE LEGENDARY ARCHER, HAWKEYE.
BRAM
SUCH WONDER IS ALSO SHARED BY THE RELUCTANT CLONE NAMED "SELBE"--
--AND THE MAN FROM WHOSE CELLS HE HAD SPRUNG, DR. PERNELL SOLOMON...
FUMP
CHUD
THLANG
...FOR ALL FIVE NOW REALIZE THAT BEHIND THE TASKMASTER'S CASUAL BRAGGADOCIO LIE A SKILL AND A RUTHLESSNESS THAT MAKE HIM DEADLY BEYOND THEIR DARKEST IMAGININGS!

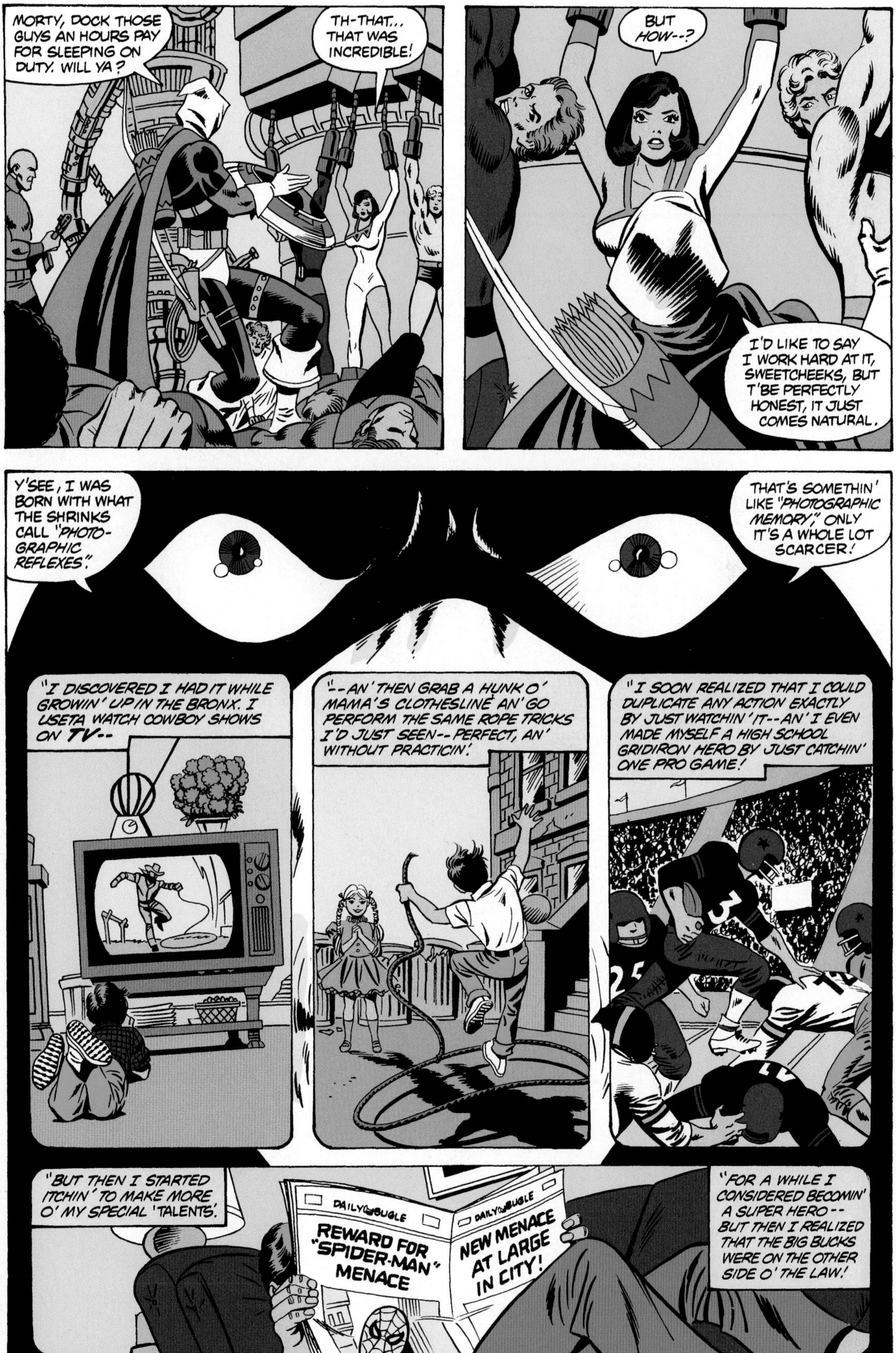
MORTY, DOCK THOSE GUYS AN HOURS PAY FOR SLEEPING ON DUTY. WILL YA?
TH-THAT... THAT WAS INCREDIBLE!
BUT HOW--?
I'D LIKE TO SAY I WORK HARD AT IT, SWEETCHEEKS, BUT T'BE PERFECTLY HONEST, IT JUST COMES NATURAL.
Y'SEE, I WAS BORN WITH WHAT THE SHRINKS CALL "PHOTO-GRAPHIC REFLEXES".
THAT'S SOMETHIN' LIKE "PHOTOGRAPHIC MEMORY," ONLY IT'S A WHOLE LOT SCARCER!
"I DISCOVERED I HAD IT WHILE GROWIN' UP IN THE BRONX. I USETA WATCH COWBOY SHOWS ON TV--
"--AN' THEN GRAB A HUNK O' MAMA'S CLOTHESLINE AN' GO PERFORM THE SAME ROPE TRICKS I'D JUST SEEN--PERFECT, AN' WITHOUT PRACTICIN'.
"I SOON REALIZED THAT I COULD DUPLICATE ANY ACTION EXACTLY BY JUST WATCHIN' IT--AN' I EVEN MADE MYSELF A HIGH SCHOOL GRIDIRON HERO BY JUST CATCHIN' ONE PRO GAME!
"BUT THEN I STARTED ITCHIN' TO MAKE MORE O' MY SPECIAL 'TALENTS'.
DAILY BUGLE
REWARD FOR "SPIDER-MAN" MENACE
DAILY BUGLE
NEW MENACE AT LARGE IN CITY!
"FOR A WHILE I CONSIDERED BECOMIN' A SUPER HERO--BUT THEN I REALIZED THAT THE BIG BUCKS WERE ON THE OTHER SIDE O' THE LAW.'

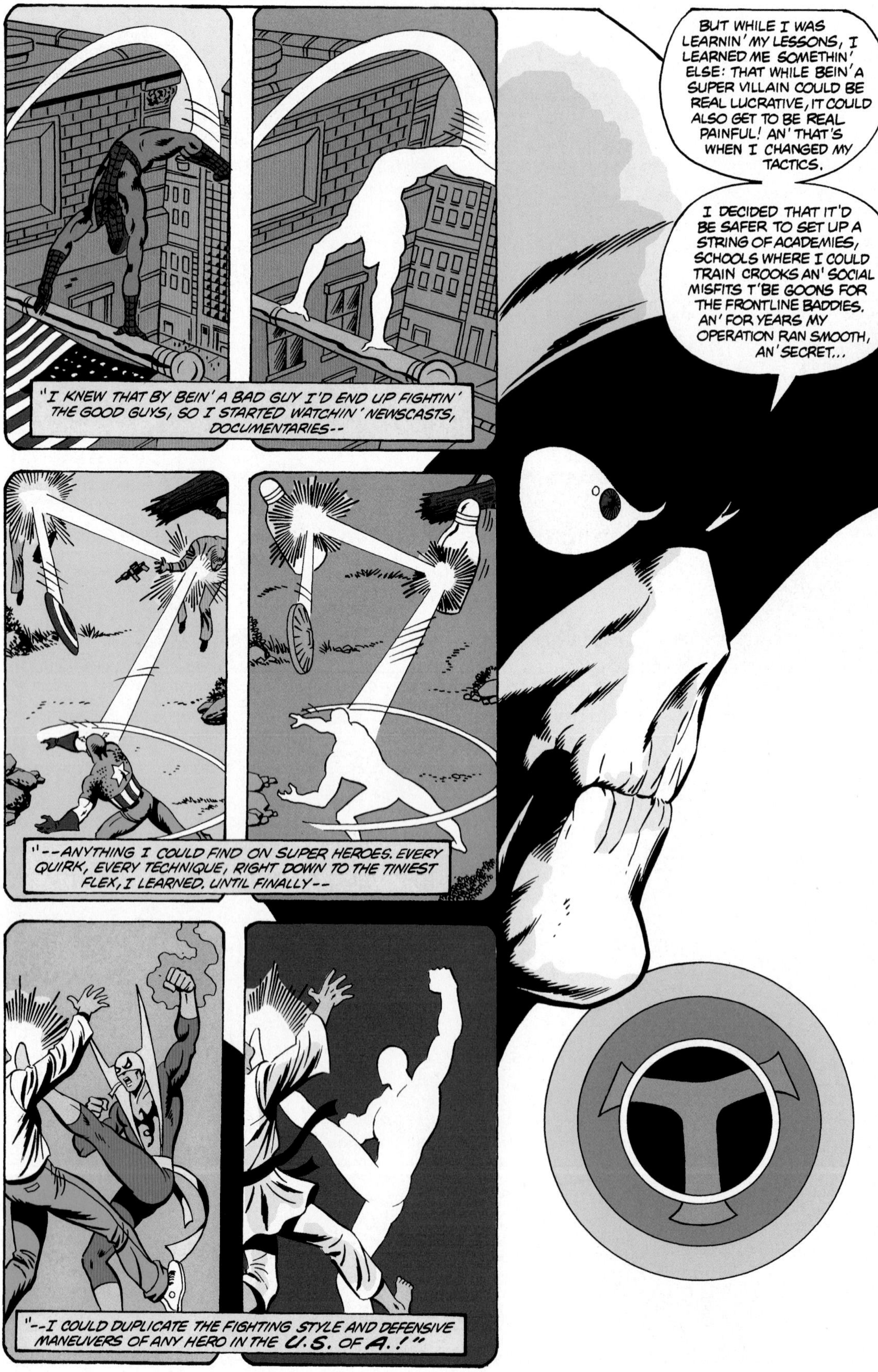
BUT WHILE I WAS LEARNIN' MY LESSONS, I LEARNED ME SOMETHIN' ELSE: THAT WHILE BEIN' A SUPER VILLAIN COULD BE REAL LUCRATIVE, IT COULD ALSO GET TO BE REAL PAINFUL! AN' THAT'S WHEN I CHANGED MY TACTICS.
I DECIDED THAT IT'D BE SAFER TO SET UP A STRING OF ACADEMIES, SCHOOLS WHERE I COULD TRAIN CROOKS AN' SOCIAL MISFITS T'BE GOONS FOR THE FRONTLINE BADDIES. AN' FOR YEARS MY OPERATION RAN SMOOTH, AN' SECRET...
"I KNEW THAT BY BEIN' A BAD GUY I'D END UP FIGHTIN' THE GOOD GUYS, SO I STARTED WATCHIN' NEWSCASTS, DOCUMENTARIES--
"--ANYTHING I COULD FIND ON SUPER HEROES. EVERY QUIRK, EVERY TECHNIQUE, RIGHT DOWN TO THE TINIEST FLEX, I LEARNED. UNTIL FINALLY--
"--I COULD DUPLICATE THE FIGHTING STYLE AND DEFENSIVE MANEUVERS OF ANY HERO IN THE U.S. OF A.!"

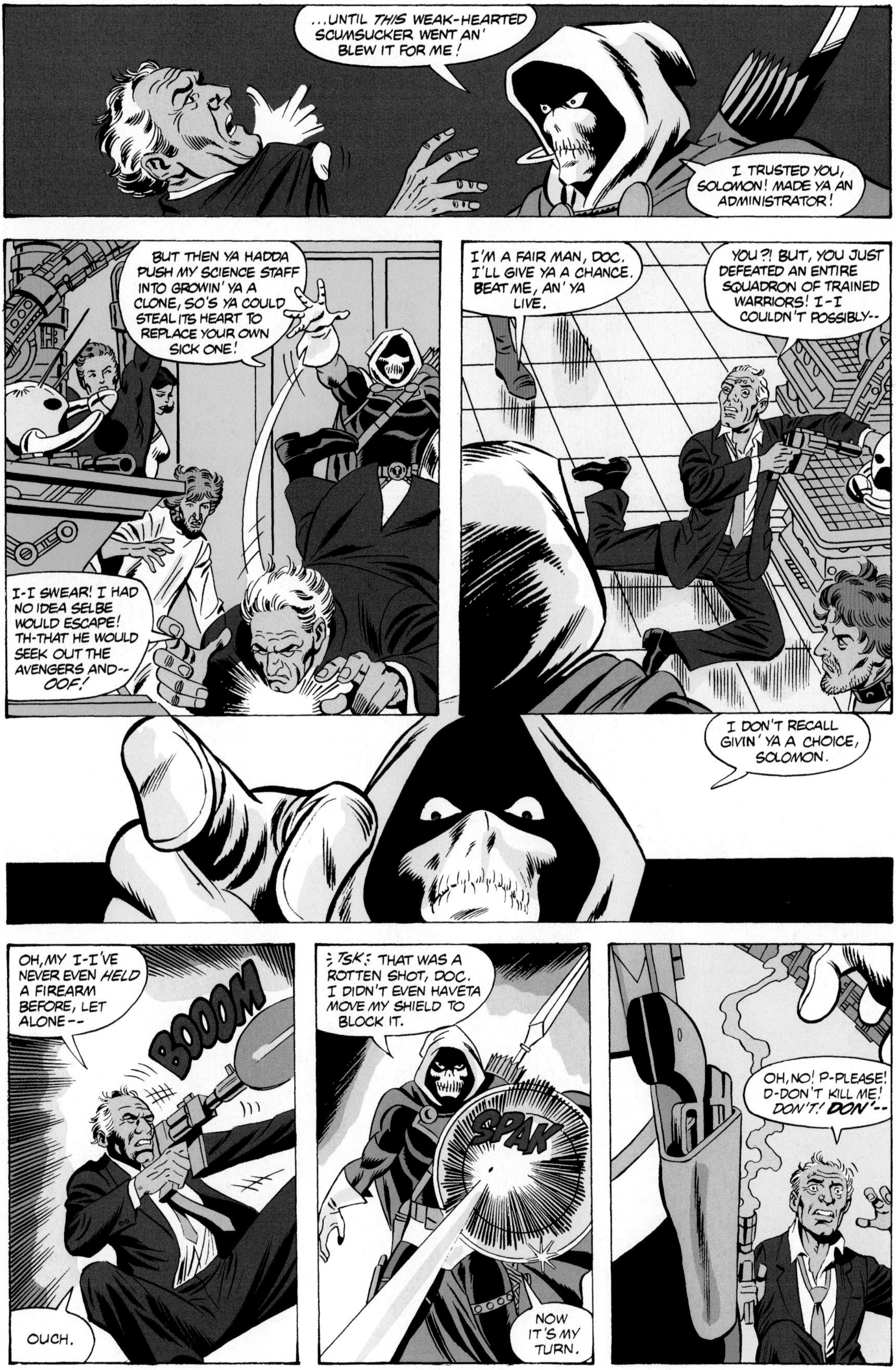
...UNTIL *THIS* WEAK-HEARTED SCUMSUCKER WENT AN' BLEW IT FOR ME!
I TRUSTED YOU, SOLOMON! MADE YA AN ADMINISTRATOR!
BUT THEN YA HADDA PUSH MY SCIENCE STAFF INTO GROWIN' YA A CLONE, SO'S YA COULD STEAL ITS HEART TO REPLACE YOUR OWN SICK ONE!
I-I SWEAR! I HAD NO IDEA SELBE WOULD ESCAPE! TH-THAT HE WOULD SEEK OUT THE AVENGERS AND-- *OOF!*
I'M A FAIR MAN, DOC. I'LL GIVE YA A CHANCE. BEAT ME, AN' YA LIVE.
YOU?! BUT, YOU JUST DEFEATED AN ENTIRE SQUADRON OF TRAINED WARRIORS! I-I COULDN'T POSSIBLY--
I DON'T RECALL GIVIN' YA A CHOICE, SOLOMON.
OH, MY I-I'VE NEVER EVEN *HELD* A FIREARM BEFORE, LET ALONE--
BOOOM
OUCH.
TSK THAT WAS A ROTTEN SHOT, DOC. I DIDN'T EVEN HAVETA MOVE MY SHIELD TO BLOCK IT.
SPAK
NOW IT'S MY TURN.
OH, NO! P-PLEASE! D-DON'T KILL ME! *DON'T! **DON'--***

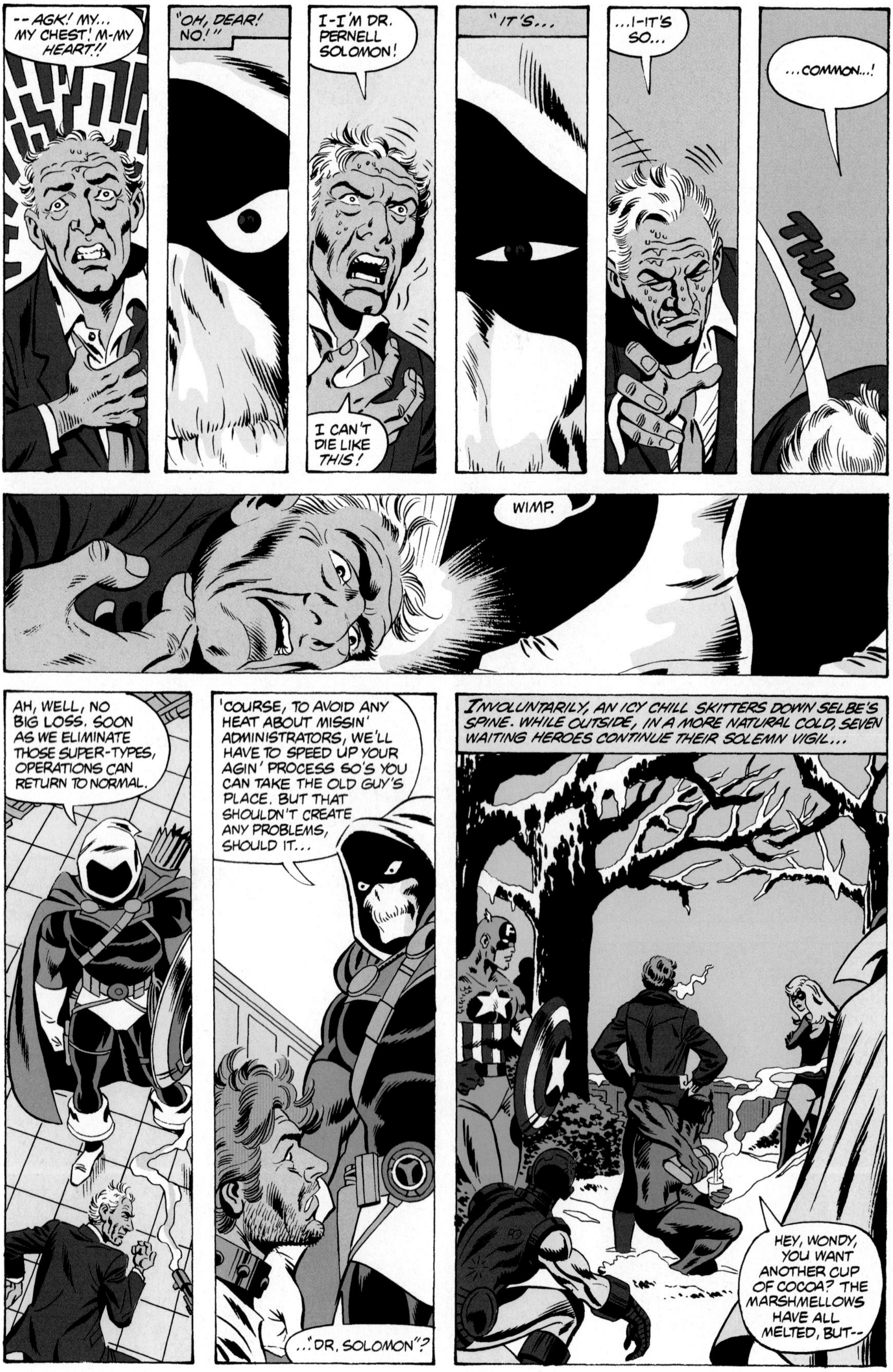
--AGK! MY... MY CHEST! M-MY HEART!!
"OH, DEAR! NO!"
I-I'M DR. PERNELL SOLOMON!
I CAN'T DIE LIKE THIS!
"IT'S...
...I-IT'S SO...
...COMMON...!
THUD
WIMP.
AH, WELL, NO BIG LOSS. SOON AS WE ELIMINATE THOSE SUPER-TYPES, OPERATIONS CAN RETURN TO NORMAL.
'COURSE, TO AVOID ANY HEAT ABOUT MISSIN' ADMINISTRATORS, WE'LL HAVE TO SPEED UP YOUR AGIN' PROCESS SO'S YOU CAN TAKE THE OLD GUY'S PLACE. BUT THAT SHOULDN'T CREATE ANY PROBLEMS, SHOULD IT...
..."DR. SOLOMON"?
INVOLUNTARILY, AN ICY CHILL SKITTERS DOWN SELBE'S SPINE. WHILE OUTSIDE, IN A MORE NATURAL COLD, SEVEN WAITING HEROES CONTINUE THEIR SOLEMN VIGIL...
HEY, WONDY, YOU WANT ANOTHER CUP OF COCOA? THE MARSHMELLOWS HAVE ALL MELTED, BUT--

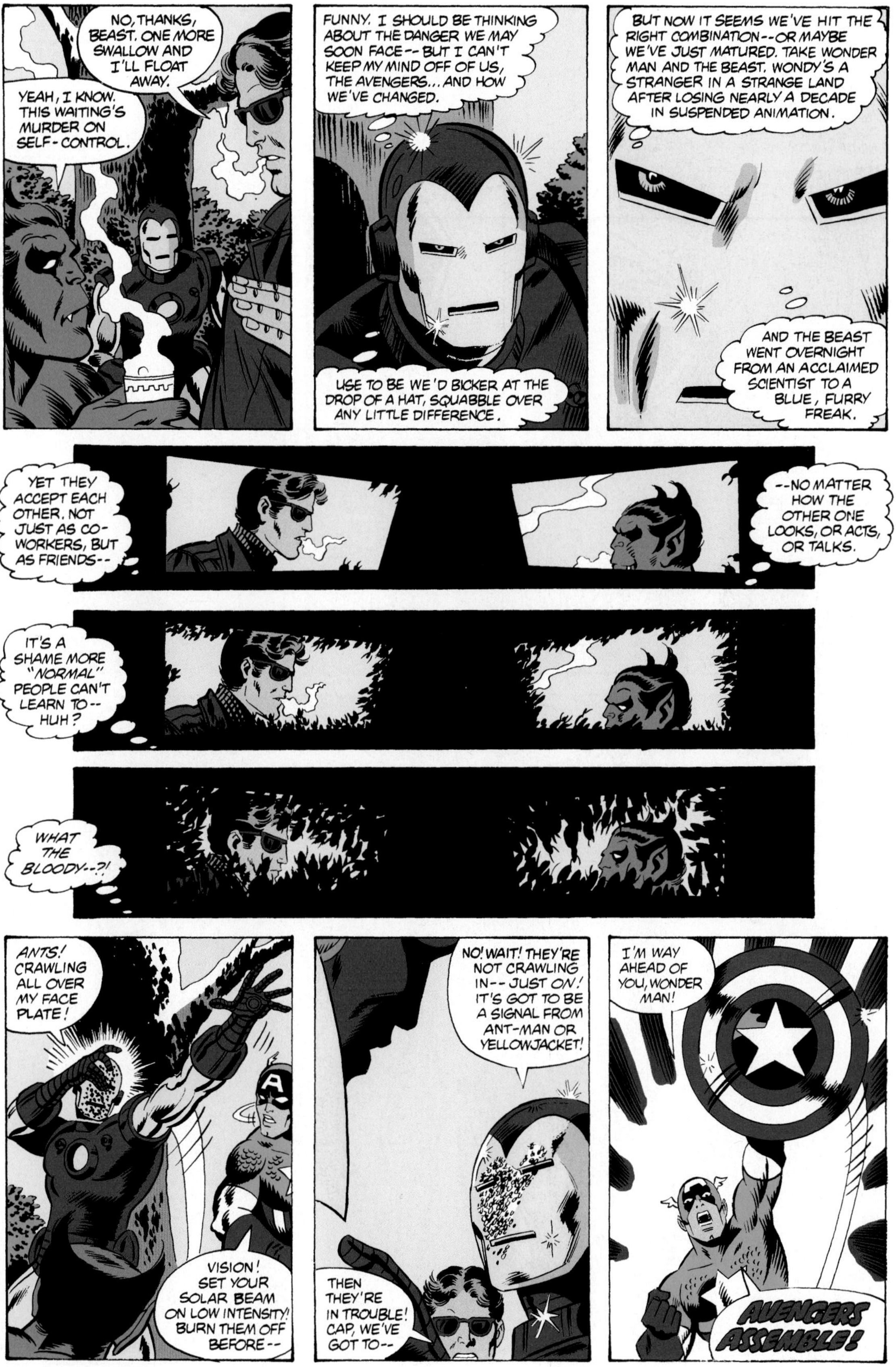

YEAH, I KNOW. THIS WAITING'S MURDER ON SELF-CONTROL.
NO, THANKS, BEAST. ONE MORE SWALLOW AND I'LL FLOAT AWAY.
FUNNY. I SHOULD BE THINKING ABOUT THE DANGER WE MAY SOON FACE-- BUT I CAN'T KEEP MY MIND OFF OF US, THE AVENGERS... AND HOW WE'VE CHANGED.
USE TO BE WE'D BICKER AT THE DROP OF A HAT, SQUABBLE OVER ANY LITTLE DIFFERENCE.
BUT NOW IT SEEMS WE'VE HIT THE RIGHT COMBINATION--OR MAYBE WE'VE JUST MATURED. TAKE WONDER MAN AND THE BEAST. WONDY'S A STRANGER IN A STRANGE LAND AFTER LOSING NEARLY A DECADE IN SUSPENDED ANIMATION.
AND THE BEAST WENT OVERNIGHT FROM AN ACCLAIMED SCIENTIST TO A BLUE, FURRY FREAK.
YET THEY ACCEPT EACH OTHER. NOT JUST AS CO-WORKERS, BUT AS FRIENDS--
--NO MATTER HOW THE OTHER ONE LOOKS, OR ACTS, OR TALKS.
IT'S A SHAME MORE "NORMAL" PEOPLE CAN'T LEARN TO-- HUH?
WHAT THE BLOODY--?!
ANTS! CRAWLING ALL OVER MY FACE PLATE!
VISION! SET YOUR SOLAR BEAM ON LOW INTENSITY! BURN THEM OFF BEFORE--
NO! WAIT! THEY'RE NOT CRAWLING IN-- JUST ON! IT'S GOT TO BE A SIGNAL FROM ANT-MAN OR YELLOWJACKET!
THEN THEY'RE IN TROUBLE! CAP, WE'VE GOT TO--
I'M WAY AHEAD OF YOU, WONDER MAN!
AVENGERS ASSEMBLE!

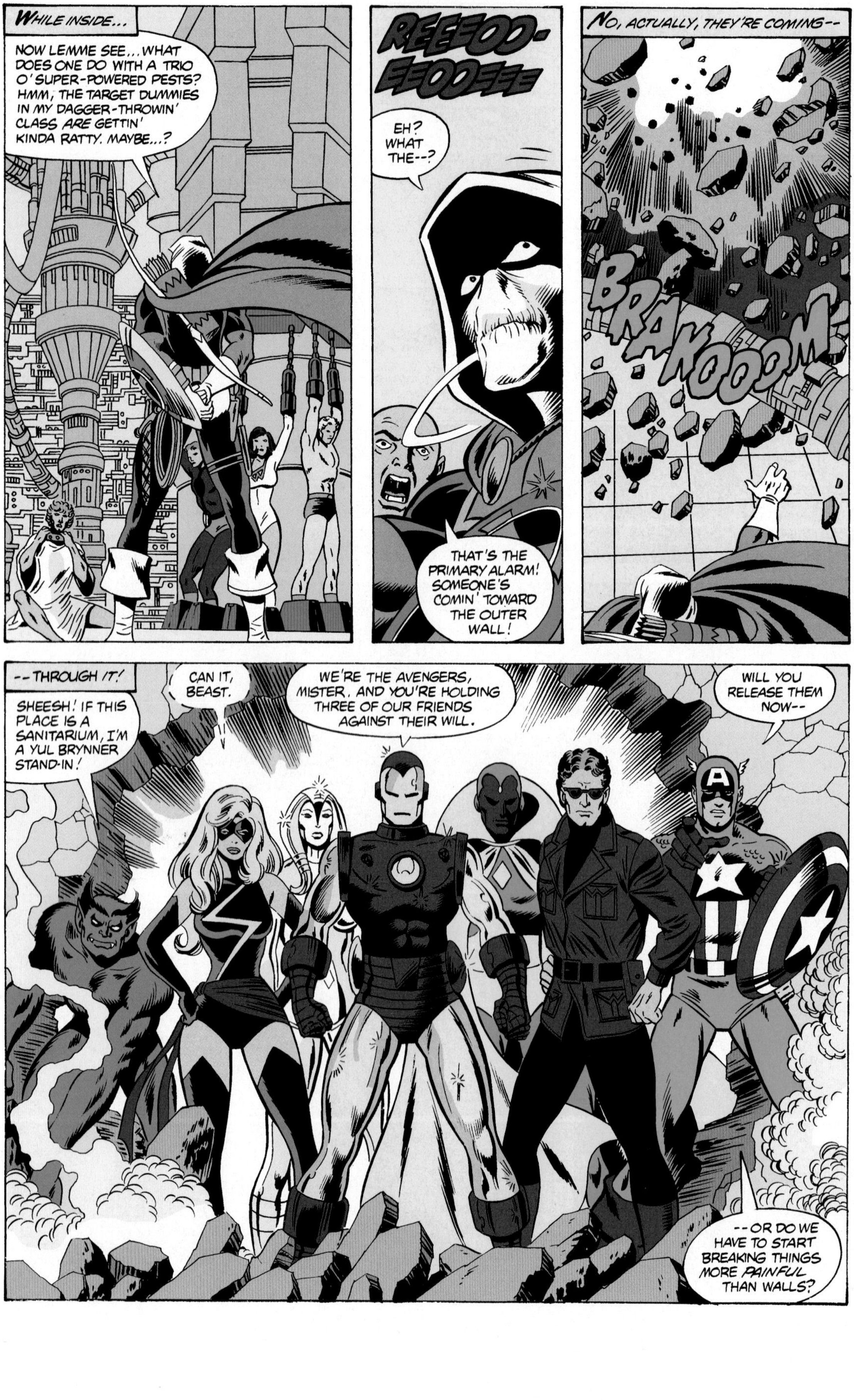
WHILE INSIDE...
NOW LEMME SEE... WHAT DOES ONE DO WITH A TRIO O' SUPER-POWERED PESTS? HMM, THE TARGET DUMMIES IN MY DAGGER-THROWIN' CLASS ARE GETTIN' KINDA RATTY. MAYBE...?
REEEOO-EEEOOEEE
EH? WHAT THE--?
THAT'S THE PRIMARY ALARM! SOMEONE'S COMIN' TOWARD THE OUTER WALL!
NO, ACTUALLY, THEY'RE COMING--
BRAKOOOM
--THROUGH IT!
SHEESH! IF THIS PLACE IS A SANITARIUM, I'M A YUL BRYNNER STAND-IN!
CAN IT, BEAST.
WE'RE THE AVENGERS, MISTER, AND YOU'RE HOLDING THREE OF OUR FRIENDS AGAINST THEIR WILL.
WILL YOU RELEASE THEM NOW--
--OR DO WE HAVE TO START BREAKING THINGS MORE PAINFUL THAN WALLS?

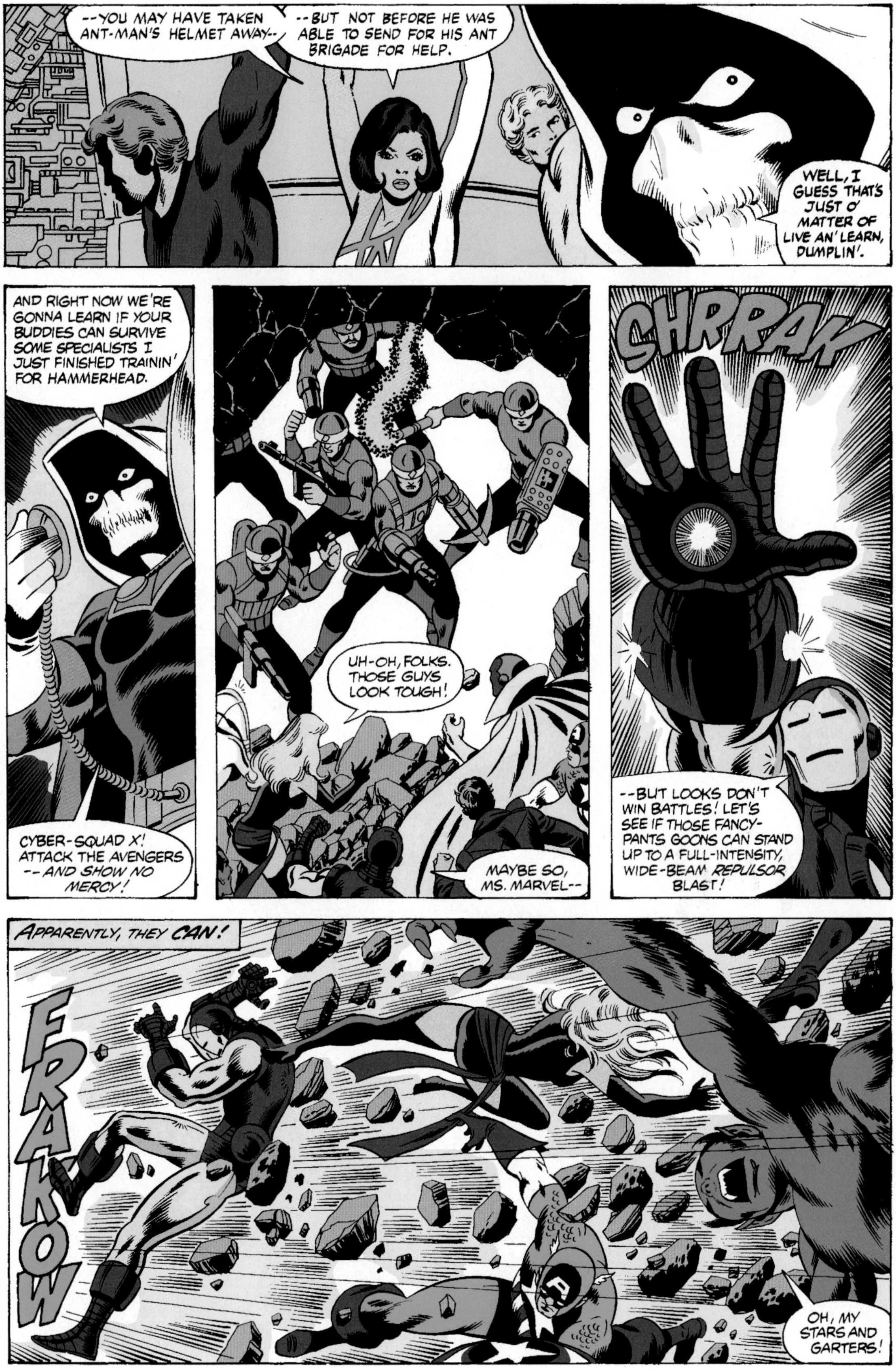
--YOU MAY HAVE TAKEN ANT-MAN'S HELMET AWAY--
--BUT NOT BEFORE HE WAS ABLE TO SEND FOR HIS ANT BRIGADE FOR HELP.
WELL, I GUESS THAT'S JUST O' MATTER OF LIVE AN' LEARN, DUMPLIN'.
AND RIGHT NOW WE'RE GONNA LEARN IF YOUR BUDDIES CAN SURVIVE SOME SPECIALISTS I JUST FINISHED TRAININ' FOR HAMMERHEAD.
CYBER-SQUAD X! ATTACK THE AVENGERS --AND SHOW NO MERCY!
UH-OH, FOLKS. THOSE GUYS LOOK TOUGH!
MAYBE SO, MS. MARVEL--
SHRRAK
--BUT LOOKS DON'T WIN BATTLES! LET'S SEE IF THOSE FANCY-PANTS GOONS CAN STAND UP TO A FULL-INTENSITY, WIDE-BEAM REPULSOR BLAST!
APPARENTLY, THEY CAN!
FRAKOW
OH, MY STARS AND GARTERS!

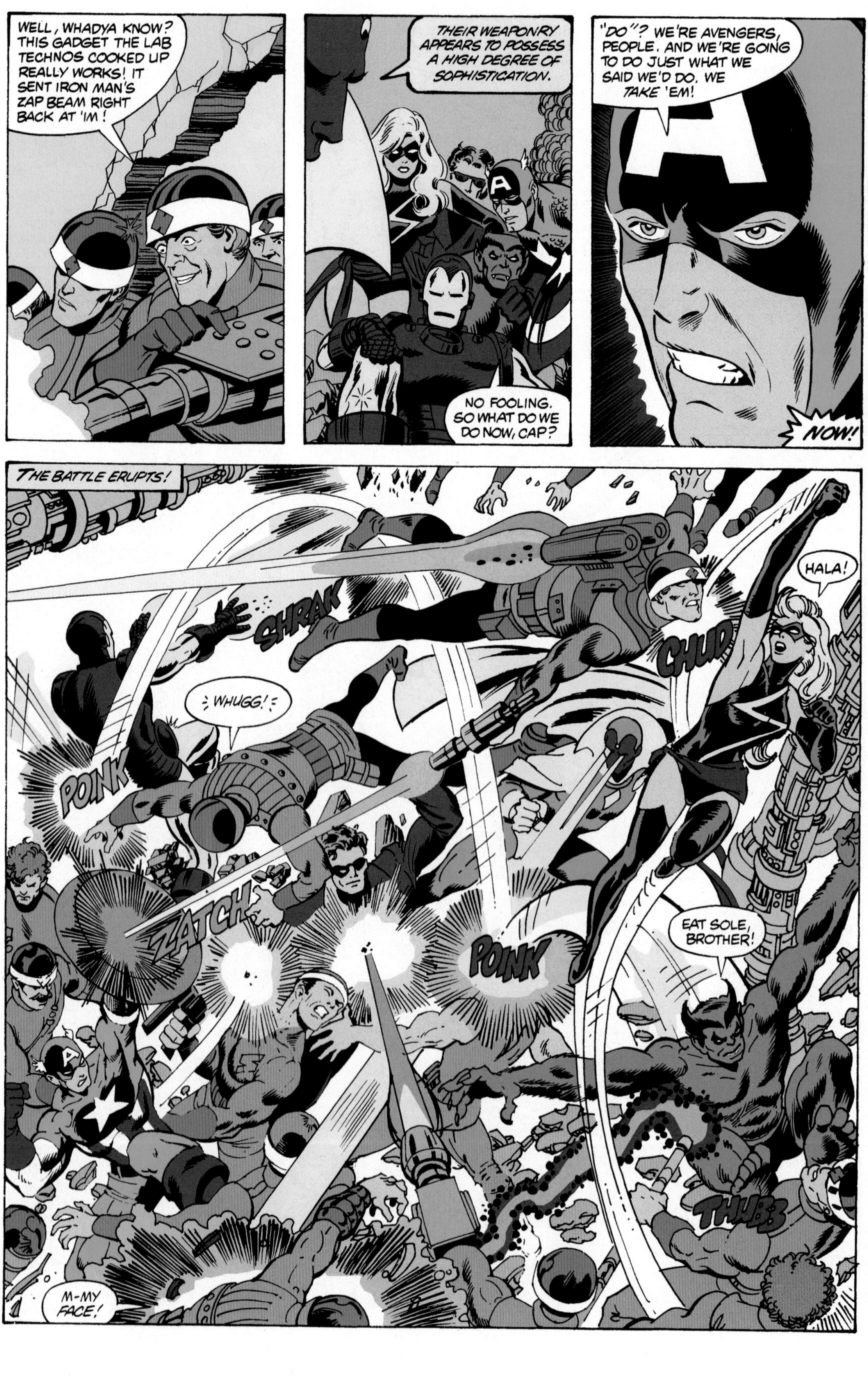
WELL, WHADYA KNOW? THIS GADGET THE LAB TECHNOS COOKED UP REALLY WORKS! IT SENT IRON MAN'S ZAP BEAM RIGHT BACK AT 'IM!
THEIR WEAPONRY APPEARS TO POSSESS A HIGH DEGREE OF SOPHISTICATION.
NO FOOLING. SO WHAT DO WE DO NOW, CAP?
"DO"? WE'RE AVENGERS, PEOPLE. AND WE'RE GOING TO DO JUST WHAT WE SAID WE'D DO. WE TAKE 'EM!
NOW!
THE BATTLE ERUPTS!
HALA!
SHRAK
CHUD
WHUGG!
POINK
ZATCH
POINK
EAT SOLE, BROTHER!
THUBB
M-MY FACE!

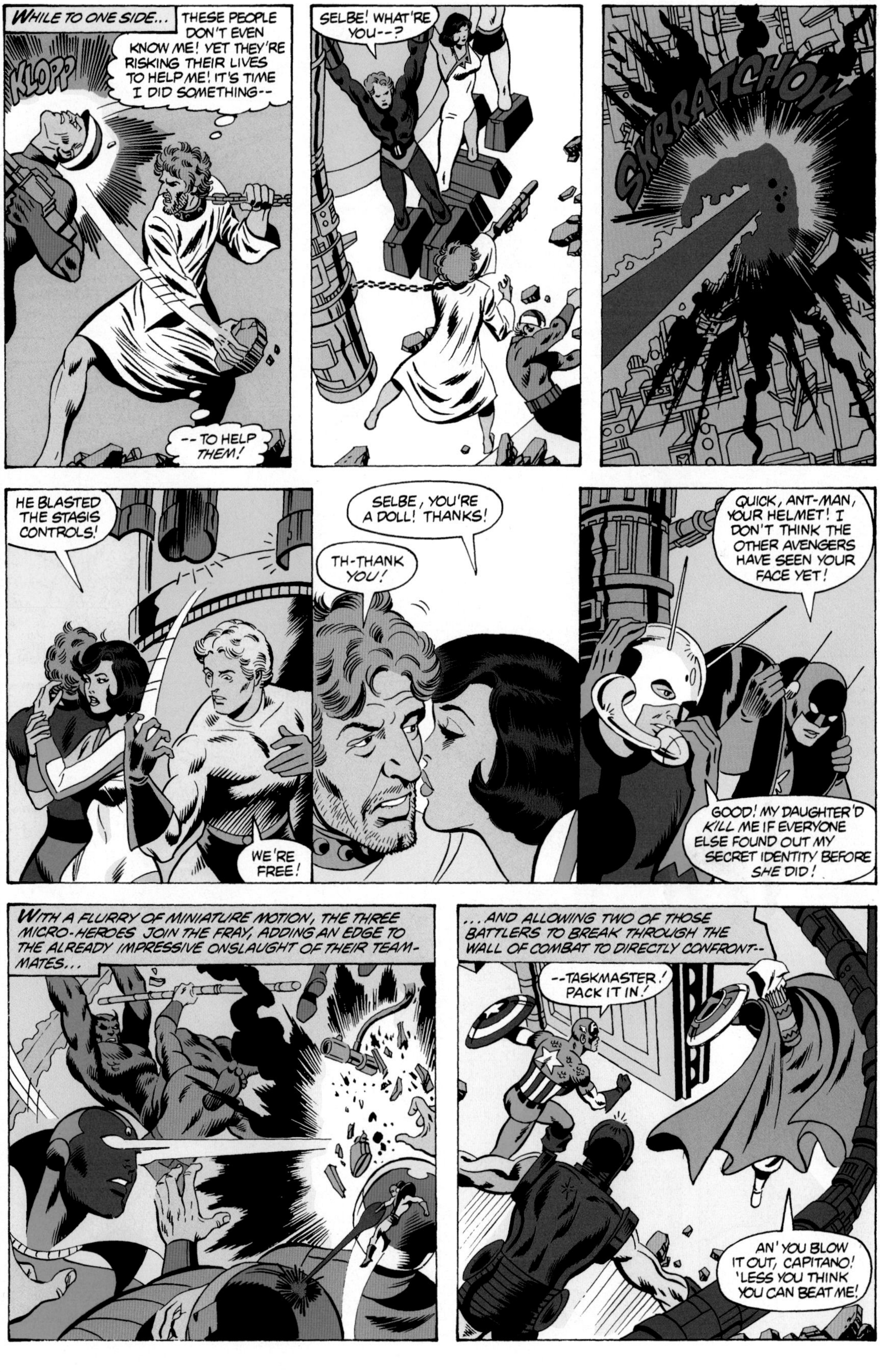

WHILE TO ONE SIDE...
THESE PEOPLE DON'T EVEN KNOW ME! YET THEY'RE RISKING THEIR LIVES TO HELP ME! IT'S TIME I DID SOMETHING--
KLOPP
--TO HELP THEM!
SELBE! WHAT'RE YOU--?
SKRRATCHOW
HE BLASTED THE STASIS CONTROLS!
WE'RE FREE!
SELBE, YOU'RE A DOLL! THANKS!
TH-THANK YOU!
QUICK, ANT-MAN, YOUR HELMET! I DON'T THINK THE OTHER AVENGERS HAVE SEEN YOUR FACE YET!
GOOD! MY DAUGHTER'D KILL ME IF EVERYONE ELSE FOUND OUT MY SECRET IDENTITY BEFORE SHE DID!
WITH A FLURRY OF MINIATURE MOTION, THE THREE MICRO-HEROES JOIN THE FRAY, ADDING AN EDGE TO THE ALREADY IMPRESSIVE ONSLAUGHT OF THEIR TEAM-MATES...
...AND ALLOWING TWO OF THOSE BATTLERS TO BREAK THROUGH THE WALL OF COMBAT TO DIRECTLY CONFRONT--
--TASKMASTER! PACK IT IN!
AN' YOU BLOW IT OUT, CAPITANO! 'LESS YOU THINK YOU CAN BEAT ME!

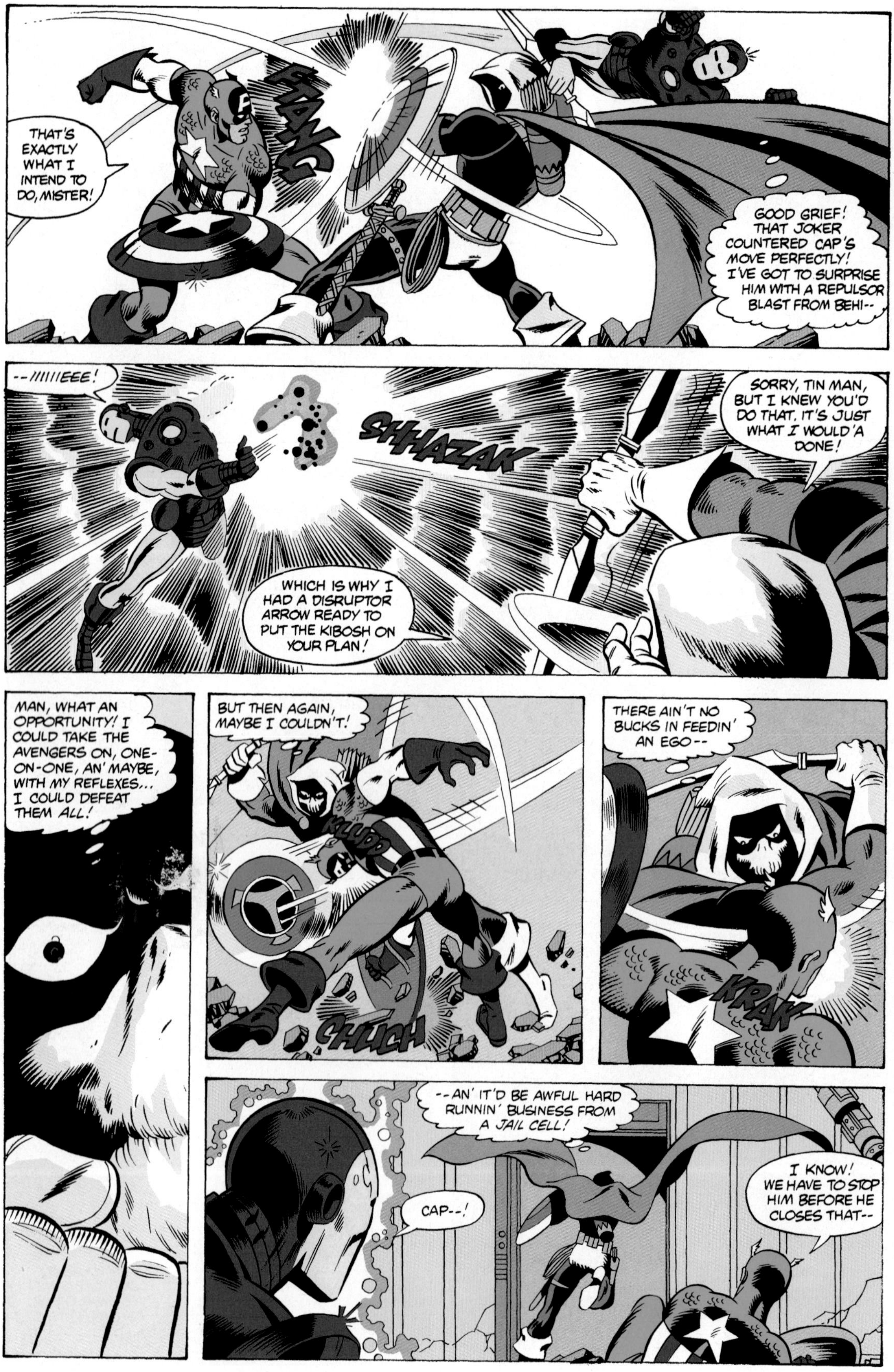

THAT'S EXACTLY WHAT I INTEND TO DO, MISTER!
GOOD GRIEF! THAT JOKER COUNTERED CAP'S MOVE PERFECTLY! I'VE GOT TO SURPRISE HIM WITH A REPULSOR BLAST FROM BEHI--
--!!!!!EEE!
SHHAZAK
SORRY, TIN MAN, BUT I KNEW YOU'D DO THAT. IT'S JUST WHAT I WOULD'A DONE!
WHICH IS WHY I HAD A DISRUPTOR ARROW READY TO PUT THE KIBOSH ON YOUR PLAN!
MAN, WHAT AN OPPORTUNITY! I COULD TAKE THE AVENGERS ON, ONE-ON-ONE, AN' MAYBE, WITH MY REFLEXES... I COULD DEFEAT THEM ALL!
BUT THEN AGAIN, MAYBE I COULDN'T!
CHUCH
THERE AIN'T NO BUCKS IN FEEDIN' AN EGO--
KRAK
--AN' IT'D BE AWFUL HARD RUNNIN' BUSINESS FROM A JAIL CELL!
CAP--!
I KNOW! WE HAVE TO STOP HIM BEFORE HE CLOSES THAT--

--DOOR.

KARREEEBANG

GOTTA GET TO CENTRAL CONTROL, FLOOD THIS PLACE WITH SLEEP GAS! THAT'LL DROP EVERYONE BUT IRON MAN AN' THE VISION!

THEN I CAN--

--HUH? A METAL WOMAN?!

THE NAME'S JOCASTA, FRIEND.

AND THE ONLY WAY YOU'RE GETTING PAST ME IS OVER MY DEACTIVATED BODY!

THAT'S FINE BY ME, BIMBO!

'CAUSE ONE SWIPE O' MY ALLOY SHIELD'S GONNA CUT YOU IN--

--WHAT?! SHE'S THROWIN' UP A FORCE FIELD ALL AROUND 'ER!

FTING

MY, LOOKS AND BRAINS. WHAT A RARE COMBINATION.

KVHZZZZ

JUST KEEP LAUGHIN', BABYBUNS. AFTER THIS ELECTRO-SHAFT SHORTS OUT YOUR DEFENSE FIELD, WE'LL SEE HOW--

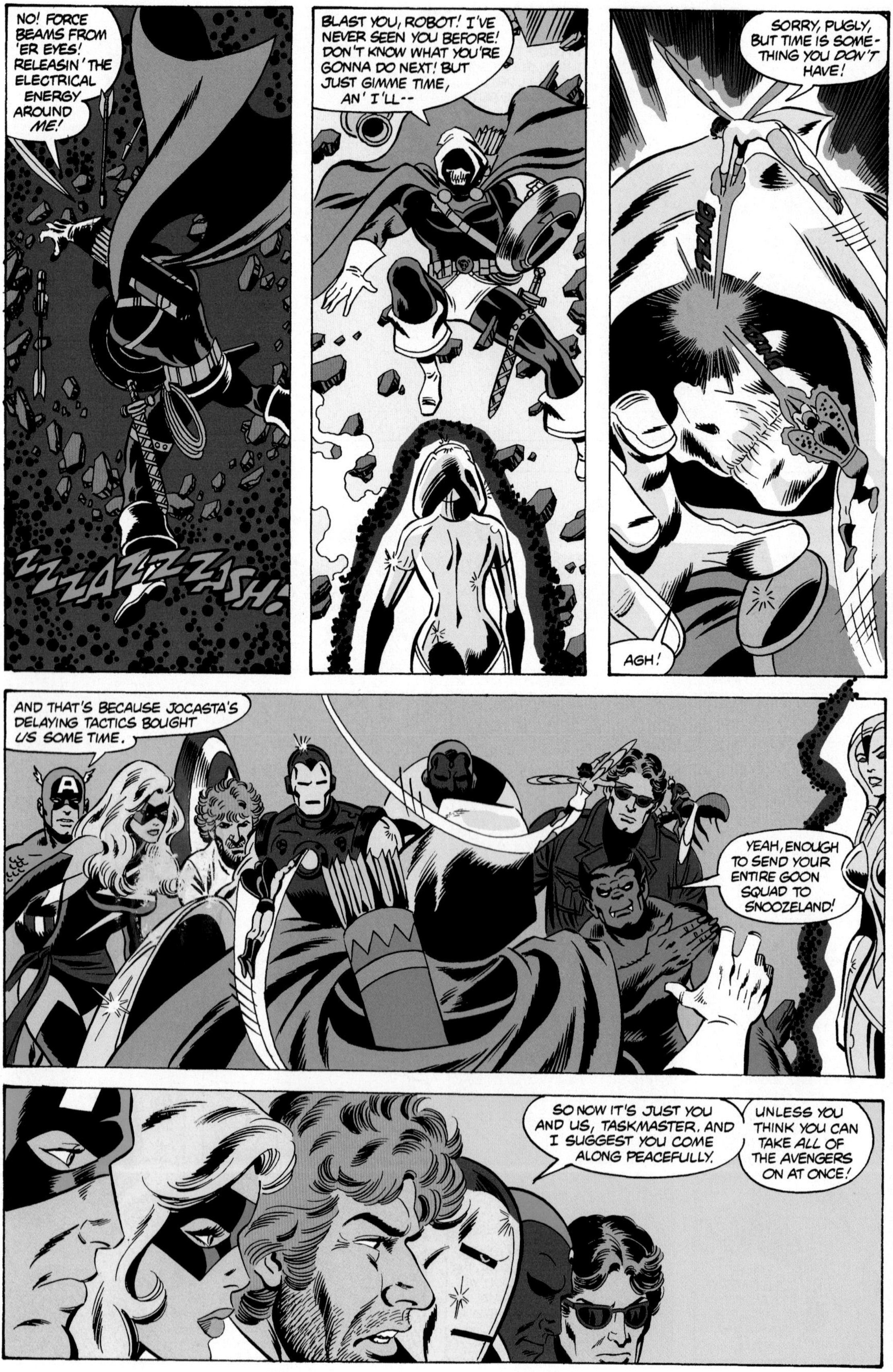
NO! FORCE BEAMS FROM 'ER EYES! RELEASIN' THE ELECTRICAL ENERGY AROUND ME!
ZZZAZZZZASH!
BLAST YOU, ROBOT! I'VE NEVER SEEN YOU BEFORE! DON'T KNOW WHAT YOU'RE GONNA DO NEXT! BUT JUST GIMME TIME, AN' I'LL--
SORRY, PUGLY, BUT TIME IS SOMETHING YOU DON'T HAVE!
THUNG
AGH!
AND THAT'S BECAUSE JOCASTA'S DELAYING TACTICS BOUGHT US SOME TIME.
YEAH, ENOUGH TO SEND YOUR ENTIRE GOON SQUAD TO SNOOZELAND!
SO NOW IT'S JUST YOU AND US, TASKMASTER, AND I SUGGEST YOU COME ALONG PEACEFULLY.
UNLESS YOU THINK YOU CAN TAKE ALL OF THE AVENGERS ON AT ONCE!

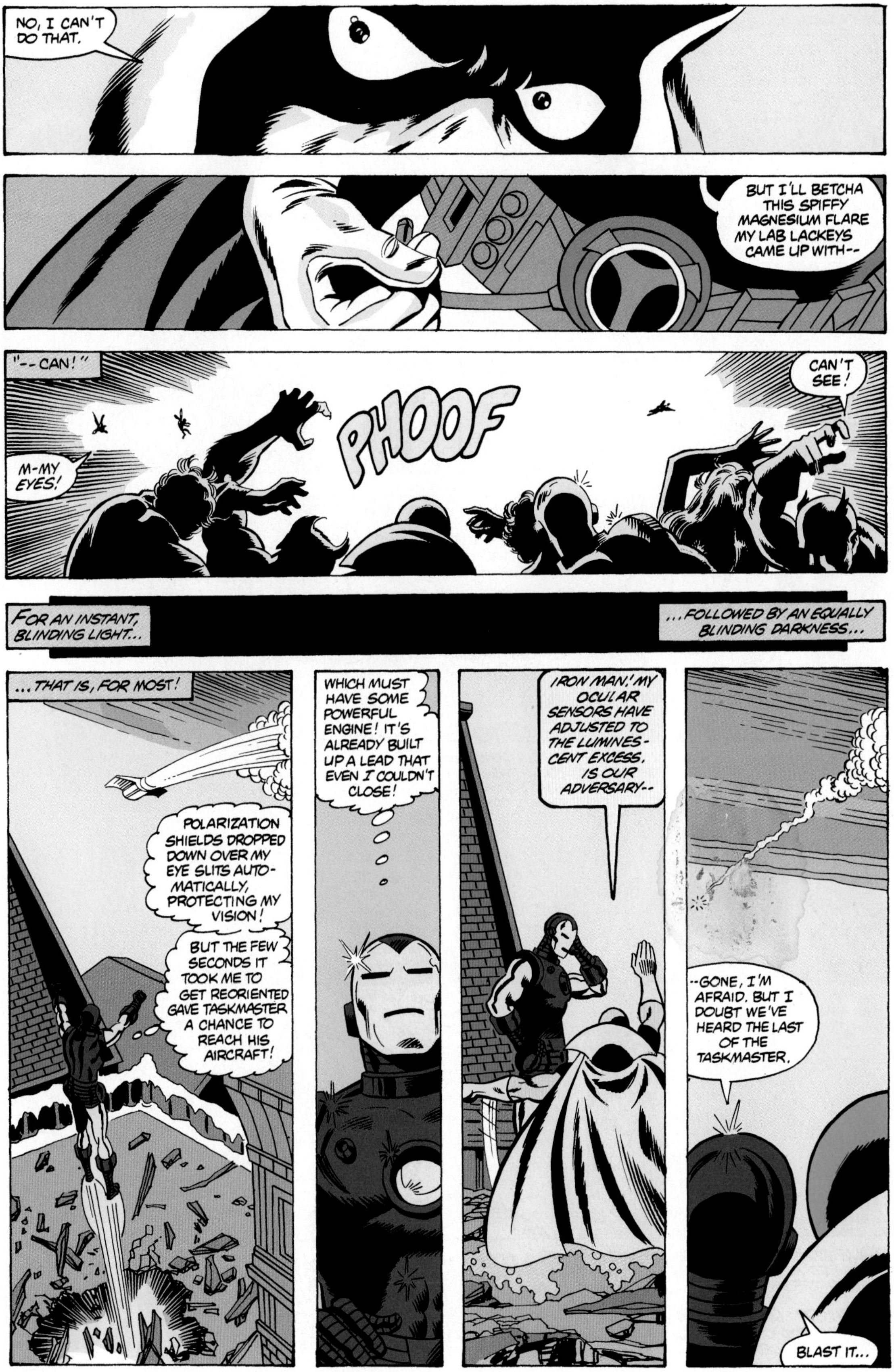
NO, I CAN'T DO THAT.
BUT I'LL BETCHA THIS SPIFFY MAGNESIUM FLARE MY LAB LACKEYS CAME UP WITH--
"--CAN!"
CAN'T SEE!
PHOOF
M-MY EYES!
FOR AN INSTANT, BLINDING LIGHT...
...FOLLOWED BY AN EQUALLY BLINDING DARKNESS...
...THAT IS, FOR MOST!
POLARIZATION SHIELDS DROPPED DOWN OVER MY EYE SLITS AUTOMATICALLY, PROTECTING MY VISION!
BUT THE FEW SECONDS IT TOOK ME TO GET REORIENTED GAVE TASKMASTER A CHANCE TO REACH HIS AIRCRAFT!
WHICH MUST HAVE SOME POWERFUL ENGINE! IT'S ALREADY BUILT UP A LEAD THAT EVEN I COULDN'T CLOSE!
IRON MAN! MY OCULAR SENSORS HAVE ADJUSTED TO THE LUMINESCENT EXCESS. IS OUR ADVERSARY--
--GONE, I'M AFRAID. BUT I DOUBT WE'VE HEARD THE LAST OF THE TASKMASTER.
BLAST IT...

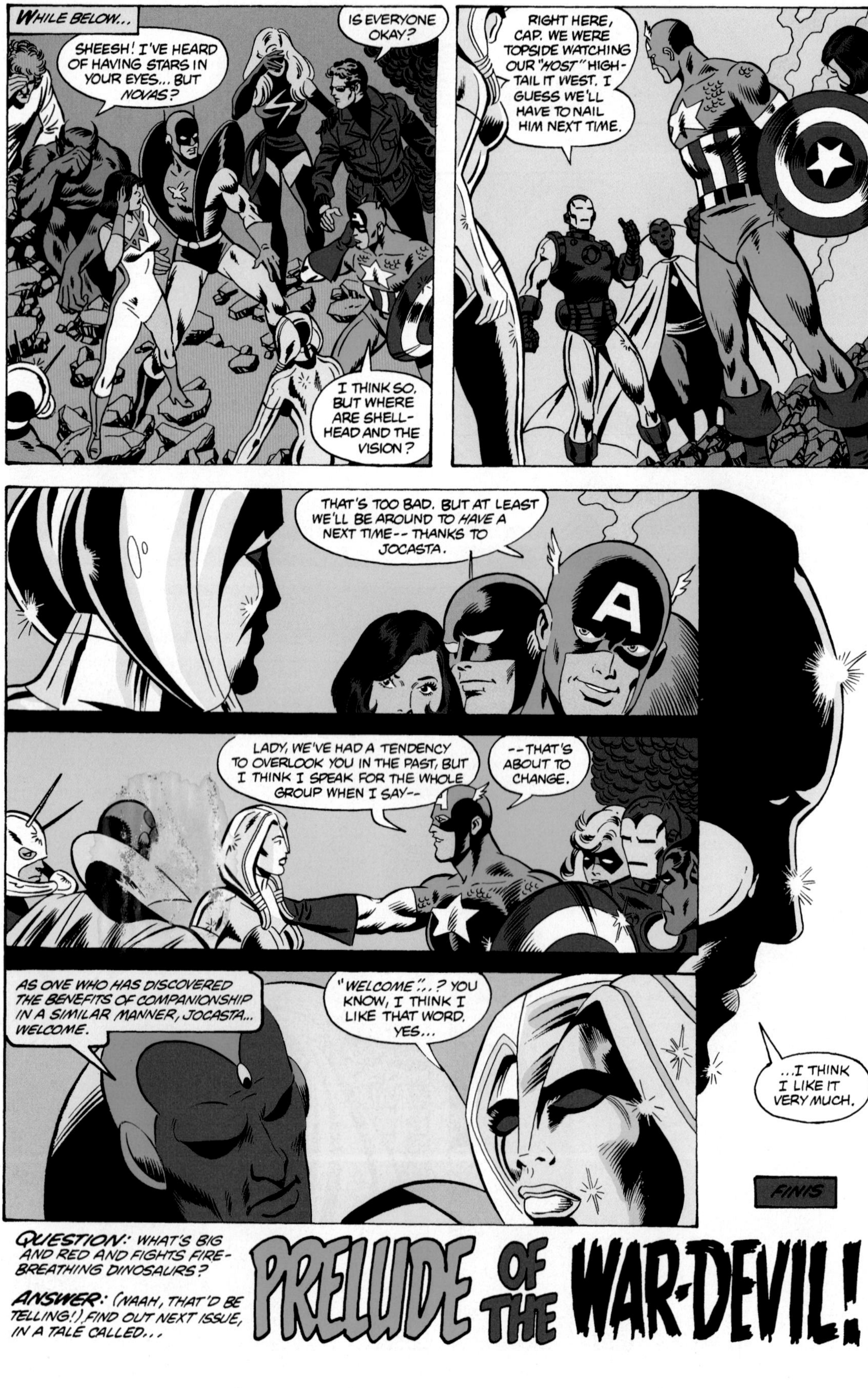
WHILE BELOW...
SHEESH! I'VE HEARD OF HAVING STARS IN YOUR EYES... BUT NOVAS?
IS EVERYONE OKAY?
I THINK SO, BUT WHERE ARE SHELL-HEAD AND THE VISION?
RIGHT HERE, CAP. WE WERE TOPSIDE WATCHING OUR "HOST" HIGH-TAIL IT WEST. I GUESS WE'LL HAVE TO NAIL HIM NEXT TIME.
THAT'S TOO BAD. BUT AT LEAST WE'LL BE AROUND TO HAVE A NEXT TIME-- THANKS TO JOCASTA.
LADY, WE'VE HAD A TENDENCY TO OVERLOOK YOU IN THE PAST, BUT I THINK I SPEAK FOR THE WHOLE GROUP WHEN I SAY--
--THAT'S ABOUT TO CHANGE.
AS ONE WHO HAS DISCOVERED THE BENEFITS OF COMPANIONSHIP IN A SIMILAR MANNER, JOCASTA... WELCOME.
"WELCOME"...? YOU KNOW, I THINK I LIKE THAT WORD. YES...
...I THINK I LIKE IT VERY MUCH.
FINIS
QUESTION: WHAT'S BIG AND RED AND FIGHTS FIRE-BREATHING DINOSAURS?
ANSWER: (NAAH, THAT'D BE TELLING!) FIND OUT NEXT ISSUE, IN A TALE CALLED...
PRELUDE OF THE WAR-DEVIL!

HANK PYM MAKES THE DISCOVERY OF HIS LIFE WITH THE PYM PARTICLES, TRANSFORMING HIMSELF AND JANET VAN DYNE INTO THE SIZE-SHIFTING HEROES ANT-MAN AND THE WASP!

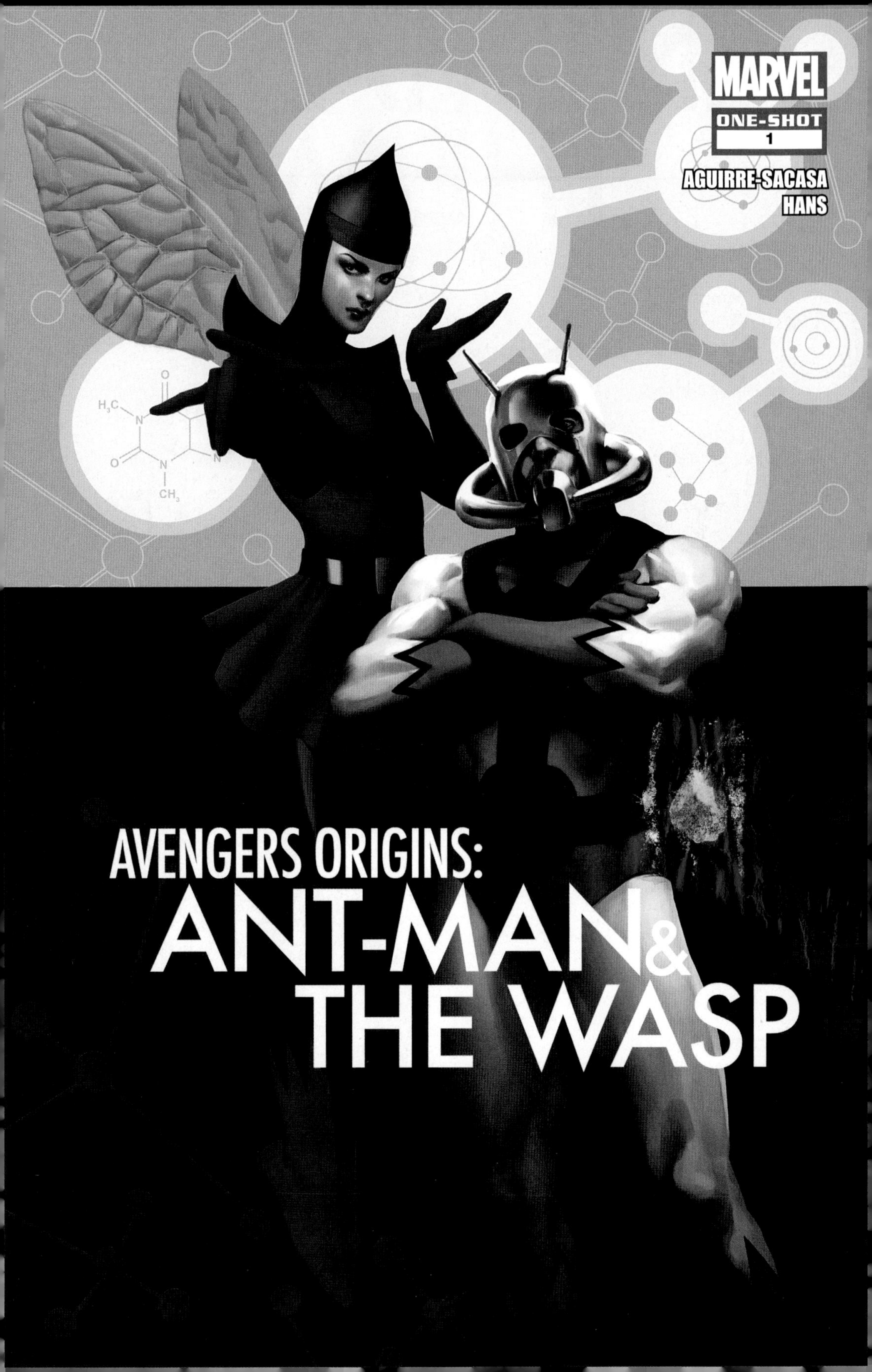
MARVEL
ONE-SHOT
1
AGUIRRE-SACASA
HANS
AVENGERS ORIGINS:
ANT-MAN & THE WASP

AVENGERS ORIGINS:
ANT-MAN & THE WASP

WRITER
ROBERTO AGUIRRE-SACASA

ARTIST
STEPHANIE HANS

LETTERER
DAVE LANPHEAR

COVER
MARKO DJURDJEVIC

PRODUCTION
MANNY MEDEROS

ASSISTANT EDITOR
JOHN DENNING

EDITOR
LAUREN SANKOVITCH

EXECUTIVE EDITOR
T

EDITOR IN CHIEF
AXEL ALONSO

CHIEF CREATIVE OFFICER
JOE QUESADA

PUBLISHER
DAN BUCKLEY

EXECUTIVE PRODUCER
ALAN FINE

Chapter One:

DO INSECTS DREAM?

WE KNOW MEN DO. WE KNOW THIS MAN, HENRY PYM, DOES.

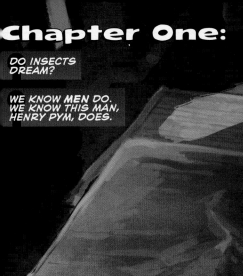

IN THE DREAM THAT RECURS MOST OFTEN, HE IS WITH HIS WIFE, MARIA.

WALKING ALONG THE BANKS OF THE DANUBE, THROUGH BUDAPEST'S OLDEST NEIGHBORHOOD.

HE IS THINKING HOW STUPID HE'D BEEN TO WORRY ABOUT COMING TO HUNGARY FOR THEIR HONEY-MOON.

YES, MARIA AND HER FATHER HAD POLITICAL ENEMIES, BUT THAT WAS YEARS AGO.

HE IS THINKING WHAT THE QUICKEST ROUTE BACK TO THEIR HOTEL MIGHT BE...

...WHEN THE CAR SCREECHES TO A HALT IN FRONT OF THEM.

THIS IS WHAT HAPPENS TO THOSE WHO ATTEMPT TO ESCAPE US!

IT'S A DREAM, SO HENRY PYM CAN DO NOTHING.

BLAMM! BLAMM! BLAMM!

HE WAKES, INVARIABLY, COATED IN SWEAT.

NO MORE SLEEP FOR HENRY PYM TONIGHT...

ANYWAY, IT'S ALMOST DAWN, AND HE HAS HIS PRESENTATION TODAY.

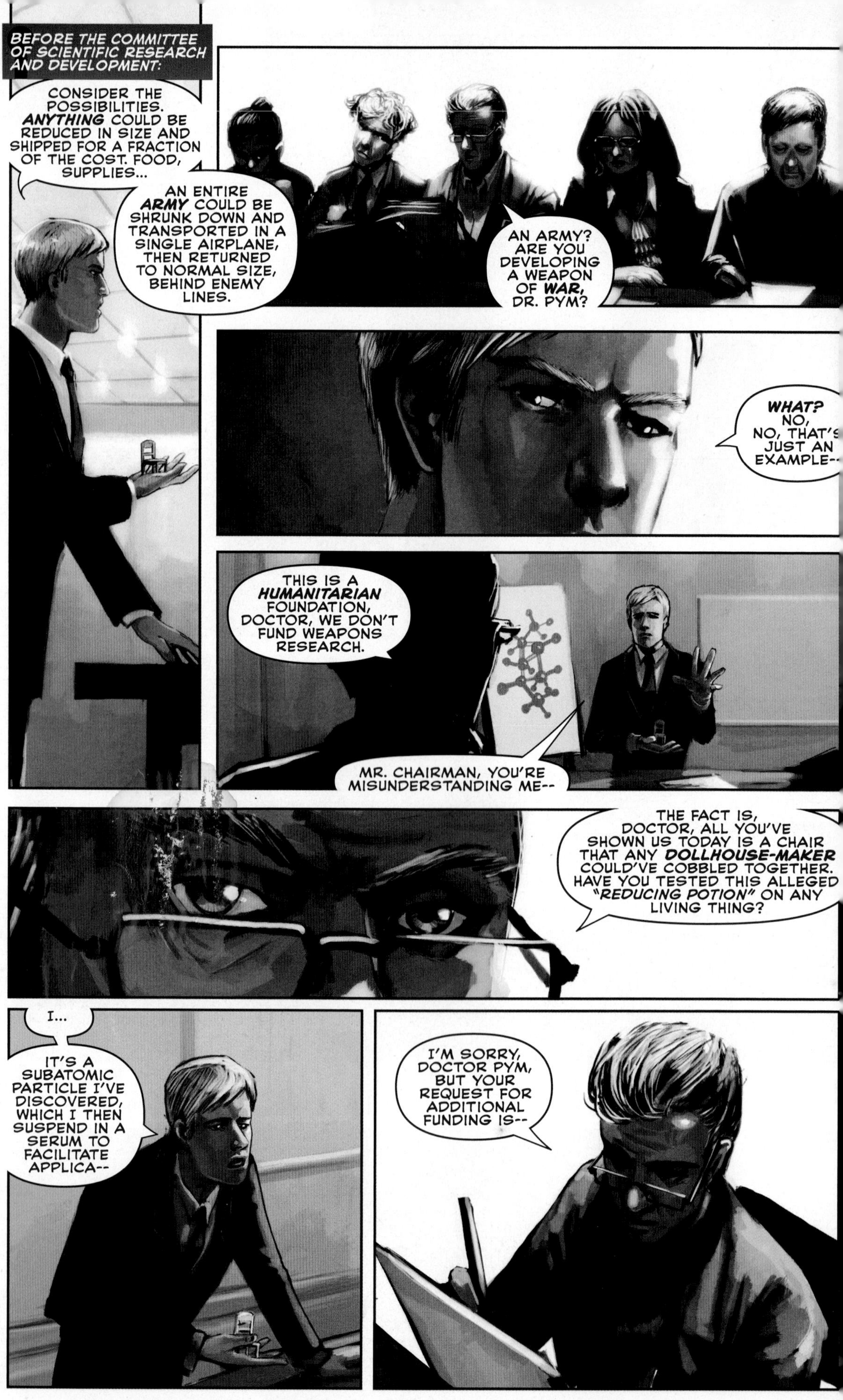
BEFORE THE COMMITTEE OF SCIENTIFIC RESEARCH AND DEVELOPMENT:
CONSIDER THE POSSIBILITIES. ANYTHING COULD BE REDUCED IN SIZE AND SHIPPED FOR A FRACTION OF THE COST. FOOD, SUPPLIES...
AN ENTIRE ARMY COULD BE SHRUNK DOWN AND TRANSPORTED IN A SINGLE AIRPLANE, THEN RETURNED TO NORMAL SIZE, BEHIND ENEMY LINES.
AN ARMY? ARE YOU DEVELOPING A WEAPON OF WAR, DR. PYM?
WHAT? NO, NO, THAT'S JUST AN EXAMPLE--
THIS IS A HUMANITARIAN FOUNDATION, DOCTOR, WE DON'T FUND WEAPONS RESEARCH.
MR. CHAIRMAN, YOU'RE MISUNDERSTANDING ME--
THE FACT IS, DOCTOR, ALL YOU'VE SHOWN US TODAY IS A CHAIR THAT ANY DOLLHOUSE-MAKER COULD'VE COBBLED TOGETHER. HAVE YOU TESTED THIS ALLEGED "REDUCING POTION" ON ANY LIVING THING?
I...
IT'S A SUBATOMIC PARTICLE I'VE DISCOVERED, WHICH I THEN SUSPEND IN A SERUM TO FACILITATE APPLICA--
I'M SORRY, DOCTOR PYM, BUT YOUR REQUEST FOR ADDITIONAL FUNDING IS--

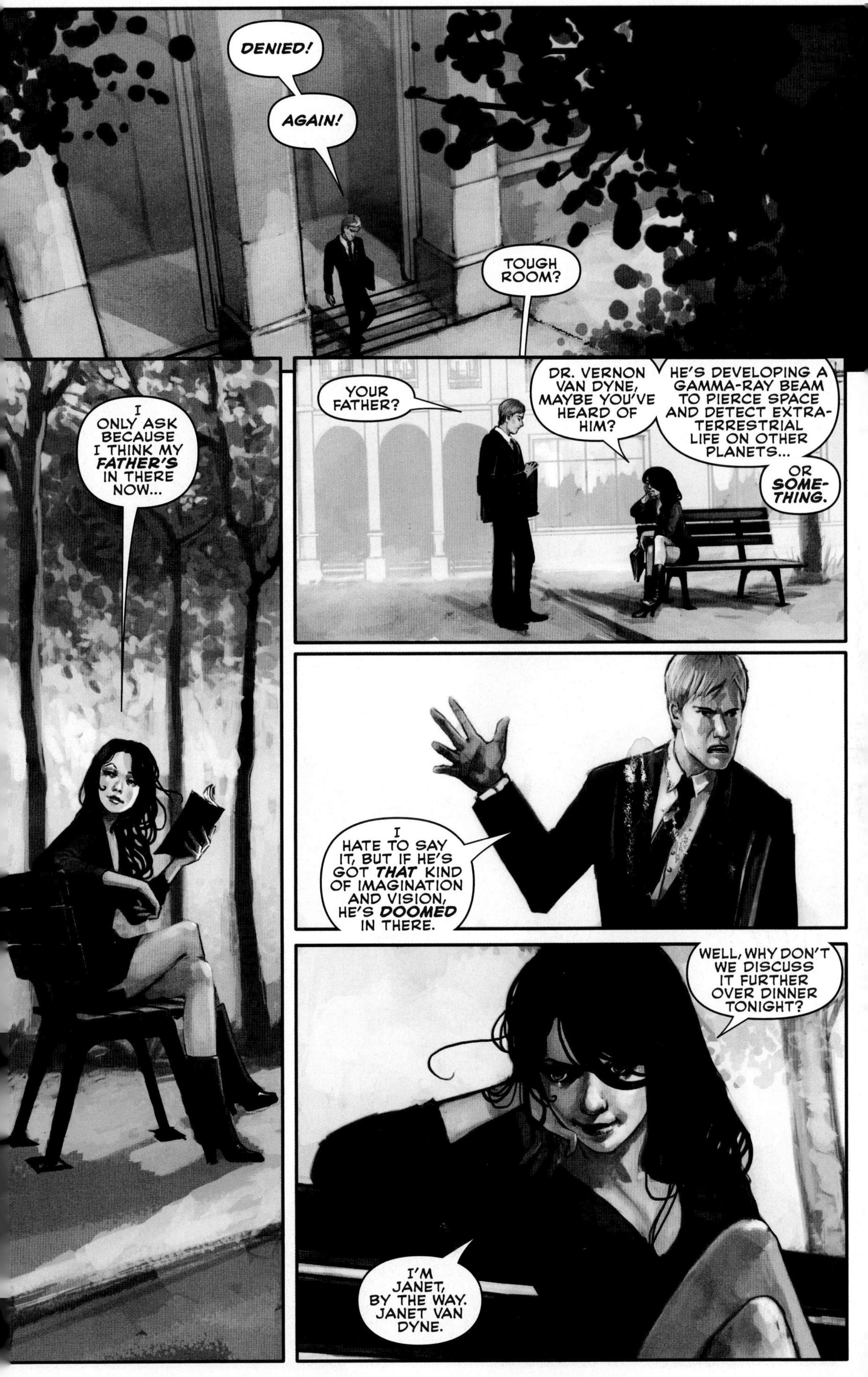
DENIED!
AGAIN!
TOUGH ROOM?
I ONLY ASK BECAUSE I THINK MY FATHER'S IN THERE NOW...
YOUR FATHER?
DR. VERNON VAN DYNE, MAYBE YOU'VE HEARD OF HIM?
HE'S DEVELOPING A GAMMA-RAY BEAM TO PIERCE SPACE AND DETECT EXTRA-TERRESTRIAL LIFE ON OTHER PLANETS...
OR SOME-THING.
I HATE TO SAY IT, BUT IF HE'S GOT THAT KIND OF IMAGINATION AND VISION, HE'S DOOMED IN THERE.
WELL, WHY DON'T WE DISCUSS IT FURTHER OVER DINNER TONIGHT?
I'M JANET, BY THE WAY. JANET VAN DYNE.

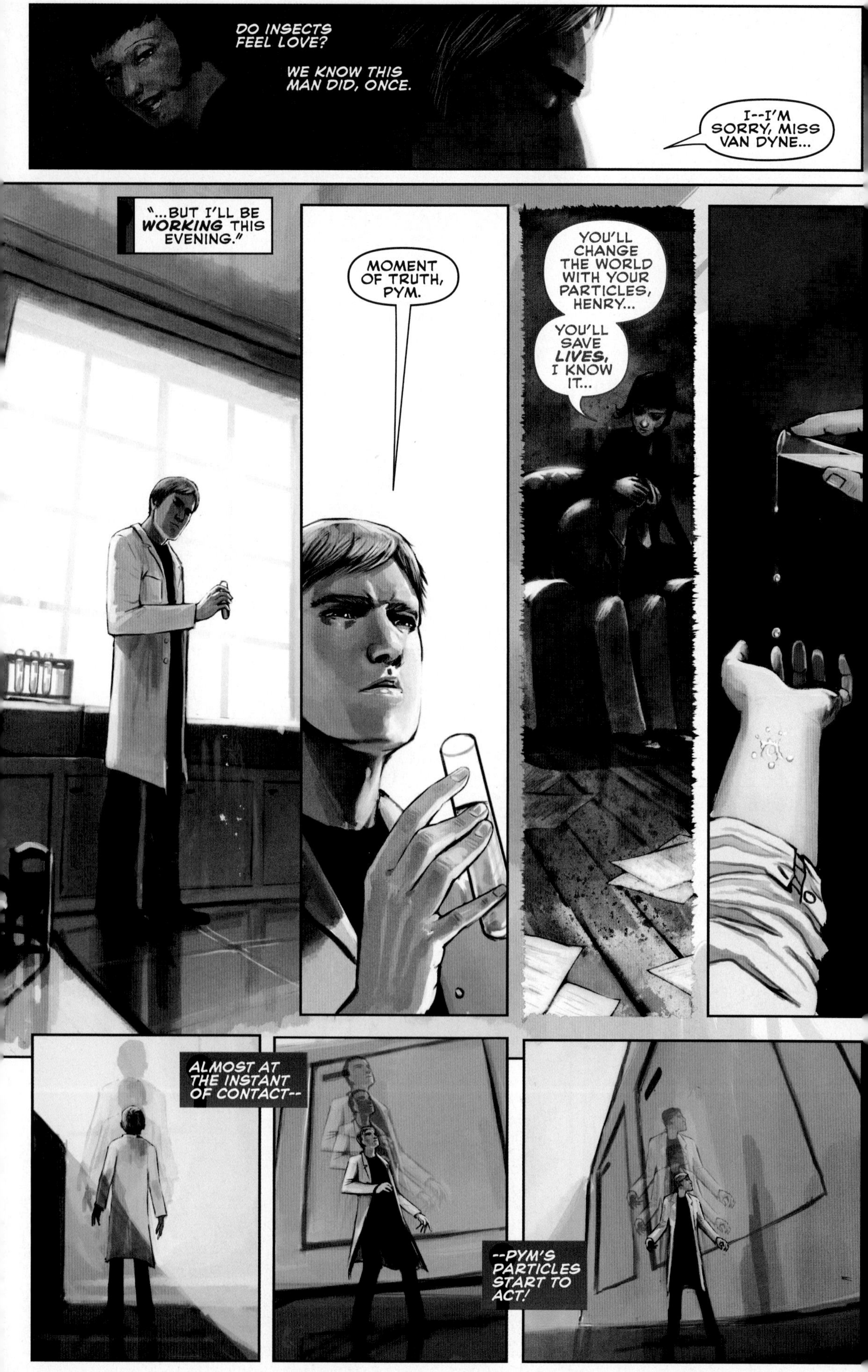
DO INSECTS FEEL LOVE?
WE KNOW THIS MAN DID, ONCE.
I--I'M SORRY, MISS VAN DYNE...
"...BUT I'LL BE WORKING THIS EVENING."
MOMENT OF TRUTH, PYM.
YOU'LL CHANGE THE WORLD WITH YOUR PARTICLES, HENRY...
YOU'LL SAVE LIVES, I KNOW IT...
ALMOST AT THE INSTANT OF CONTACT--
--PYM'S PARTICLES START TO ACT!

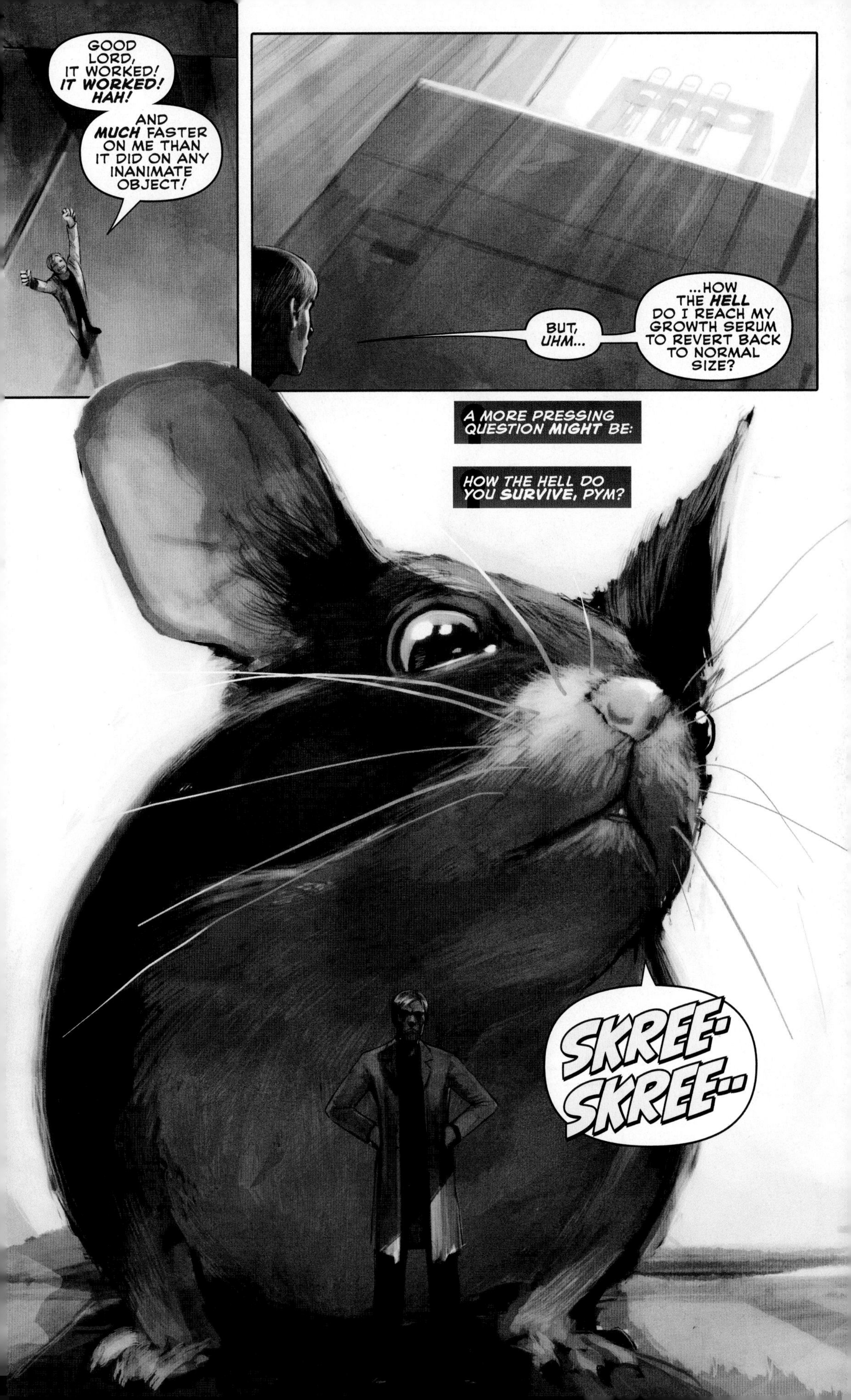
GOOD LORD, IT WORKED! IT WORKED! HAH!
AND MUCH FASTER ON ME THAN IT DID ON ANY INANIMATE OBJECT!
BUT, UHM...
...HOW THE HELL DO I REACH MY GROWTH SERUM TO REVERT BACK TO NORMAL SIZE?
A MORE PRESSING QUESTION MIGHT BE:
HOW THE HELL DO YOU SURVIVE, PYM?
SKREE-SKREE..

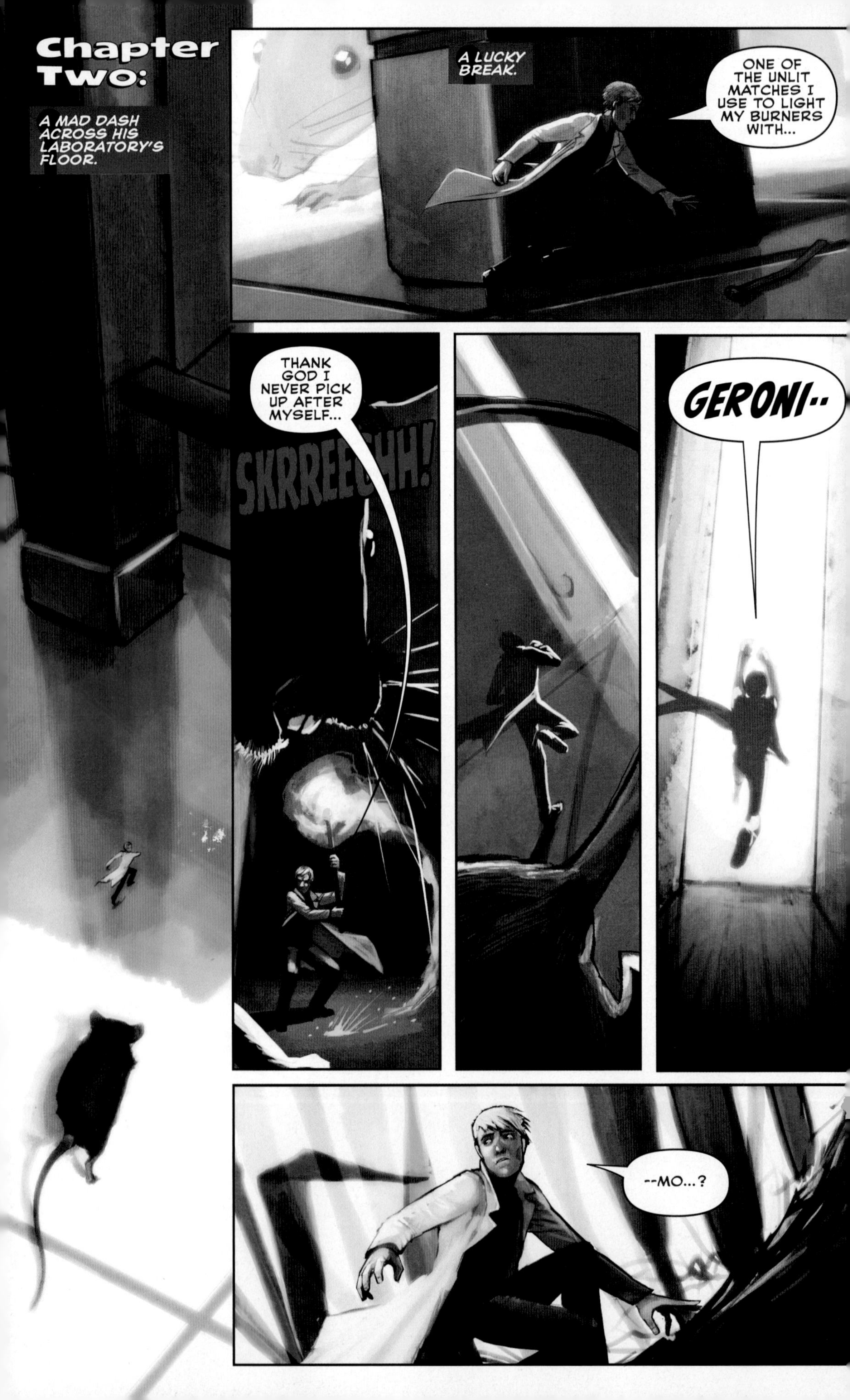
Chapter Two:
A MAD DASH ACROSS HIS LABORATORY'S FLOOR.
A LUCKY BREAK.
ONE OF THE UNLIT MATCHES I USE TO LIGHT MY BURNERS WITH...
THANK GOD I NEVER PICK UP AFTER MYSELF...
SKRREECHH!
GERONI..
--MO...?

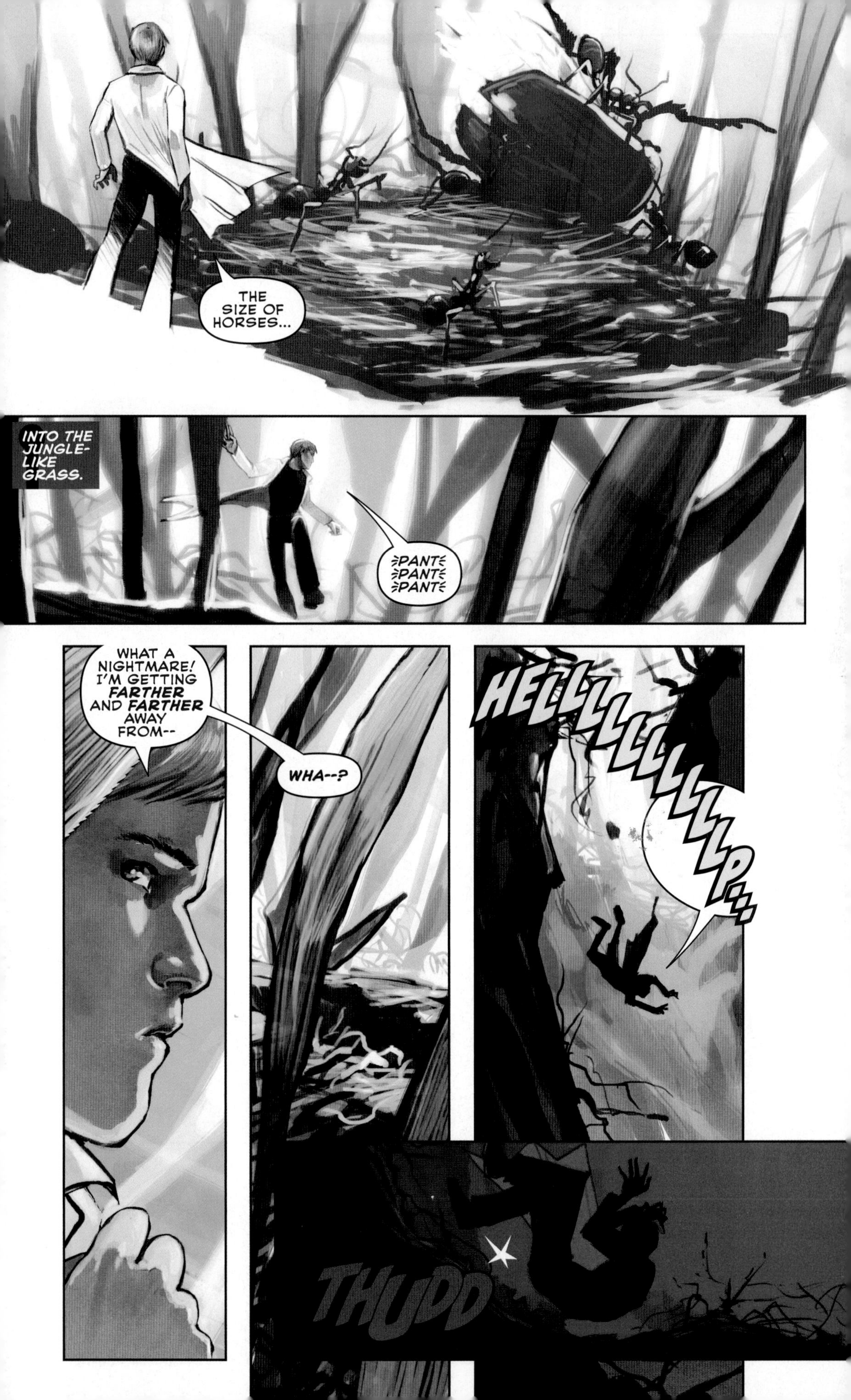
THE SIZE OF HORSES...
INTO THE JUNGLE-LIKE GRASS.
PANT PANT PANT
WHAT A NIGHTMARE! I'M GETTING FARTHER AND FARTHER AWAY FROM--
WHA--?
HELLLLLLLLLP...
THUDD

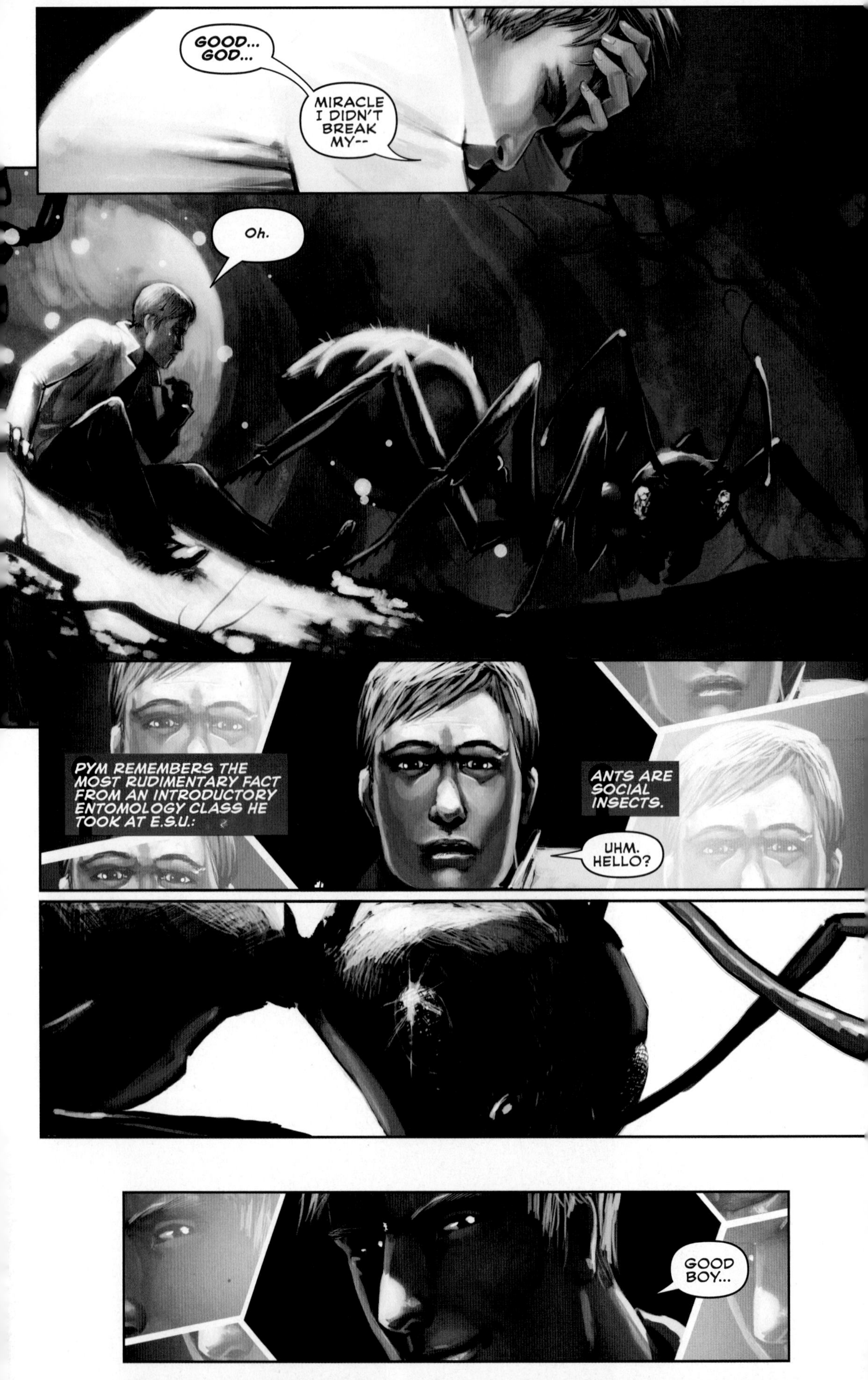
GOOD... GOD...
MIRACLE I DIDN'T BREAK MY--
Oh.
PYM REMEMBERS THE MOST RUDIMENTARY FACT FROM AN INTRODUCTORY ENTOMOLOGY CLASS HE TOOK AT E.S.U.:
ANTS ARE SOCIAL INSECTS.
UHM. HELLO?
GOOD BOY...

Chapter Three:

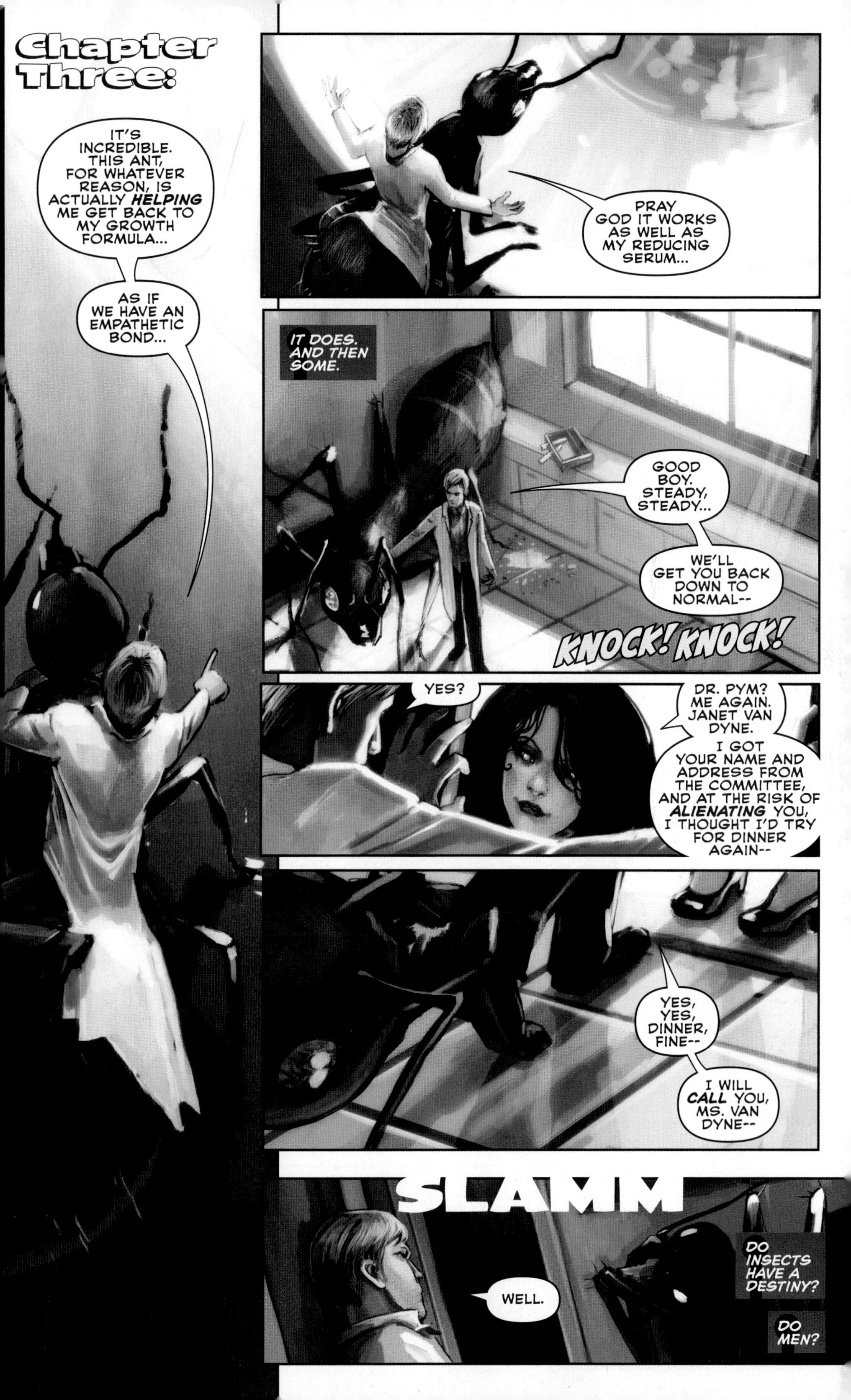

IT'S INCREDIBLE. THIS ANT, FOR WHATEVER REASON, IS ACTUALLY *HELPING* ME GET BACK TO MY GROWTH FORMULA...
PRAY GOD IT WORKS AS WELL AS MY REDUCING SERUM...
AS IF WE HAVE AN EMPATHETIC BOND...
IT DOES. AND THEN SOME.
GOOD BOY. STEADY, STEADY...
WE'LL GET YOU BACK DOWN TO NORMAL--
KNOCK! KNOCK!
YES?
DR. PYM? ME AGAIN. JANET VAN DYNE.
I GOT YOUR NAME AND ADDRESS FROM THE COMMITTEE, AND AT THE RISK OF *ALIENATING* YOU, I THOUGHT I'D TRY FOR DINNER AGAIN--
YES, YES, DINNER, FINE--
I WILL *CALL* YOU, MS. VAN DYNE--
SLAMM
WELL.
DO INSECTS HAVE A DESTINY?
DO MEN?

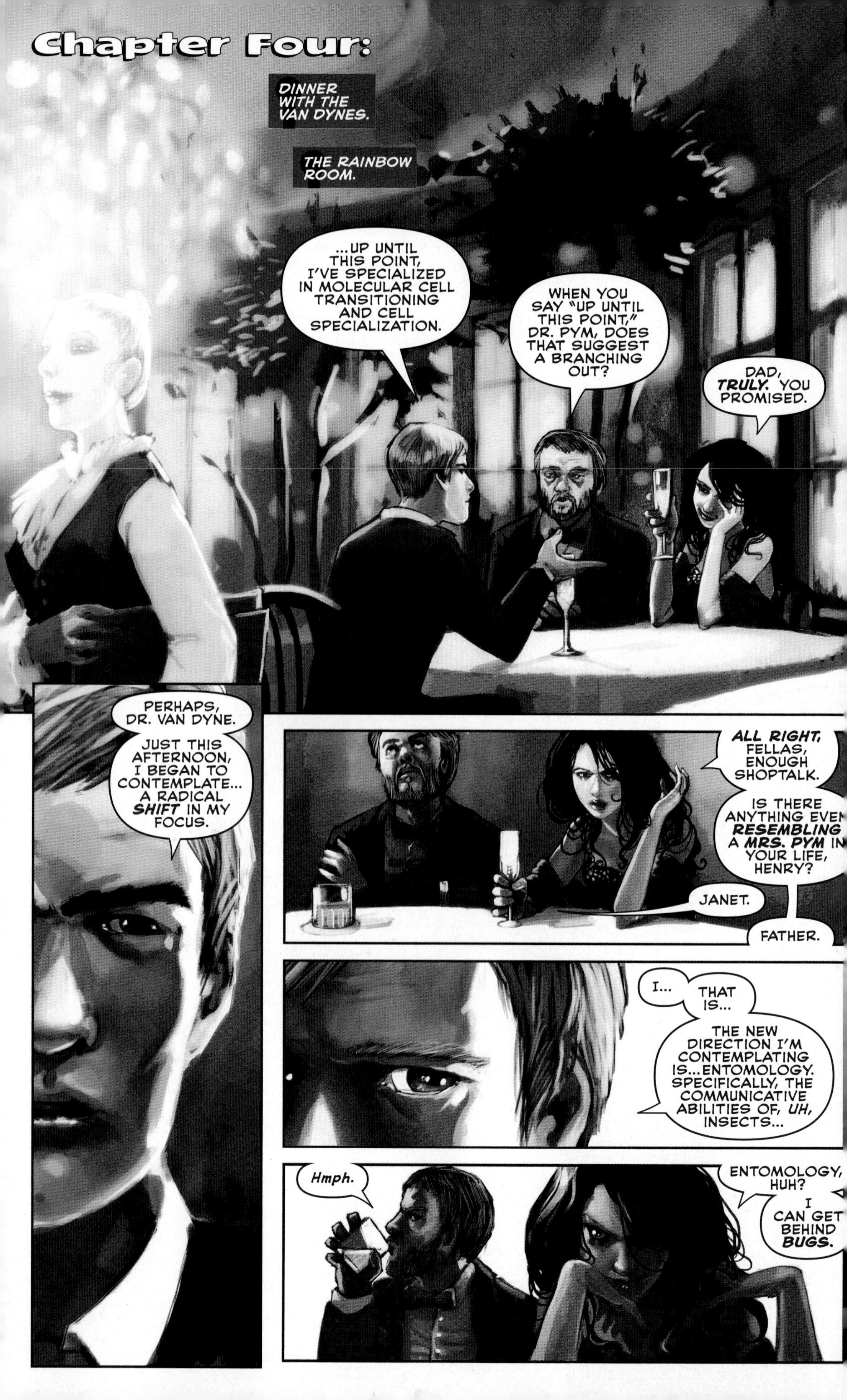

Chapter Four:
DINNER WITH THE VAN DYNES.
THE RAINBOW ROOM.
...UP UNTIL THIS POINT, I'VE SPECIALIZED IN MOLECULAR CELL TRANSITIONING AND CELL SPECIALIZATION.
WHEN YOU SAY "UP UNTIL THIS POINT," DR. PYM, DOES THAT SUGGEST A BRANCHING OUT?
DAD, TRULY. YOU PROMISED.
PERHAPS, DR. VAN DYNE.
JUST THIS AFTERNOON, I BEGAN TO CONTEMPLATE... A RADICAL SHIFT IN MY FOCUS.
ALL RIGHT, FELLAS, ENOUGH SHOPTALK.
IS THERE ANYTHING EVEN RESEMBLING A MRS. PYM IN YOUR LIFE, HENRY?
JANET.
FATHER.
I...
THAT IS...
THE NEW DIRECTION I'M CONTEMPLATING IS...ENTOMOLOGY. SPECIFICALLY, THE COMMUNICATIVE ABILITIES OF, UH, INSECTS...
Hmph.
ENTOMOLOGY, HUH?
I CAN GET BEHIND BUGS.

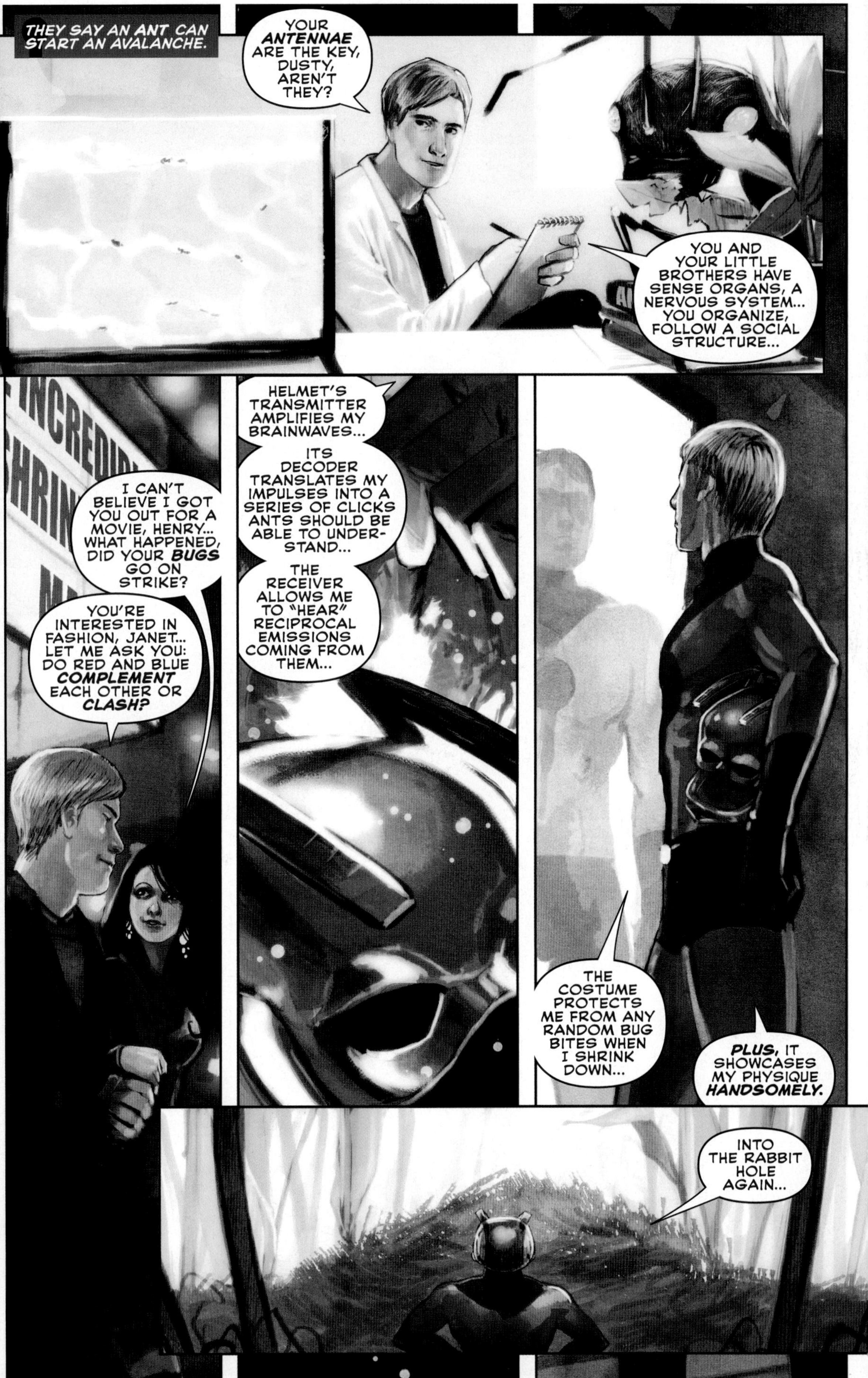
THEY SAY AN ANT CAN START AN AVALANCHE.
YOUR ANTENNAE ARE THE KEY, DUSTY, AREN'T THEY?
YOU AND YOUR LITTLE BROTHERS HAVE SENSE ORGANS, A NERVOUS SYSTEM... YOU ORGANIZE, FOLLOW A SOCIAL STRUCTURE...
I CAN'T BELIEVE I GOT YOU OUT FOR A MOVIE, HENRY... WHAT HAPPENED, DID YOUR BUGS GO ON STRIKE?
YOU'RE INTERESTED IN FASHION, JANET... LET ME ASK YOU: DO RED AND BLUE COMPLEMENT EACH OTHER OR CLASH?
HELMET'S TRANSMITTER AMPLIFIES MY BRAINWAVES...
ITS DECODER TRANSLATES MY IMPULSES INTO A SERIES OF CLICKS ANTS SHOULD BE ABLE TO UNDER-STAND...
THE RECEIVER ALLOWS ME TO "HEAR" RECIPROCAL EMISSIONS COMING FROM THEM...
THE COSTUME PROTECTS ME FROM ANY RANDOM BUG BITES WHEN I SHRINK DOWN...
PLUS, IT SHOWCASES MY PHYSIQUE HANDSOMELY.
INTO THE RABBIT HOLE AGAIN...

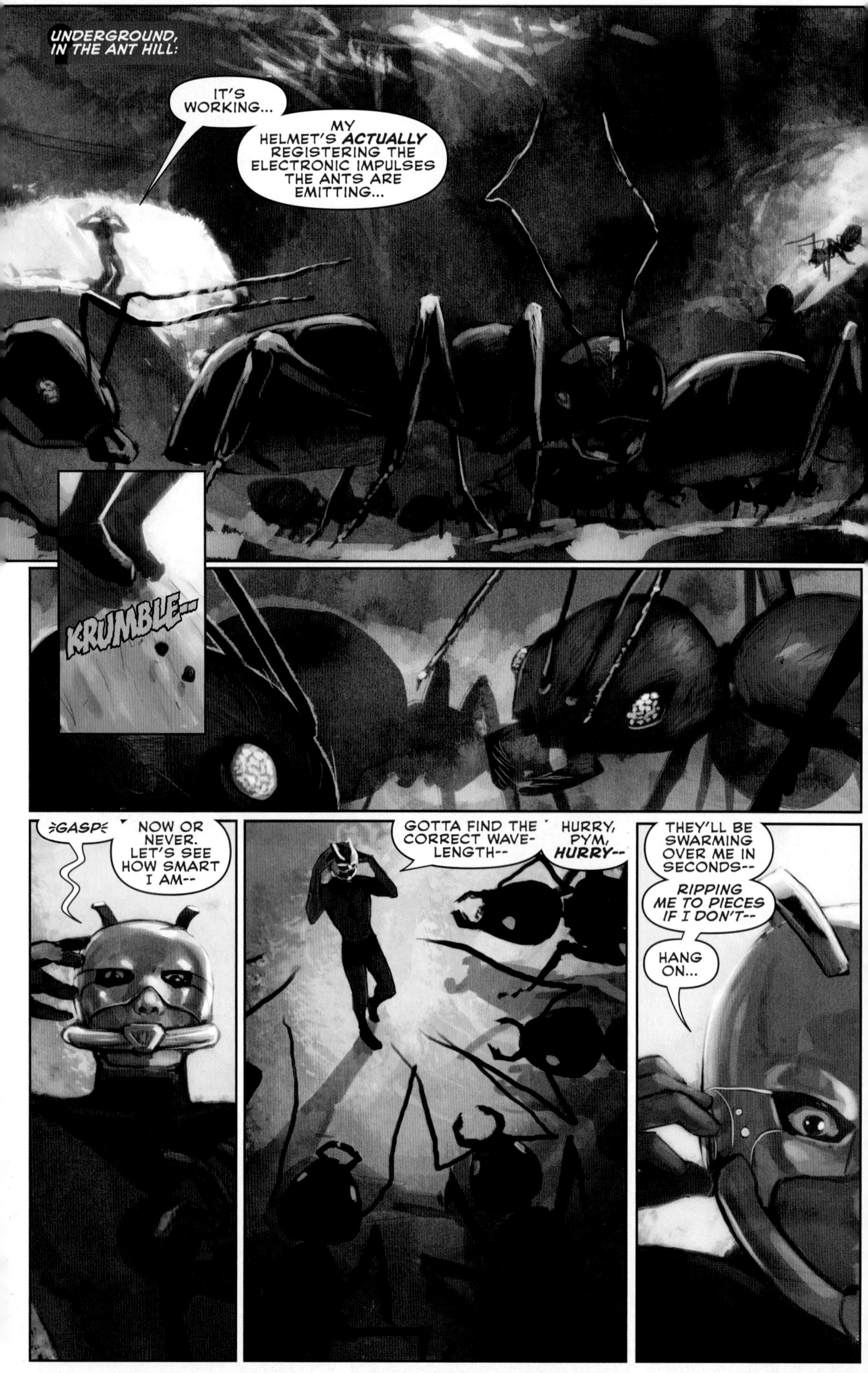
UNDERGROUND, IN THE ANT HILL:
IT'S WORKING...
MY HELMET'S ACTUALLY REGISTERING THE ELECTRONIC IMPULSES THE ANTS ARE EMITTING...
KRUMBLE--
GASP
NOW OR NEVER. LET'S SEE HOW SMART I AM--
GOTTA FIND THE CORRECT WAVE-LENGTH--
HURRY, PYM, HURRY--
THEY'LL BE SWARMING OVER ME IN SECONDS--
RIPPING ME TO PIECES IF I DON'T--
HANG ON...

THERE WE GO...

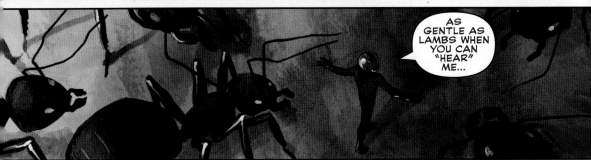

AS GENTLE AS LAMBS WHEN YOU CAN "HEAR" ME...

EXCEPT FOR ONE PARTICULARLY SINGLE-MINDED WORKER.

BACK OFF, DRONE!

OWW!!

THE HELL--!

AT THIS POINT...

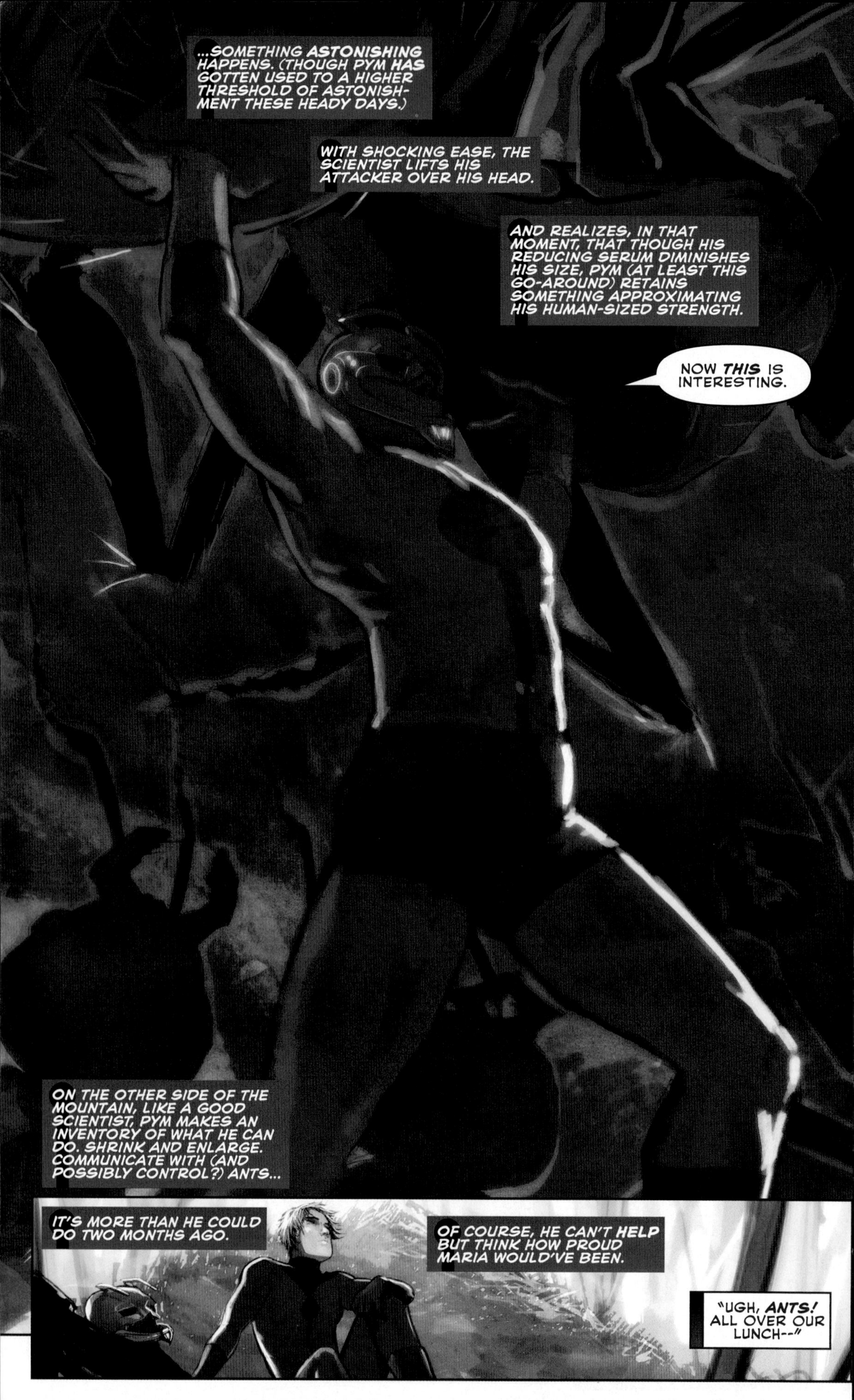
...SOMETHING ASTONISHING HAPPENS. (THOUGH PYM HAS GOTTEN USED TO A HIGHER THRESHOLD OF ASTONISHMENT THESE HEADY DAYS.)
WITH SHOCKING EASE, THE SCIENTIST LIFTS HIS ATTACKER OVER HIS HEAD.
AND REALIZES, IN THAT MOMENT, THAT THOUGH HIS REDUCING SERUM DIMINISHES HIS SIZE, PYM (AT LEAST THIS GO-AROUND) RETAINS SOMETHING APPROXIMATING HIS HUMAN-SIZED STRENGTH.
NOW THIS IS INTERESTING.
ON THE OTHER SIDE OF THE MOUNTAIN, LIKE A GOOD SCIENTIST, PYM MAKES AN INVENTORY OF WHAT HE CAN DO. SHRINK AND ENLARGE. COMMUNICATE WITH (AND POSSIBLY CONTROL?) ANTS...
IT'S MORE THAN HE COULD DO TWO MONTHS AGO.
OF COURSE, HE CAN'T HELP BUT THINK HOW PROUD MARIA WOULD'VE BEEN.
"UGH, ANTS! ALL OVER OUR LUNCH--"

Chapter Five:

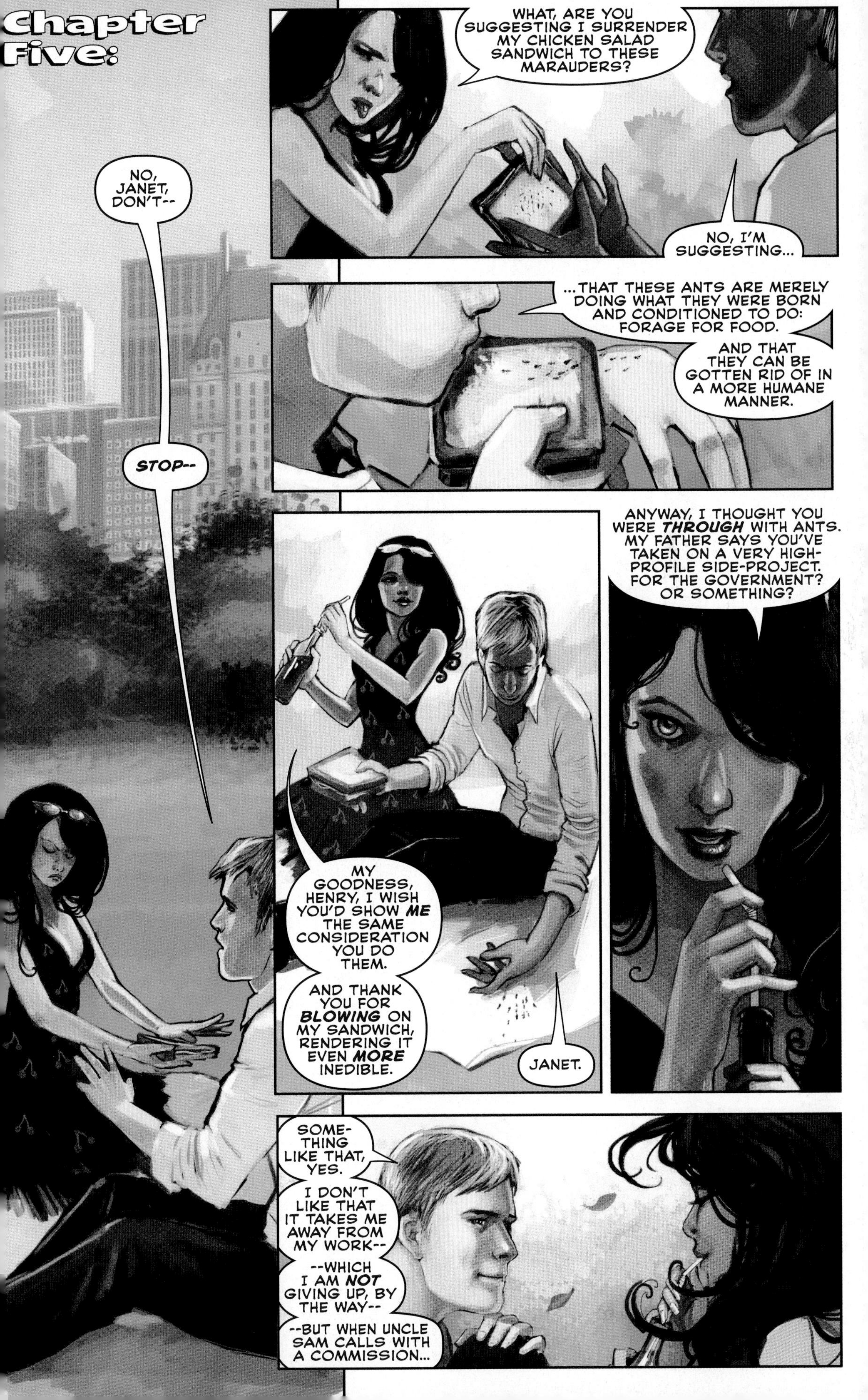

WHAT, ARE YOU SUGGESTING I SURRENDER MY CHICKEN SALAD SANDWICH TO THESE MARAUDERS?
NO, I'M SUGGESTING...
...THAT THESE ANTS ARE MERELY DOING WHAT THEY WERE BORN AND CONDITIONED TO DO: FORAGE FOR FOOD.
AND THAT THEY CAN BE GOTTEN RID OF IN A MORE HUMANE MANNER.
MY GOODNESS, HENRY, I WISH YOU'D SHOW ME THE SAME CONSIDERATION YOU DO THEM.
AND THANK YOU FOR BLOWING ON MY SANDWICH, RENDERING IT EVEN MORE INEDIBLE.
JANET.
ANYWAY, I THOUGHT YOU WERE THROUGH WITH ANTS. MY FATHER SAYS YOU'VE TAKEN ON A VERY HIGH-PROFILE SIDE-PROJECT. FOR THE GOVERNMENT? OR SOMETHING?
SOME-THING LIKE THAT, YES.
I DON'T LIKE THAT IT TAKES ME AWAY FROM MY WORK--
--WHICH I AM NOT GIVING UP, BY THE WAY--
--BUT WHEN UNCLE SAM CALLS WITH A COMMISSION...
NO, JANET, DON'T--
STOP--

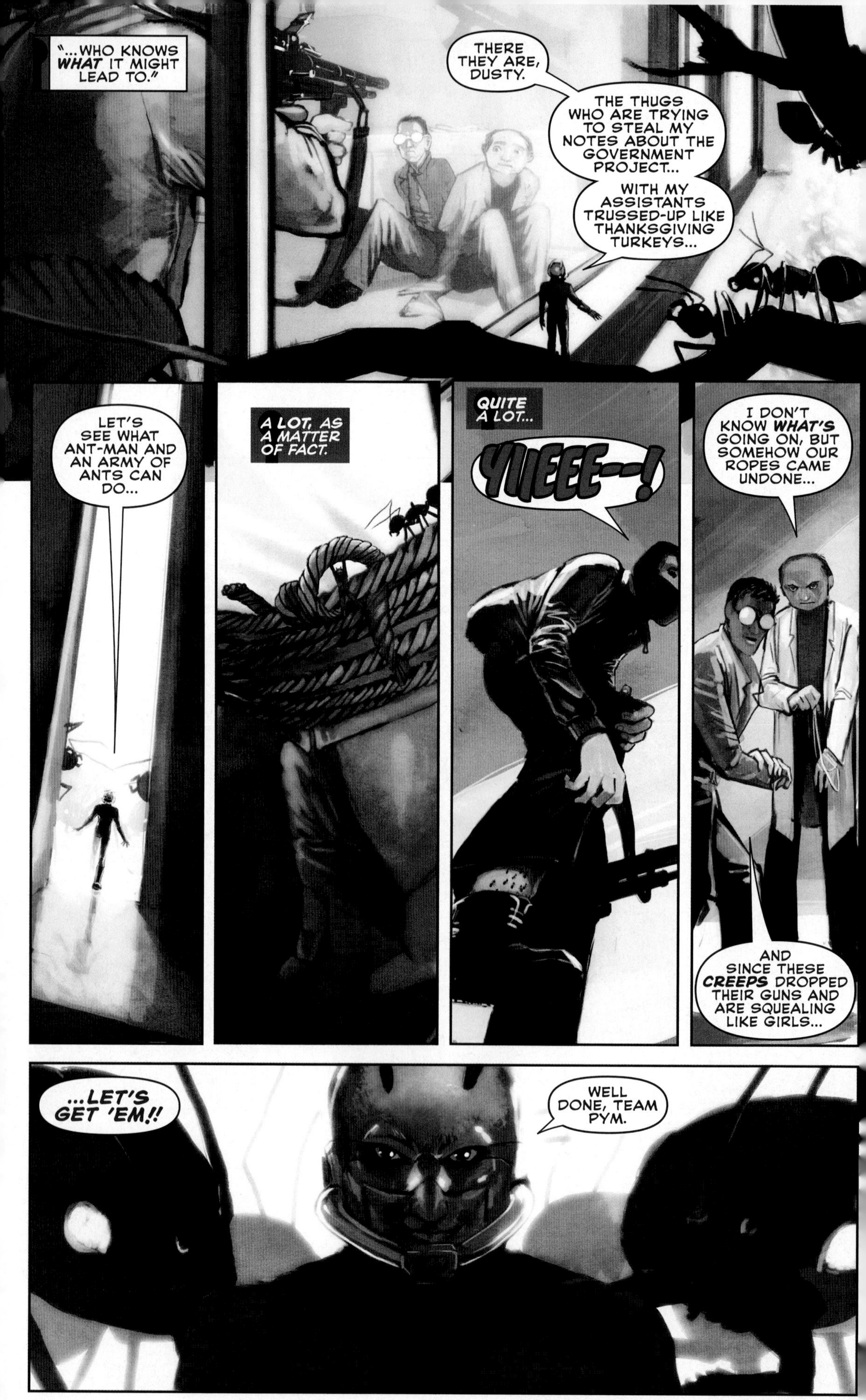
"...WHO KNOWS WHAT IT MIGHT LEAD TO."
THERE THEY ARE, DUSTY.
THE THUGS WHO ARE TRYING TO STEAL MY NOTES ABOUT THE GOVERNMENT PROJECT...
WITH MY ASSISTANTS TRUSSED-UP LIKE THANKSGIVING TURKEYS...
LET'S SEE WHAT ANT-MAN AND AN ARMY OF ANTS CAN DO...
A LOT, AS A MATTER OF FACT.
QUITE A LOT...
YIIEEE--!
I DON'T KNOW WHAT'S GOING ON, BUT SOMEHOW OUR ROPES CAME UNDONE...
AND SINCE THESE CREEPS DROPPED THEIR GUNS AND ARE SQUEALING LIKE GIRLS...
...LET'S GET 'EM!!
WELL DONE, TEAM PYM.

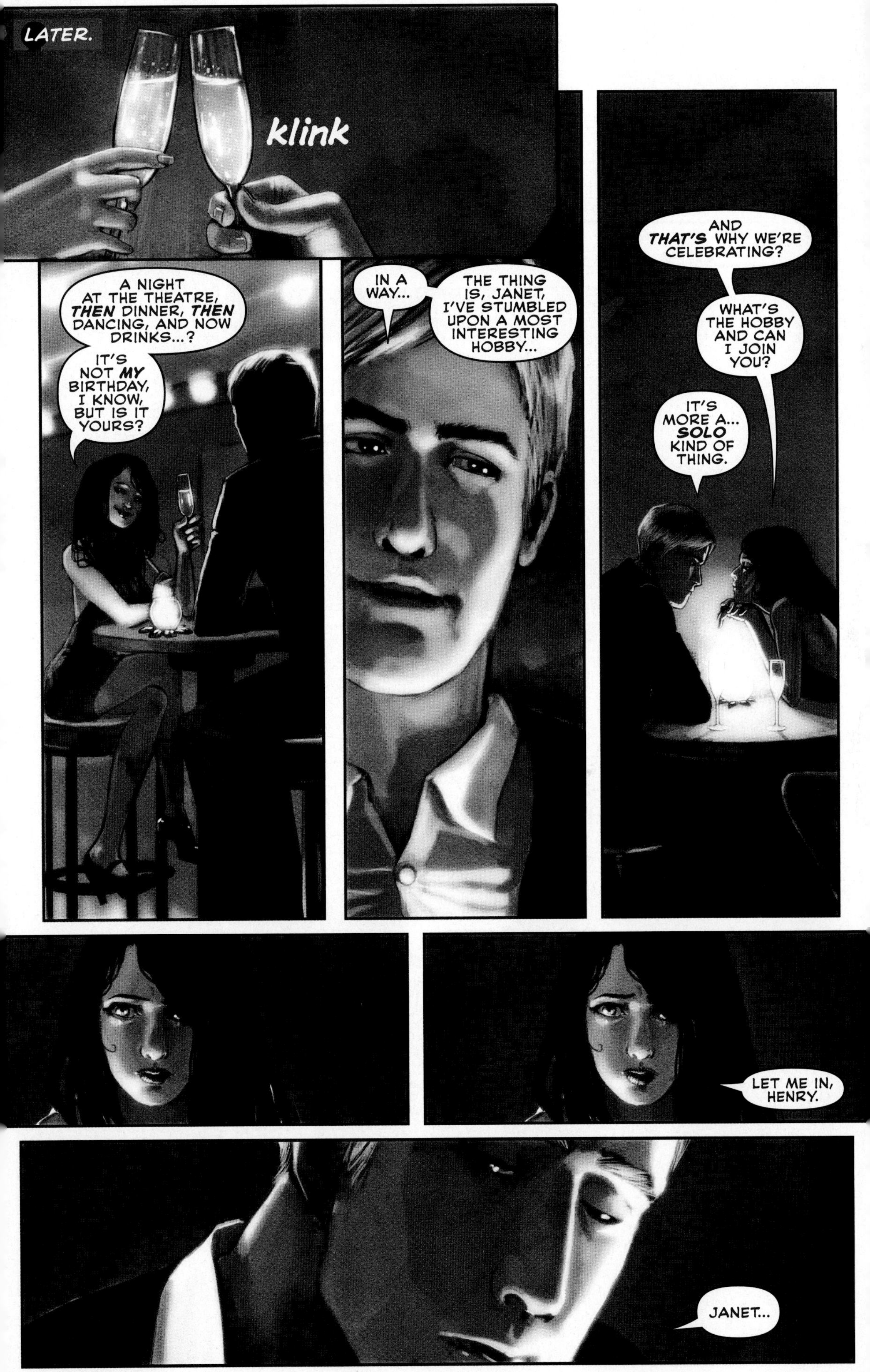
LATER.
klink
A NIGHT AT THE THEATRE, THEN DINNER, THEN DANCING, AND NOW DRINKS...?
IT'S NOT MY BIRTHDAY, I KNOW, BUT IS IT YOURS?
IN A WAY...
THE THING IS, JANET, I'VE STUMBLED UPON A MOST INTERESTING HOBBY...
AND THAT'S WHY WE'RE CELEBRATING?
WHAT'S THE HOBBY AND CAN I JOIN YOU?
IT'S MORE A... SOLO KIND OF THING.
LET ME IN, HENRY.
JANET...

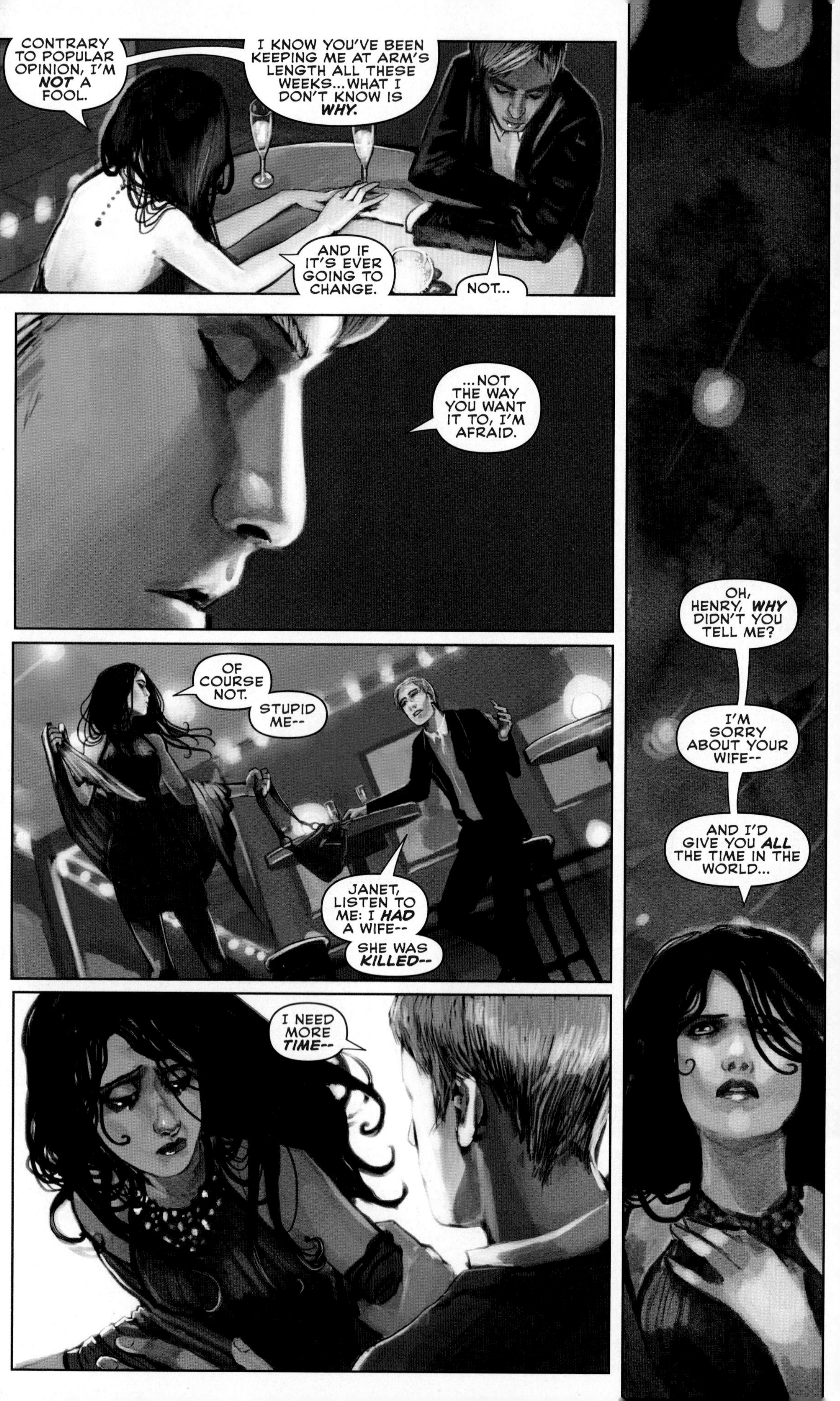
CONTRARY TO POPULAR OPINION, I'M *NOT* A FOOL.
I KNOW YOU'VE BEEN KEEPING ME AT ARM'S LENGTH ALL THESE WEEKS...WHAT I DON'T KNOW IS *WHY.*
AND IF IT'S EVER GOING TO CHANGE.
NOT...
...NOT THE WAY YOU WANT IT TO, I'M AFRAID.
OF COURSE NOT.
STUPID ME--
JANET, LISTEN TO ME: I *HAD* A WIFE--
SHE WAS *KILLED--*
I NEED MORE *TIME--*
OH, HENRY, *WHY* DIDN'T YOU TELL ME?
I'M SORRY ABOUT YOUR WIFE--
AND I'D GIVE YOU *ALL* THE TIME IN THE WORLD...

Chapter Six:

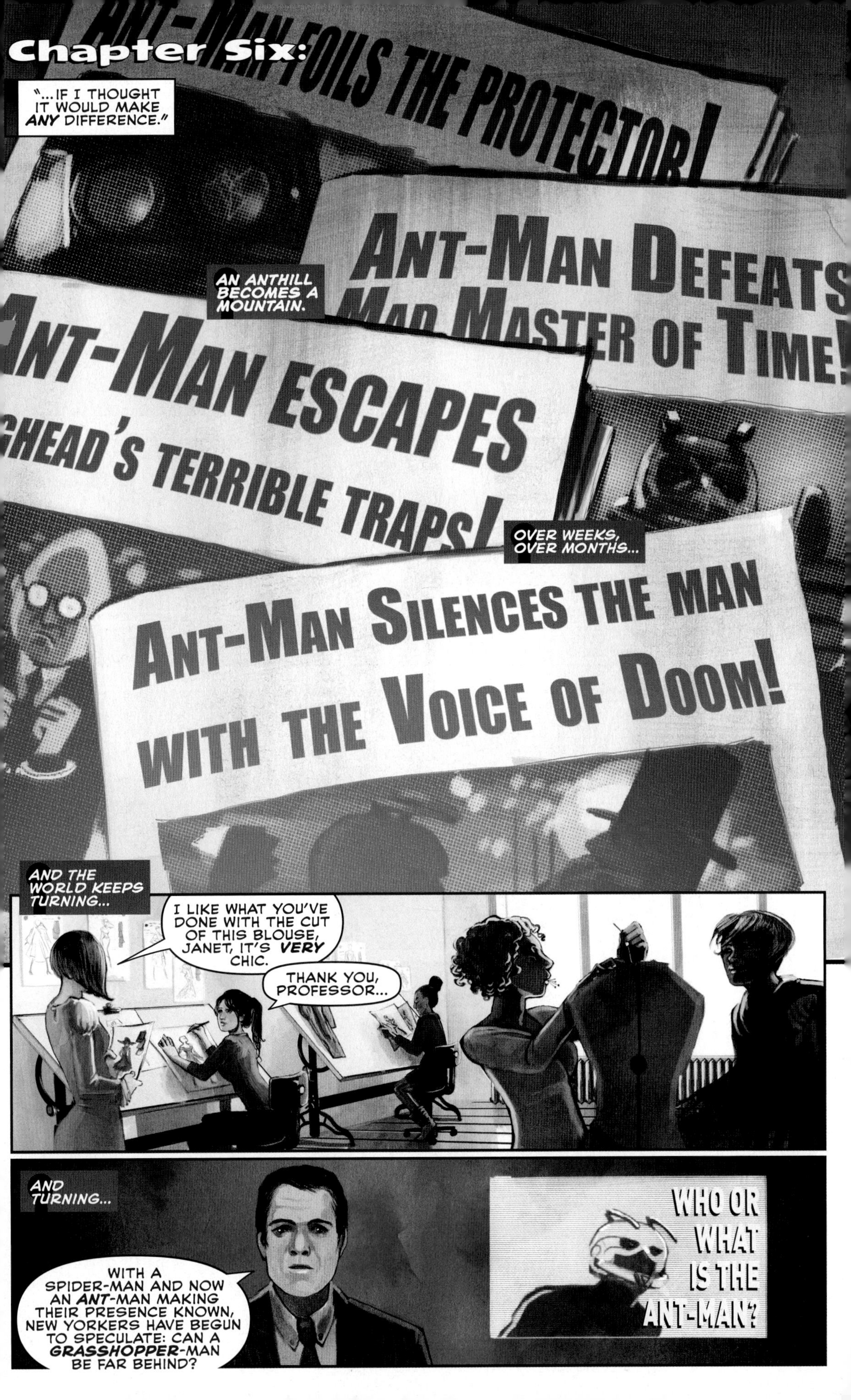
ANT-MAN FOILS THE PROTECTOR!
"...IF I THOUGHT IT WOULD MAKE ANY DIFFERENCE."
ANT-MAN DEFEATS MAD MASTER OF TIME!
AN ANTHILL BECOMES A MOUNTAIN.
NT-MAN ESCAPES
HEAD'S TERRIBLE TRAPS!
OVER WEEKS, OVER MONTHS...
ANT-MAN SILENCES THE MAN WITH THE VOICE OF DOOM!
AND THE WORLD KEEPS TURNING...
I LIKE WHAT YOU'VE DONE WITH THE CUT OF THIS BLOUSE, JANET, IT'S VERY CHIC.
THANK YOU, PROFESSOR...
AND TURNING...
WITH A SPIDER-MAN AND NOW AN ANT-MAN MAKING THEIR PRESENCE KNOWN, NEW YORKERS HAVE BEGUN TO SPECULATE: CAN A GRASSHOPPER-MAN BE FAR BEHIND?
WHO OR WHAT IS THE ANT-MAN?

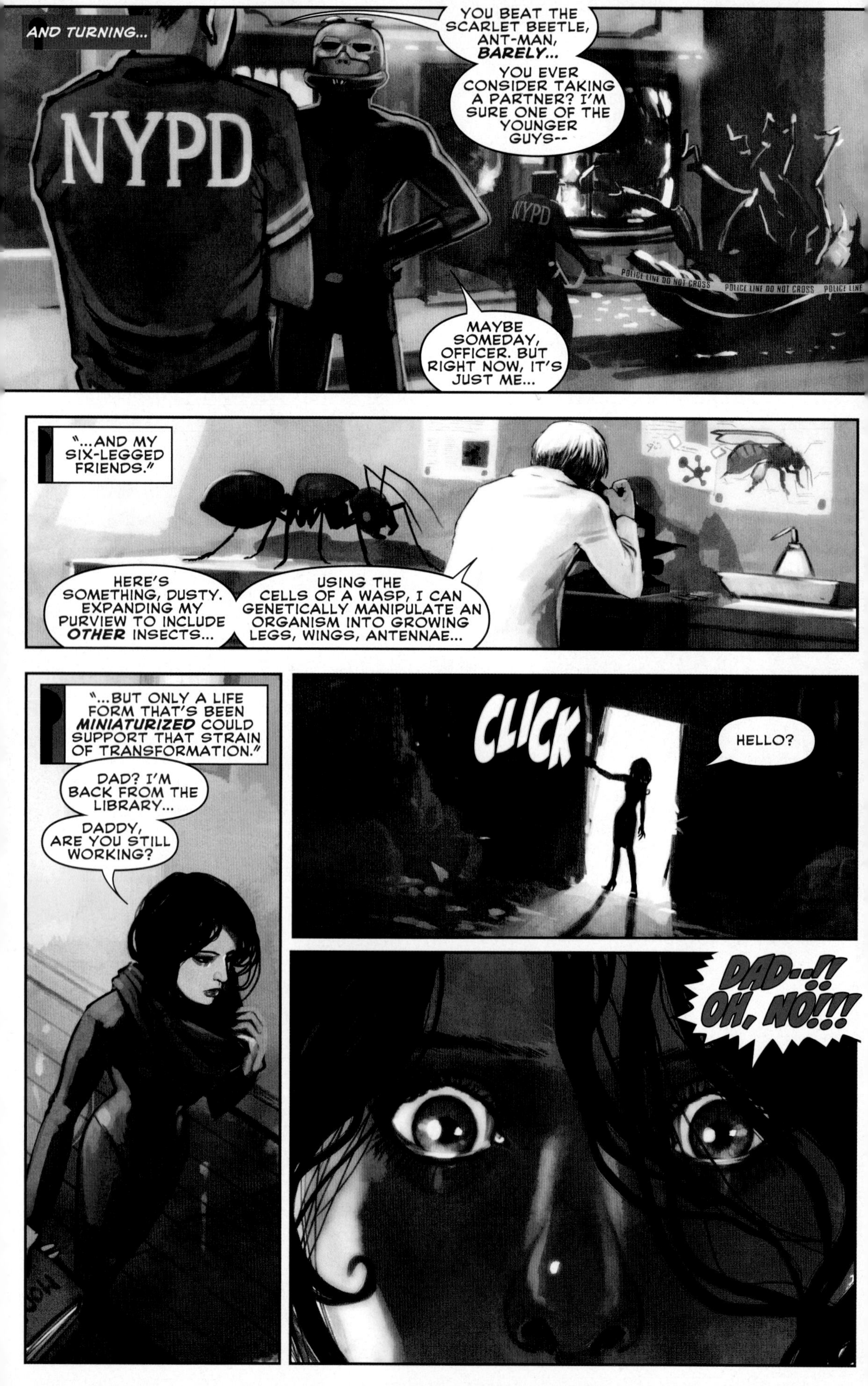

AND TURNING...
NYPD
YOU BEAT THE SCARLET BEETLE, ANT-MAN, **BARELY...**
YOU EVER CONSIDER TAKING A PARTNER? I'M SURE ONE OF THE YOUNGER GUYS--
NYPD
POLICE LINE DO NOT CROSS
MAYBE SOMEDAY, OFFICER. BUT RIGHT NOW, IT'S JUST ME...
"...AND MY SIX-LEGGED FRIENDS."
HERE'S SOMETHING, DUSTY. EXPANDING MY PURVIEW TO INCLUDE ***OTHER*** INSECTS...
USING THE CELLS OF A WASP, I CAN GENETICALLY MANIPULATE AN ORGANISM INTO GROWING LEGS, WINGS, ANTENNAE...
"...BUT ONLY A LIFE FORM THAT'S BEEN ***MINIATURIZED*** COULD SUPPORT THAT STRAIN OF TRANSFORMATION."
DAD? I'M BACK FROM THE LIBRARY...
DADDY, ARE YOU STILL WORKING?
CLICK
HELLO?
DAD--!? OH, NO!?!

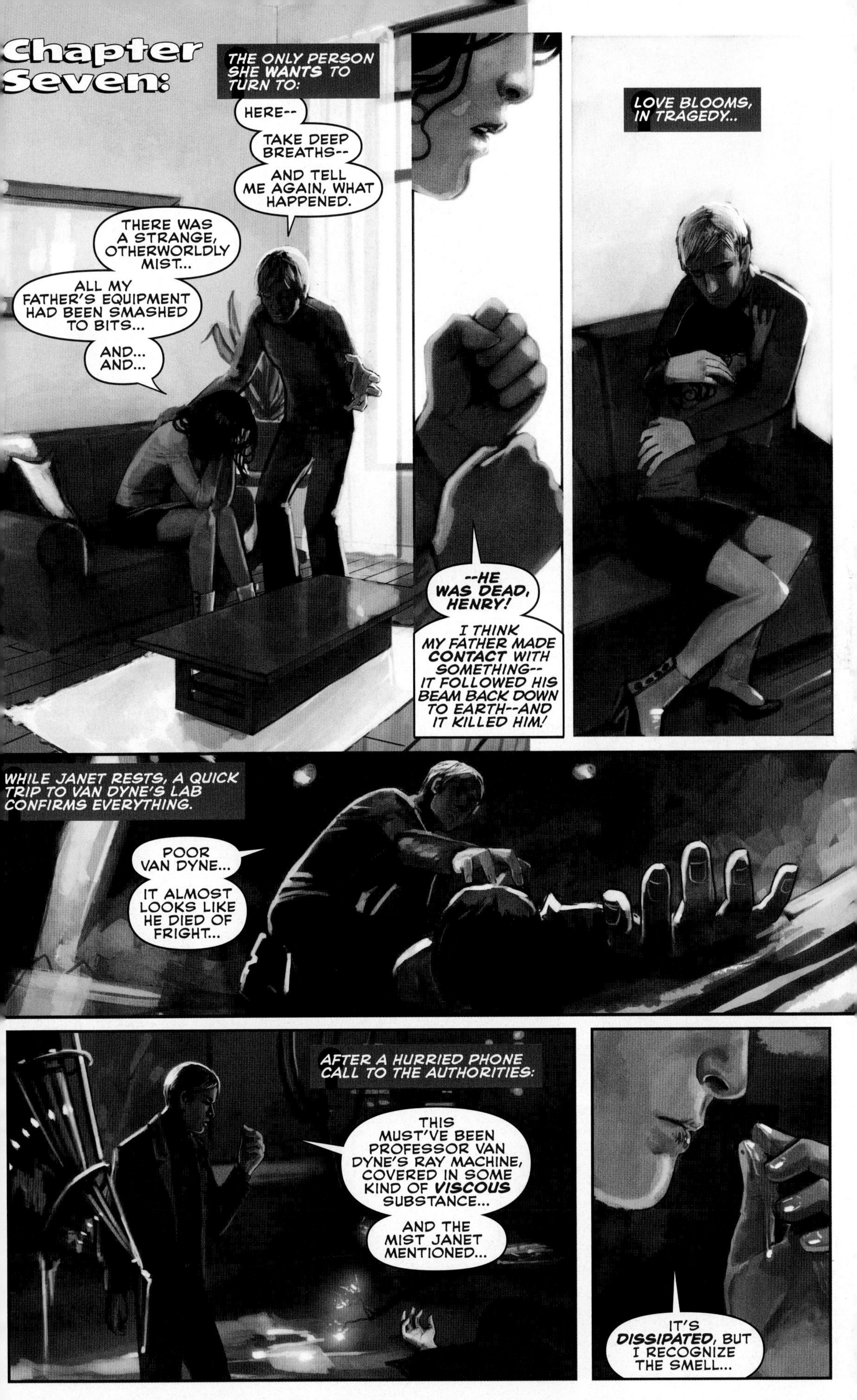
Chapter Seven:
THE ONLY PERSON SHE WANTS TO TURN TO:
HERE--
TAKE DEEP BREATHS--
AND TELL ME AGAIN, WHAT HAPPENED.
THERE WAS A STRANGE, OTHERWORLDLY MIST...
ALL MY FATHER'S EQUIPMENT HAD BEEN SMASHED TO BITS...
AND... AND...
--HE WAS DEAD, HENRY!
I THINK MY FATHER MADE CONTACT WITH SOMETHING-- IT FOLLOWED HIS BEAM BACK DOWN TO EARTH--AND IT KILLED HIM!
LOVE BLOOMS, IN TRAGEDY...
WHILE JANET RESTS, A QUICK TRIP TO VAN DYNE'S LAB CONFIRMS EVERYTHING.
POOR VAN DYNE...
IT ALMOST LOOKS LIKE HE DIED OF FRIGHT...
AFTER A HURRIED PHONE CALL TO THE AUTHORITIES:
THIS MUST'VE BEEN PROFESSOR VAN DYNE'S RAY MACHINE, COVERED IN SOME KIND OF VISCOUS SUBSTANCE...
AND THE MIST JANET MENTIONED...
IT'S DISSIPATED, BUT I RECOGNIZE THE SMELL...

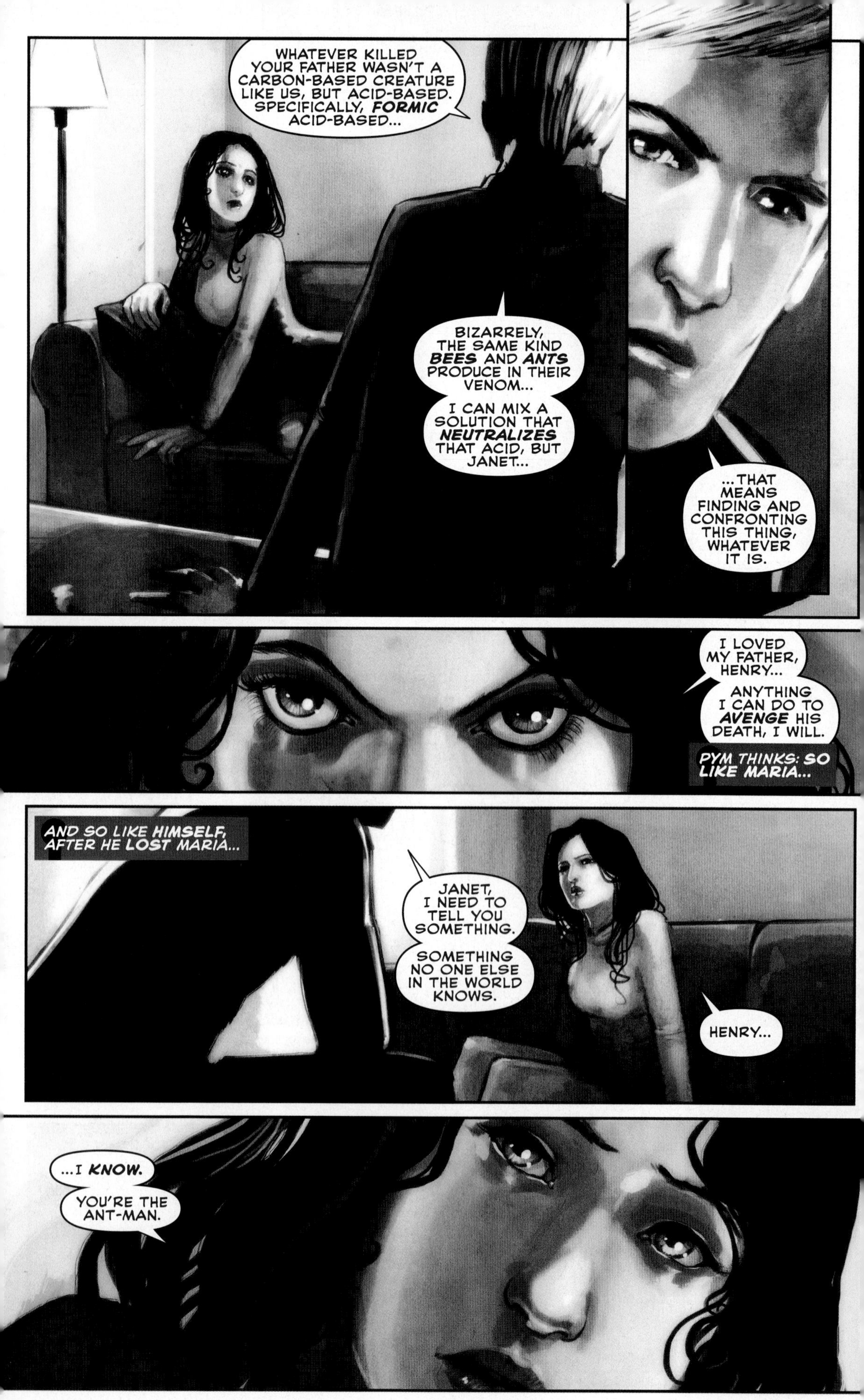
WHATEVER KILLED YOUR FATHER WASN'T A CARBON-BASED CREATURE LIKE US, BUT ACID-BASED. SPECIFICALLY, *FORMIC* ACID-BASED...
BIZARRELY, THE SAME KIND *BEES* AND *ANTS* PRODUCE IN THEIR VENOM...
I CAN MIX A SOLUTION THAT *NEUTRALIZES* THAT ACID, BUT JANET...
...THAT MEANS FINDING AND CONFRONTING THIS THING, WHATEVER IT IS.
I LOVED MY FATHER, HENRY...
ANYTHING I CAN DO TO *AVENGE* HIS DEATH, I WILL.
PYM THINKS: SO LIKE MARIA...
AND SO LIKE HIMSELF, AFTER HE LOST MARIA...
JANET, I NEED TO TELL YOU SOMETHING.
SOMETHING NO ONE ELSE IN THE WORLD KNOWS.
HENRY...
...I *KNOW.*
YOU'RE THE ANT-MAN.

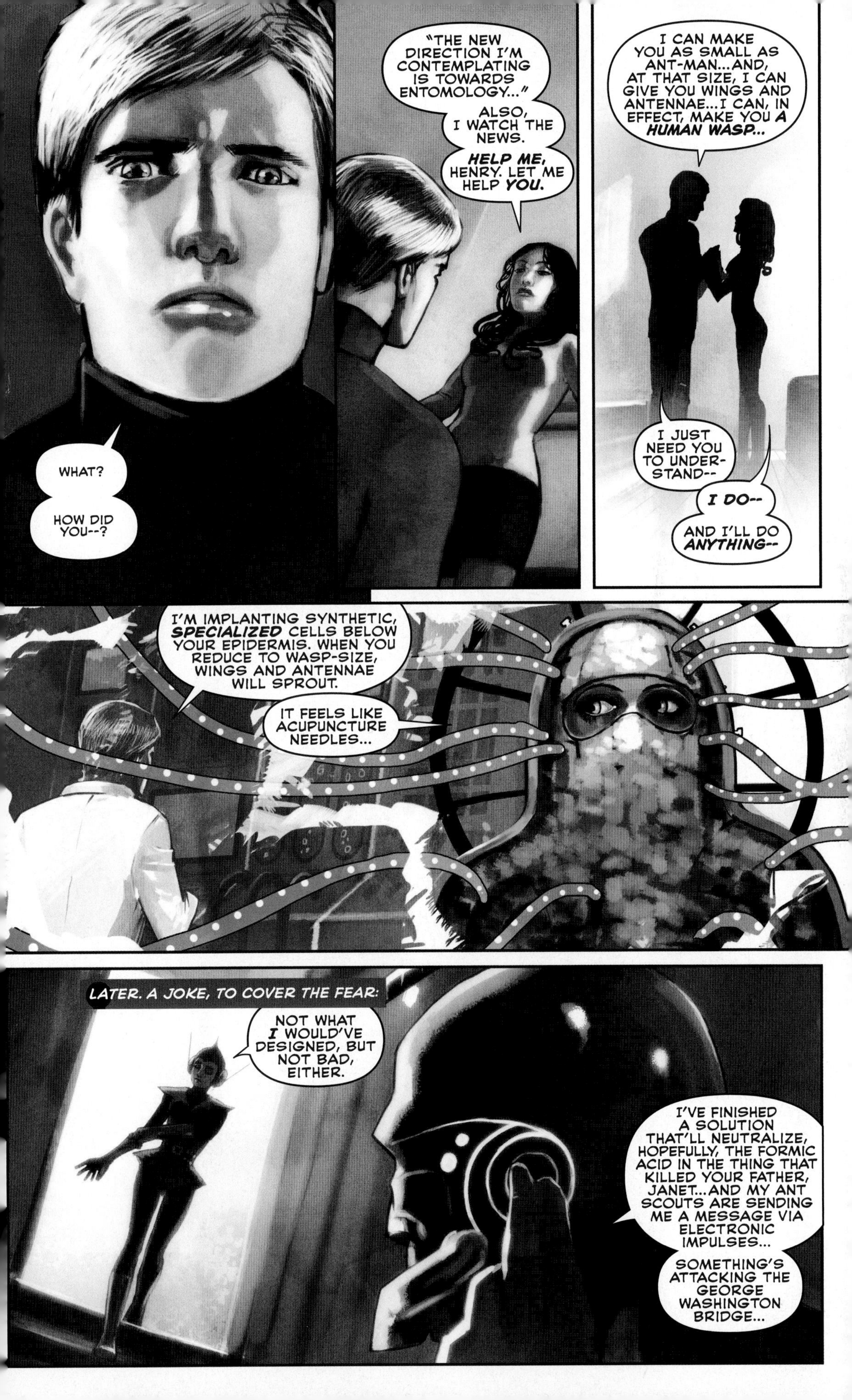

WHAT?
HOW DID YOU--?
"THE NEW DIRECTION I'M CONTEMPLATING IS TOWARDS ENTOMOLOGY..."
ALSO, I WATCH THE NEWS.
HELP ME, HENRY. LET ME HELP YOU.
I CAN MAKE YOU AS SMALL AS ANT-MAN...AND, AT THAT SIZE, I CAN GIVE YOU WINGS AND ANTENNAE...I CAN, IN EFFECT, MAKE YOU A HUMAN WASP...
I JUST NEED YOU TO UNDER-STAND--
I DO--
AND I'LL DO ANYTHING--
I'M IMPLANTING SYNTHETIC, SPECIALIZED CELLS BELOW YOUR EPIDERMIS. WHEN YOU REDUCE TO WASP-SIZE, WINGS AND ANTENNAE WILL SPROUT.
IT FEELS LIKE ACUPUNCTURE NEEDLES...
LATER. A JOKE, TO COVER THE FEAR:
NOT WHAT I WOULD'VE DESIGNED, BUT NOT BAD, EITHER.
I'VE FINISHED A SOLUTION THAT'LL NEUTRALIZE, HOPEFULLY, THE FORMIC ACID IN THE THING THAT KILLED YOUR FATHER, JANET...AND MY ANT SCOUTS ARE SENDING ME A MESSAGE VIA ELECTRONIC IMPULSES...
SOMETHING'S ATTACKING THE GEORGE WASHINGTON BRIDGE...

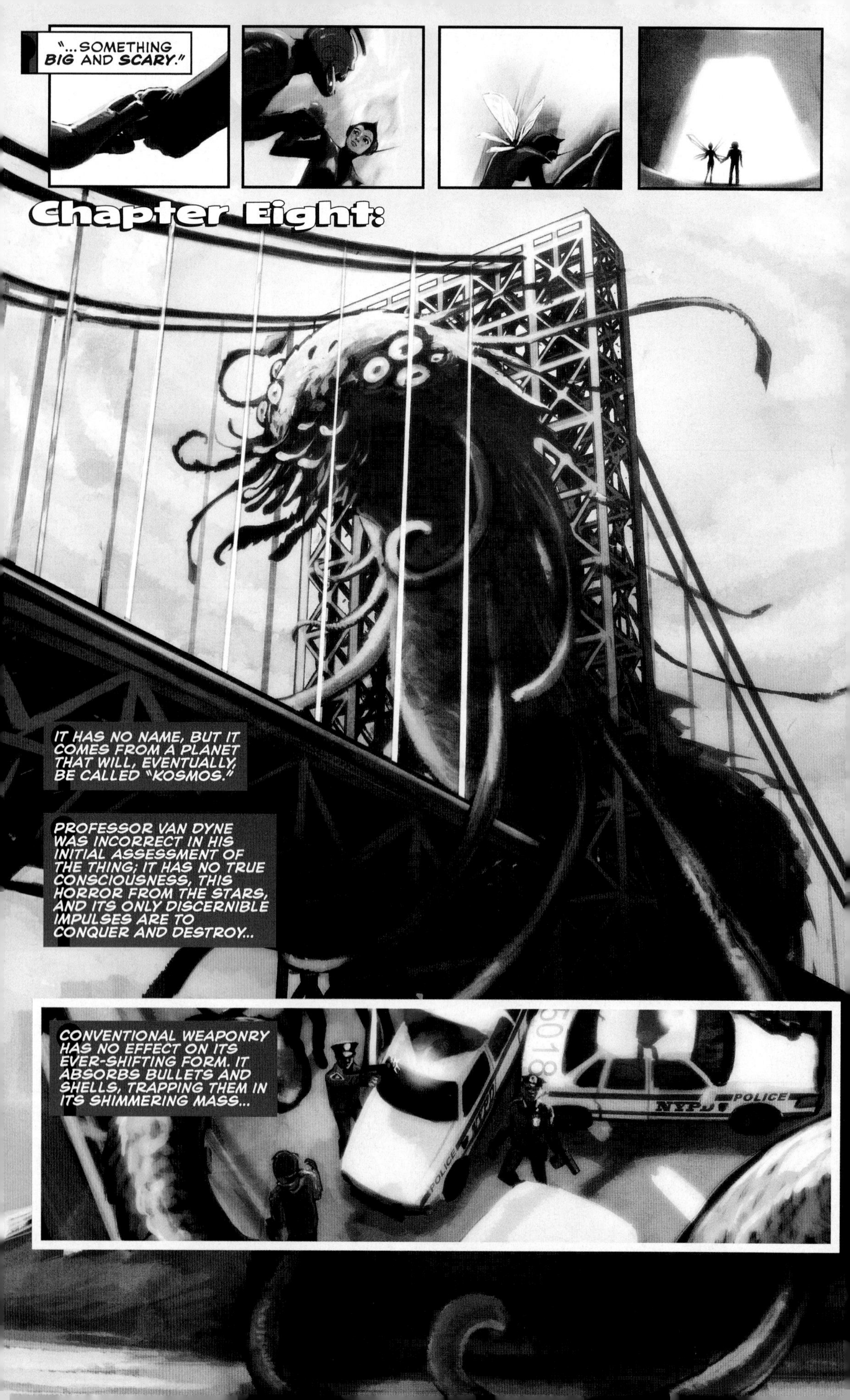
"...SOMETHING BIG AND SCARY."
Chapter Eight:
IT HAS NO NAME, BUT IT COMES FROM A PLANET THAT WILL, EVENTUALLY, BE CALLED "KOSMOS."
PROFESSOR VAN DYNE WAS INCORRECT IN HIS INITIAL ASSESSMENT OF THE THING; IT HAS NO TRUE CONSCIOUSNESS, THIS HORROR FROM THE STARS, AND ITS ONLY DISCERNIBLE IMPULSES ARE TO CONQUER AND DESTROY...
CONVENTIONAL WEAPONRY HAS NO EFFECT ON ITS EVER-SHIFTING FORM. IT ABSORBS BULLETS AND SHELLS, TRAPPING THEM IN ITS SHIMMERING MASS...
NYPD
POLICE

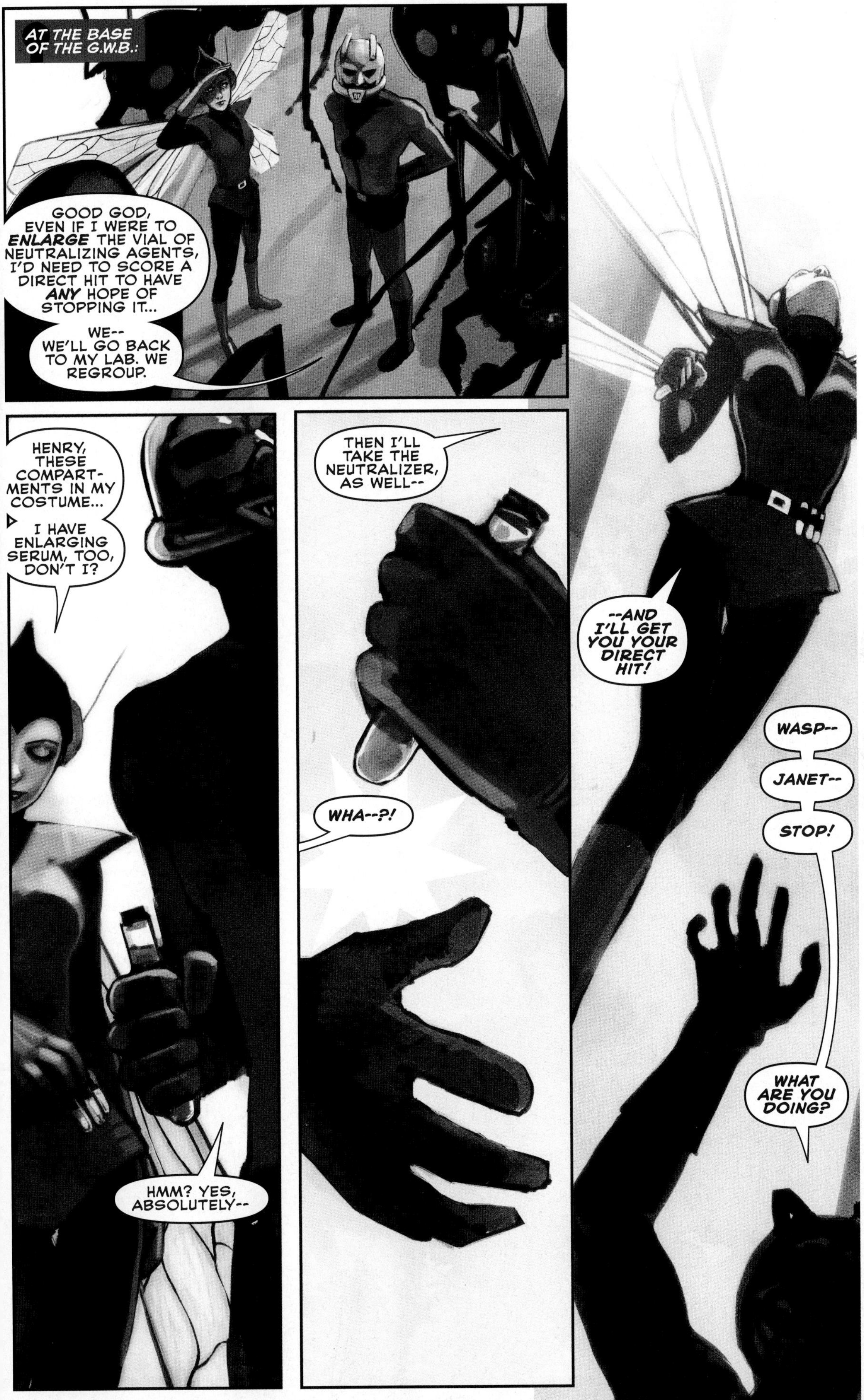
AT THE BASE OF THE G.W.B.:
GOOD GOD, EVEN IF I WERE TO ENLARGE THE VIAL OF NEUTRALIZING AGENTS, I'D NEED TO SCORE A DIRECT HIT TO HAVE ANY HOPE OF STOPPING IT...
WE-- WE'LL GO BACK TO MY LAB. WE REGROUP.
HENRY, THESE COMPART-MENTS IN MY COSTUME...
I HAVE ENLARGING SERUM, TOO, DON'T I?
HMM? YES, ABSOLUTELY--
THEN I'LL TAKE THE NEUTRALIZER, AS WELL--
WHA--?!
--AND I'LL GET YOU YOUR DIRECT HIT!
WASP--
JANET--
STOP!
WHAT ARE YOU DOING?

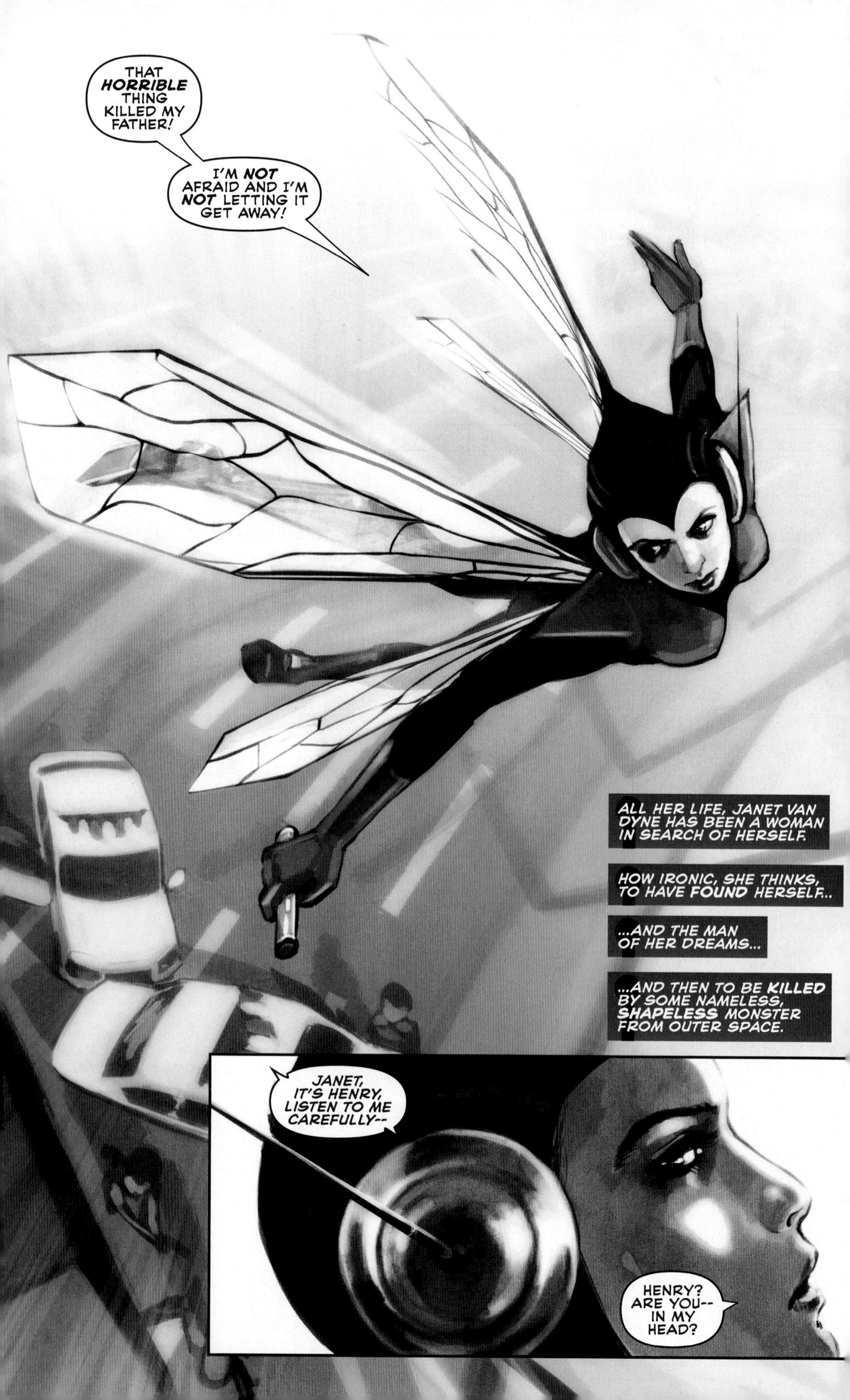
THAT HORRIBLE THING KILLED MY FATHER!
I'M NOT AFRAID AND I'M NOT LETTING IT GET AWAY!
ALL HER LIFE, JANET VAN DYNE HAS BEEN A WOMAN IN SEARCH OF HERSELF.
HOW IRONIC, SHE THINKS, TO HAVE FOUND HERSELF..
...AND THE MAN OF HER DREAMS...
...AND THEN TO BE KILLED BY SOME NAMELESS, SHAPELESS MONSTER FROM OUTER SPACE.
JANET, IT'S HENRY, LISTEN TO ME CAREFULLY--
HENRY? ARE YOU-- IN MY HEAD?

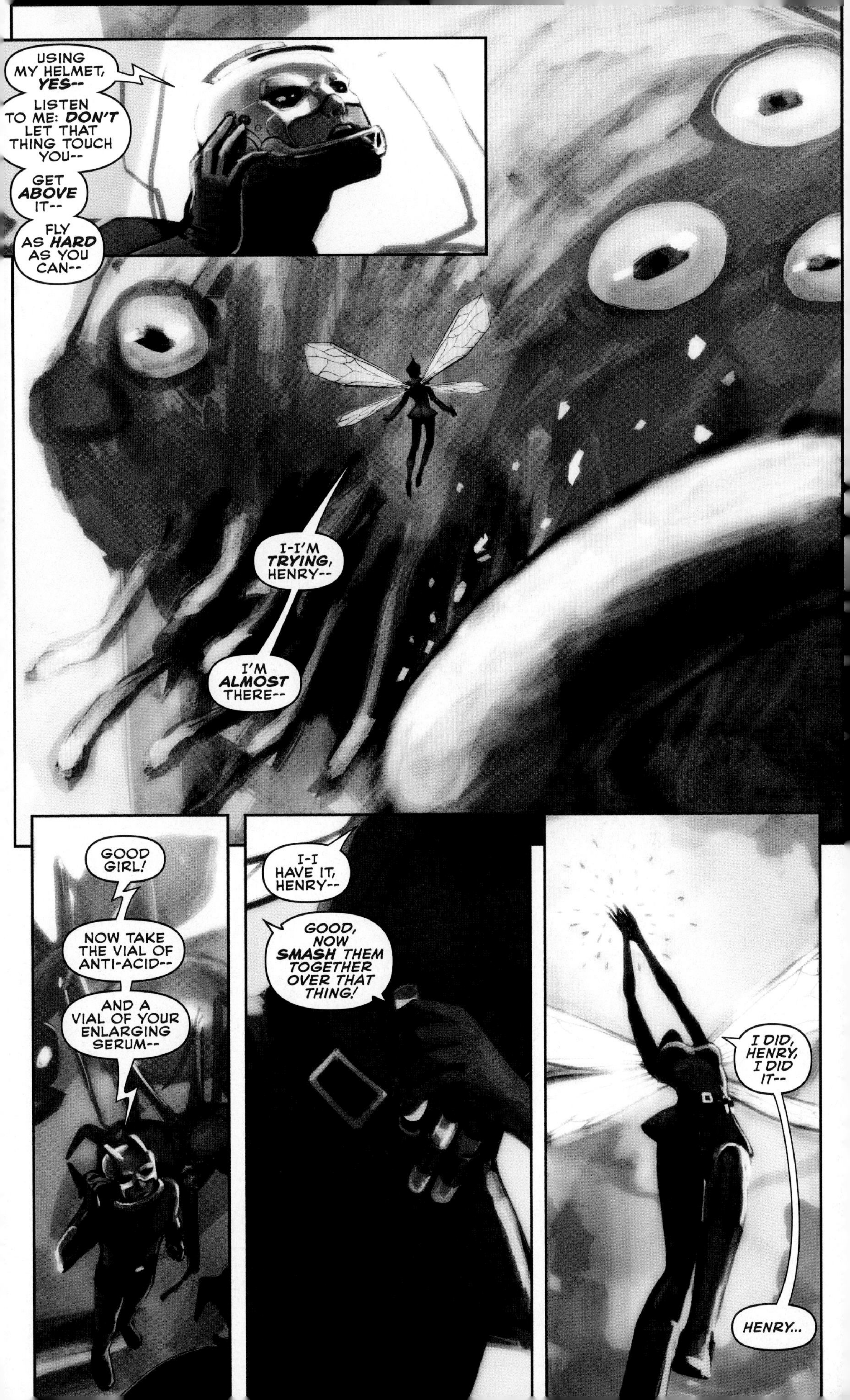
USING MY HELMET, YES--
LISTEN TO ME: DON'T LET THAT THING TOUCH YOU--
GET ABOVE IT--
FLY AS HARD AS YOU CAN--
I-I'M TRYING, HENRY--
I'M ALMOST THERE--
GOOD GIRL!
NOW TAKE THE VIAL OF ANTI-ACID--
AND A VIAL OF YOUR ENLARGING SERUM--
I-I HAVE IT, HENRY--
GOOD, NOW SMASH THEM TOGETHER OVER THAT THING!
I DID, HENRY, I DID IT--
HENRY...

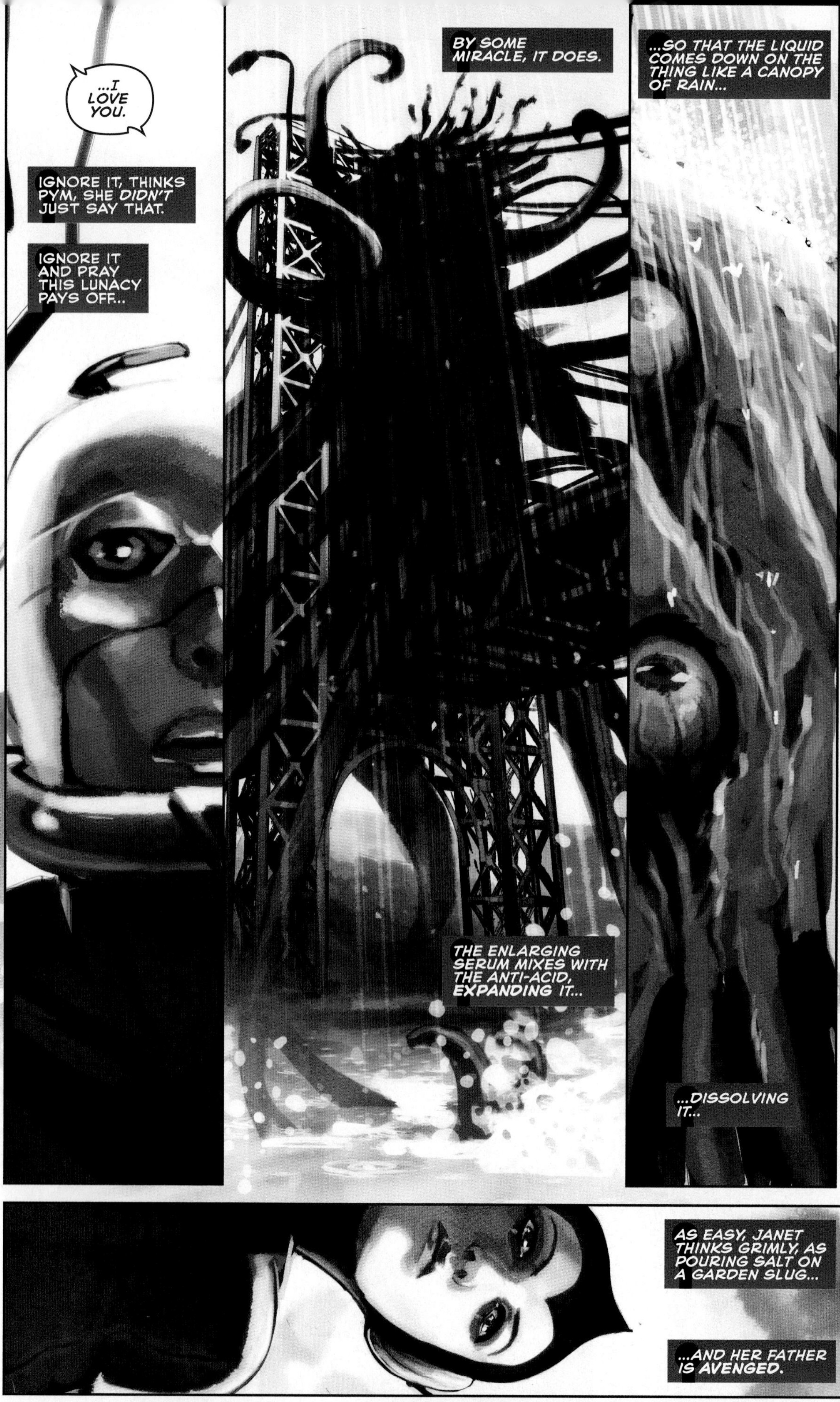
...I LOVE YOU.
IGNORE IT, THINKS PYM, SHE *DIDN'T* JUST SAY THAT.
IGNORE IT AND PRAY THIS LUNACY PAYS OFF...
BY SOME MIRACLE, IT DOES.
THE ENLARGING SERUM MIXES WITH THE ANTI-ACID, **EXPANDING** IT...
...SO THAT THE LIQUID COMES DOWN ON THE THING LIKE A CANOPY OF RAIN...
...**DISSOLVING** IT...
AS EASY, JANET THINKS GRIMLY, AS POURING SALT ON A GARDEN SLUG...
...AND HER FATHER IS **AVENGED.**

Chapter Nine

DO YOU REALIZE HOW *FOOLISH* THAT WAS?

FOR GOD'S SAKE, JANET, YOU COULD'VE BEEN *KILLED!*

HENRY, PLEASE...

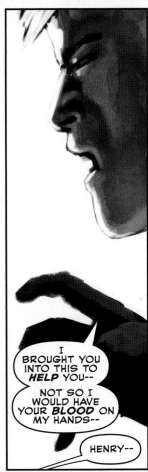

I BROUGHT YOU INTO THIS TO *HELP* YOU--

NOT SO I WOULD HAVE YOUR *BLOOD* ON MY HANDS--

HENRY--

IF THIS IS GOING TO WORK--

IF YOU'RE GOING TO HELP ME--

YOU'RE GOING TO NEED TO *LISTEN* TO--

HENRY--

MY...MY *FATHER*...

MY FATHER'S... *GONE*...

FINALLY, SHE'S LETTING HERSELF *FEEL* IT.

SO LIKE MARIA...

SO LIKE *ME*, AFTER MARIA...

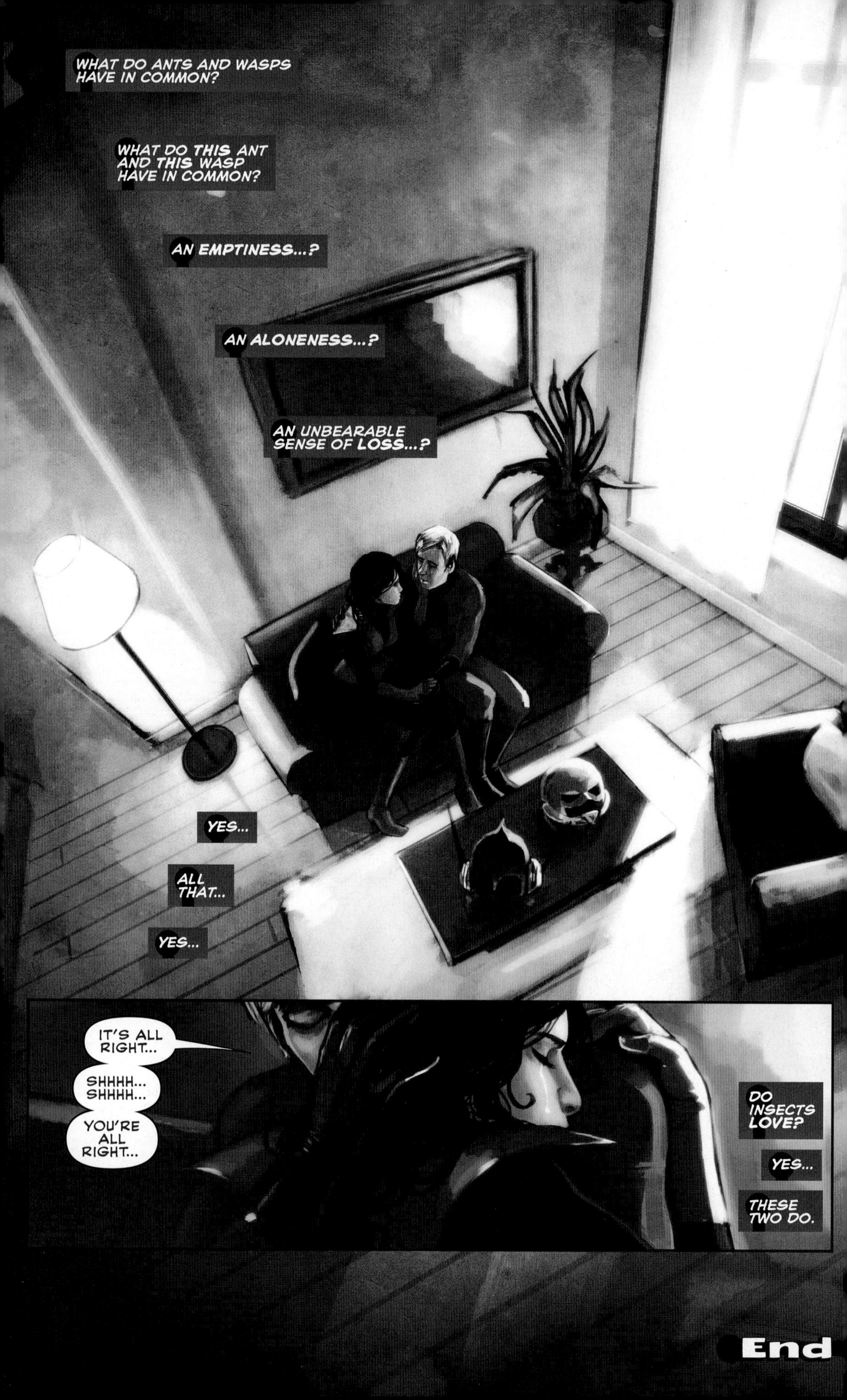
WHAT DO ANTS AND WASPS HAVE IN COMMON?
WHAT DO THIS ANT AND THIS WASP HAVE IN COMMON?
AN EMPTINESS...?
AN ALONENESS...?
AN UNBEARABLE SENSE OF LOSS...?
YES...
ALL THAT...
YES...
IT'S ALL RIGHT...
SHHHH... SHHHH...
YOU'RE ALL RIGHT...
DO INSECTS LOVE?
YES...
THESE TWO DO.
End

AS SCOTT LANG STRUGGLES TO BALANCE HIS PERSONAL AND SUPER HERO LIVES, HE IS TEMPTED TO RETURN TO A LIFE OF CRIME IN NICK SPENCER'S *ASTONISHING ANT-MAN*!

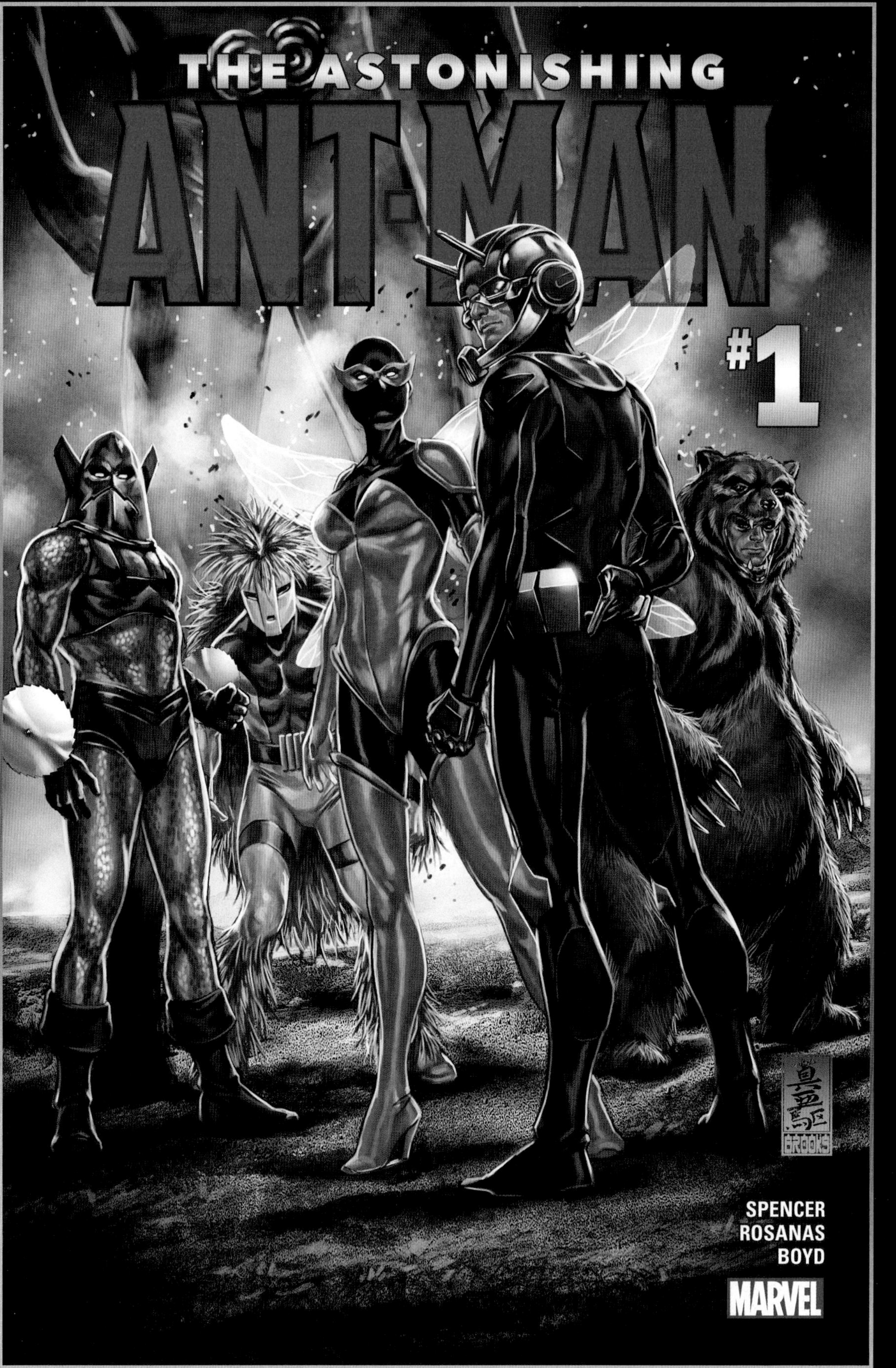
THE ASTONISHING
ANT-MAN
#1
SPENCER
ROSANAS
BOYD
MARVEL

THE ASTONISHING ANT-MAN

SCOTT LANG IS A MIAMI-AREA SMALL BUSINESS OWNER
WITH A TEENAGE DAUGHTER AND AN EX-WIFE.

OH, AND HE'S ANT-MAN!

NICK SPENCER
WRITER

RAMON ROSANAS
ARTIST

JORDAN BOYD
COLOR ARTIST

VC'S TRAVIS LANHAM
LETTERER

IDETTE WINECOOR
DESIGNER

MARK BROOKS
COVER ARTIST

MICHAEL & LAURA ALLRED; MARK BROOKS; TRADD MOORE; SOLOROBOTO INDUSTRIES (COSPLAY) & JUDY STEPHENS (PHOTOGRAPHY); SKOTTIE YOUNG
VARIANT COVER ARTISTS

CHRIS ROBINSON
ASST. EDITOR

WIL MOSS
EDITOR

TOM BREVOORT
EXEC. EDITOR

AXEL ALONSO
EDITOR IN CHIEF

JOE QUESADA
CHIEF CREATIVE OFFICER

DAN BUCKLEY
PUBLISHER

ALAN FINE
EXEC. PRODUCER

ANT-MAN CREATED BY **STAN LEE, LARRY LIEBER** & **JACK KIRBY**

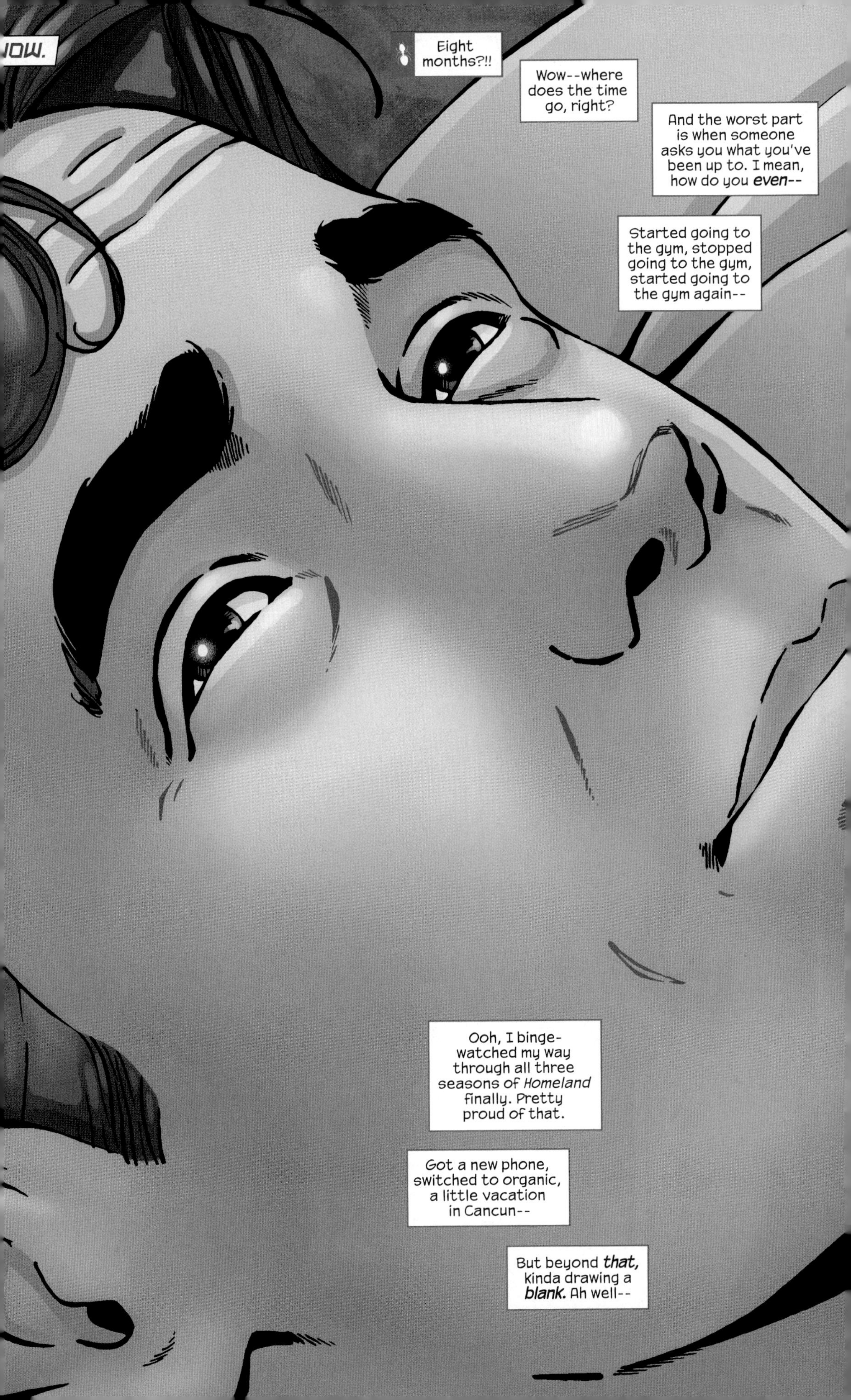

...NOW.
Eight months?!!
Wow--where does the time go, right?
And the worst part is when someone asks you what you've been up to. I mean, how do you *even*--
Started going to the gym, stopped going to the gym, started going to the gym again--
Ooh, I binge-watched my way through all three seasons of *Homeland* finally. Pretty proud of that.
Got a new phone, switched to organic, a little vacation in Cancun--
But beyond *that,* kinda drawing a *blank.* Ah well--

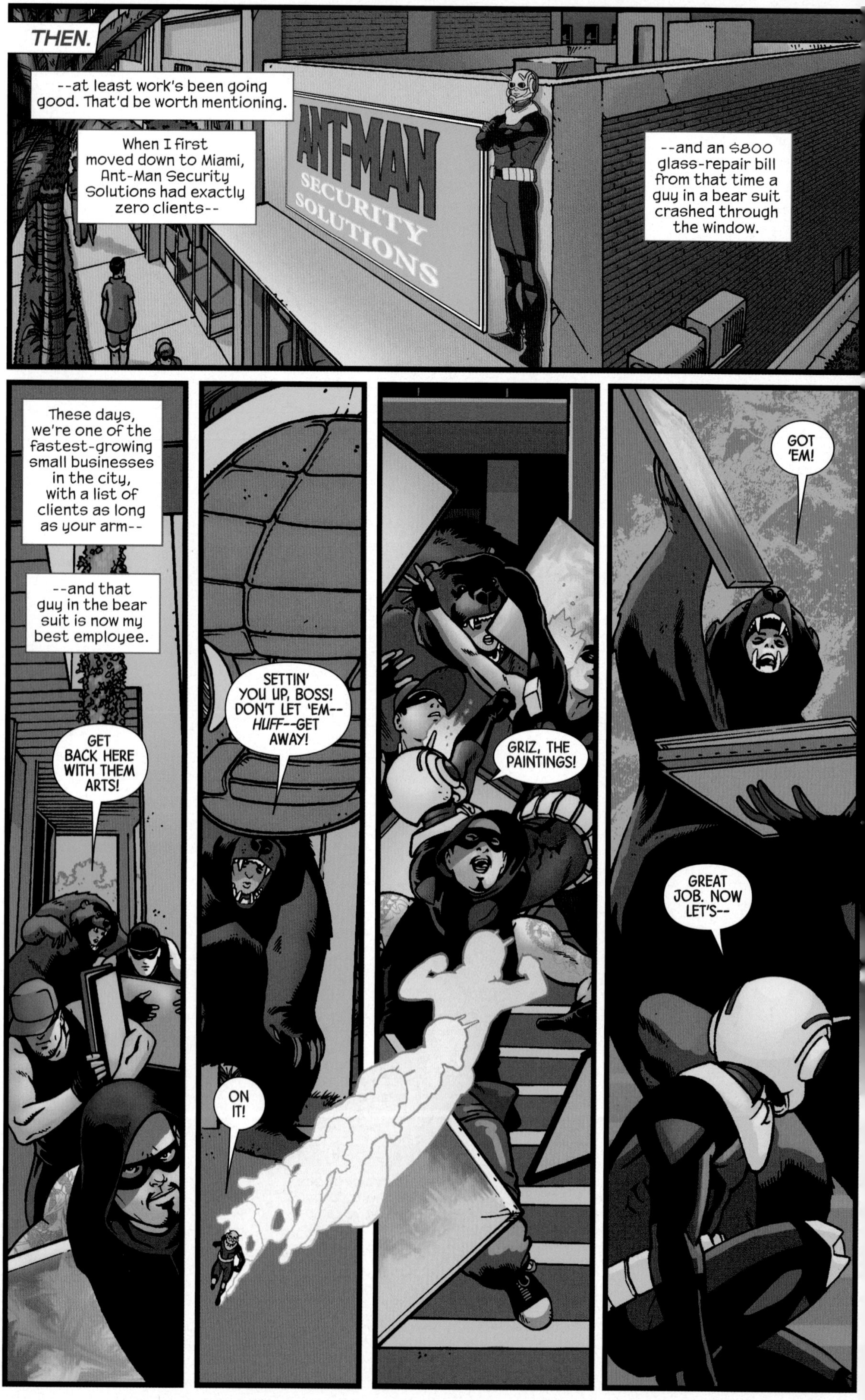
THEN.
--at least work's been going good. That'd be worth mentioning.
When I first moved down to Miami, Ant-Man Security Solutions had exactly zero clients--
ANT-MAN SECURITY SOLUTIONS
--and an $800 glass-repair bill from that time a guy in a bear suit crashed through the window.
These days, we're one of the fastest-growing small businesses in the city, with a list of clients as long as your arm--
--and that guy in the bear suit is now my best employee.
GET BACK HERE WITH THEM ARTS!
SETTIN' YOU UP, BOSS! DON'T LET 'EM--HUFF--GET AWAY!
ON IT!
GRIZ, THE PAINTINGS!
GOT 'EM!
GREAT JOB. NOW LET'S--

CEL-E-BRATE ♪♪♪ GOOD TIMES. COME ON! ♪

WA-HOO!

♪♪ IT'S A CEL-E-BRA-TION...

UH... SMITH?!!!

OH, UM...SORRY, GENTLEMEN. MUST'VE RUN A PROGRAM FROM THE *PERSONAL* COLLECTION BY ACCIDENT.

YEAH, "ACCIDENT"... SURE.

OH, COME ON. THIS IS THE FIFTEENTH SIMULATION YOU'VE HAD ME RUN TODAY. SUE ME FOR TRYING TO SPICE THINGS UP A LITTLE. BESIDES--

THIS IS MIAMI. YOU REALLY THINK YOU'RE NEVER GETTING ROBBED BY MALE STRIPPERS?

This is my other employee, *Machinesmith.* Smith for short. Our resident cyber-security expert.

Sure, he's on parole for various acts of terrorism and hacking. And sure, he maybe still golfs with Arnim Zola or whatever--

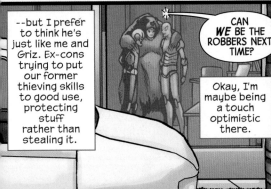

--but I prefer to think he's just like me and Griz. Ex-cons trying to put our former thieving skills to good use, protecting stuff rather than stealing it.

CAN *WE* BE THE ROBBERS NEXT TIME?

Okay, I'm maybe being a touch optimistic there.

COME ON, GUYS, I KNOW THIS IS GETTING TIRING, BUT THIS IS A BIG MEETING WE'VE GOT COMING UP. A LOT IS RIDING ON THIS.

NOT TO MENTION IF WE SCREW IT UP--

"--MS. MORGENSTERN IS GONNA BE PISSED."

YOU BETTER NOT SCREW THIS UP, LANG!

So yeah, this is Ms. Morgenstern, my kinda-sorta boss.

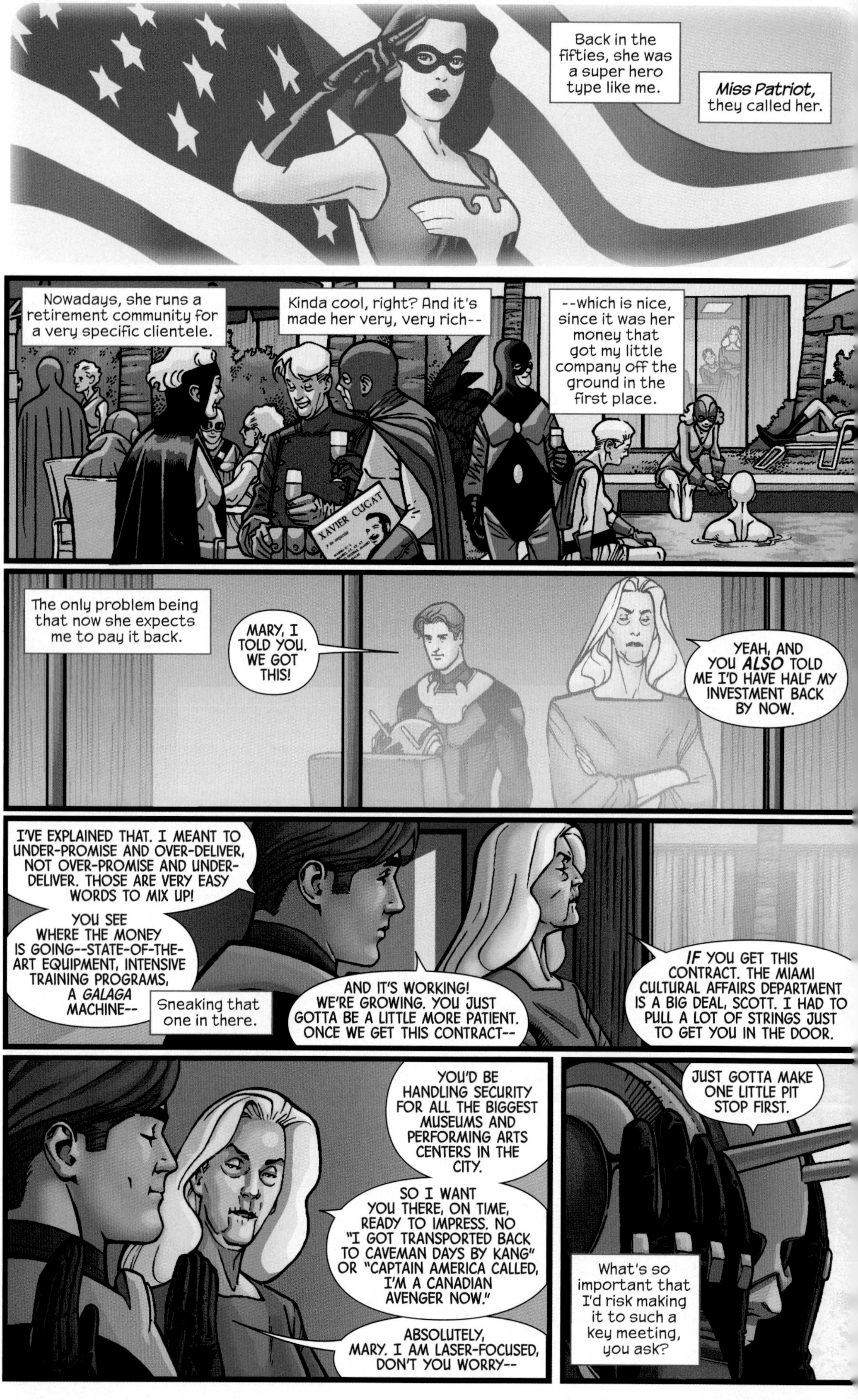

Back in the fifties, she was a super hero type like me.
Miss Patriot, they called her.
Nowadays, she runs a retirement community for a very specific clientele.
Kinda cool, right? And it's made her very, very rich--
--which is nice, since it was her money that got my little company off the ground in the first place.
XAVIER CUGAT
The only problem being that now she expects me to pay it back.
MARY, I TOLD YOU. WE GOT THIS!
YEAH, AND YOU *ALSO* TOLD ME I'D HAVE HALF MY INVESTMENT BACK BY NOW.
I'VE EXPLAINED THAT. I MEANT TO UNDER-PROMISE AND OVER-DELIVER, NOT OVER-PROMISE AND UNDER-DELIVER. THOSE ARE VERY EASY WORDS TO MIX UP!
YOU SEE WHERE THE MONEY IS GOING--STATE-OF-THE-ART EQUIPMENT, INTENSIVE TRAINING PROGRAMS, A *GALAGA* MACHINE--
Sneaking that one in there.
AND IT'S WORKING! WE'RE GROWING. YOU JUST GOTTA BE A LITTLE MORE PATIENT. ONCE WE GET THIS CONTRACT--
IF YOU GET THIS CONTRACT. THE MIAMI CULTURAL AFFAIRS DEPARTMENT IS A BIG DEAL, SCOTT. I HAD TO PULL A LOT OF STRINGS JUST TO GET YOU IN THE DOOR.
YOU'D BE HANDLING SECURITY FOR ALL THE BIGGEST MUSEUMS AND PERFORMING ARTS CENTERS IN THE CITY.
SO I WANT YOU THERE, ON TIME, READY TO IMPRESS. NO "I GOT TRANSPORTED BACK TO CAVEMAN DAYS BY KANG" OR "CAPTAIN AMERICA CALLED, I'M A CANADIAN AVENGER NOW."
ABSOLUTELY, MARY. I AM LASER-FOCUSED, DON'T YOU WORRY--
JUST GOTTA MAKE ONE LITTLE PIT STOP FIRST.
What's so important that I'd risk making it to such a key meeting, you ask?

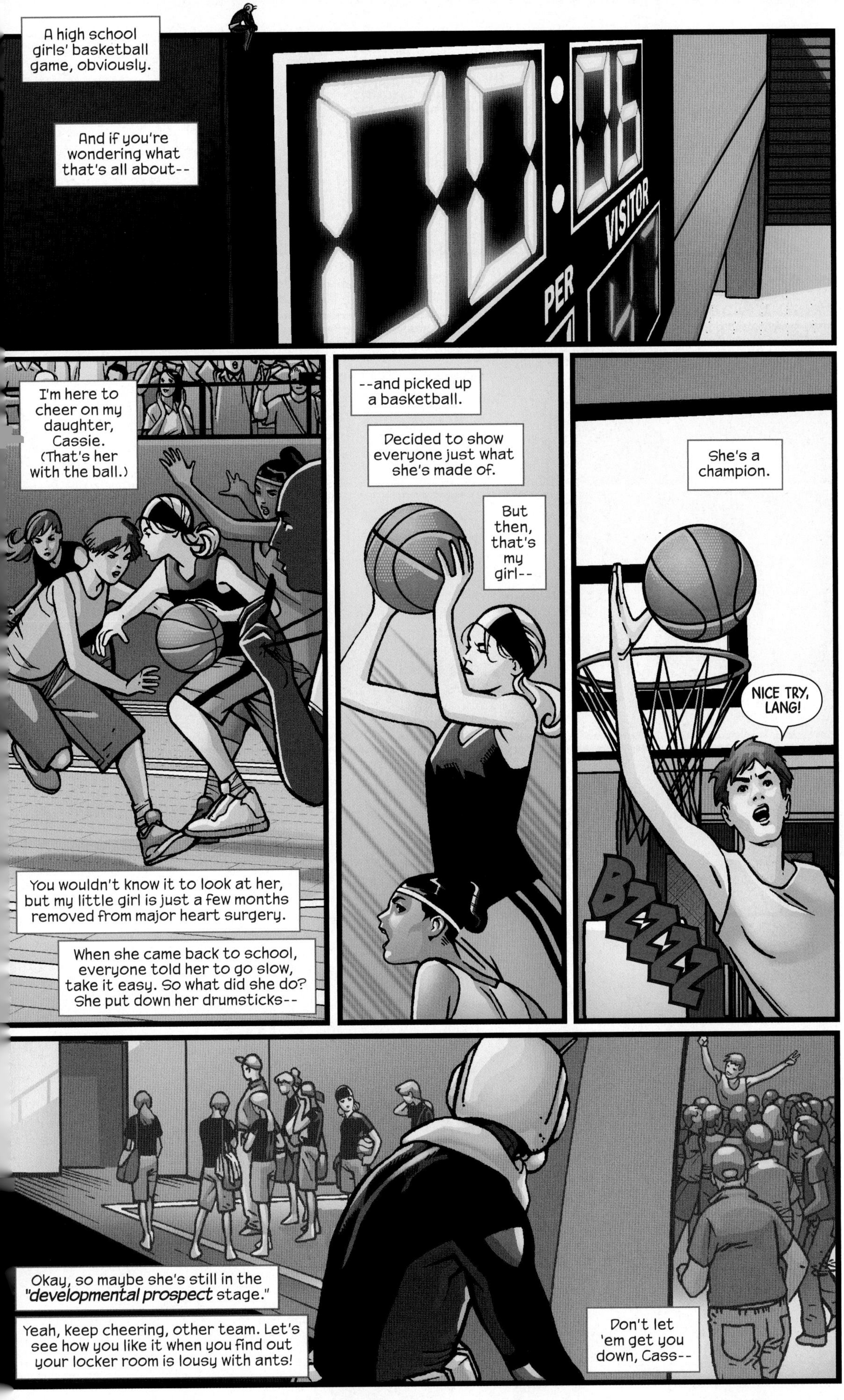
A high school girls' basketball game, obviously.
And if you're wondering what that's all about--
PER
VISITOR
I'm here to cheer on my daughter, Cassie. (That's her with the ball.)
You wouldn't know it to look at her, but my little girl is just a few months removed from major heart surgery.
When she came back to school, everyone told her to go slow, take it easy. So what did she do? She put down her drumsticks--
--and picked up a basketball.
Decided to show everyone just what she's made of.
But then, that's my girl--
She's a champion.
NICE TRY, LANG!
BZZZZ
Okay, so maybe she's still in the "*developmental prospect* stage."
Yeah, keep cheering, other team. Let's see how you like it when you find out your locker room is lousy with ants!
Don't let 'em get you down, Cass--

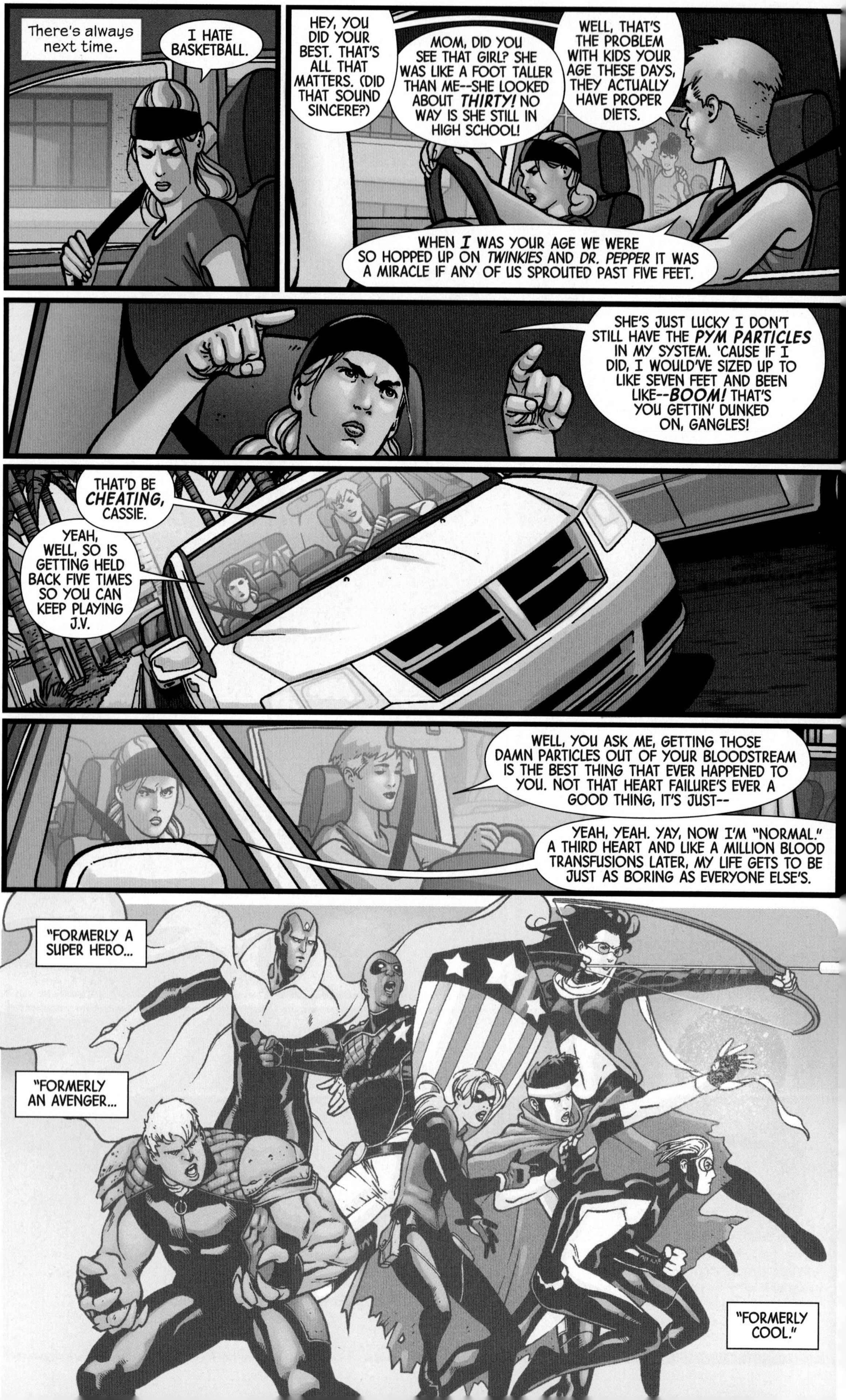
There's always next time.
I HATE BASKETBALL.
HEY, YOU DID YOUR BEST. THAT'S ALL THAT MATTERS. (DID THAT SOUND SINCERE?)
MOM, DID YOU SEE THAT GIRL? SHE WAS LIKE A FOOT TALLER THAN ME--SHE LOOKED ABOUT THIRTY! NO WAY IS SHE STILL IN HIGH SCHOOL!
WELL, THAT'S THE PROBLEM WITH KIDS YOUR AGE THESE DAYS, THEY ACTUALLY HAVE PROPER DIETS.
WHEN I WAS YOUR AGE WE WERE SO HOPPED UP ON TWINKIES AND DR. PEPPER IT WAS A MIRACLE IF ANY OF US SPROUTED PAST FIVE FEET.
SHE'S JUST LUCKY I DON'T STILL HAVE THE PYM PARTICLES IN MY SYSTEM. 'CAUSE IF I DID, I WOULD'VE SIZED UP TO LIKE SEVEN FEET AND BEEN LIKE--BOOM! THAT'S YOU GETTIN' DUNKED ON, GANGLES!
THAT'D BE CHEATING, CASSIE.
YEAH, WELL, SO IS GETTING HELD BACK FIVE TIMES SO YOU CAN KEEP PLAYING J.V.
WELL, YOU ASK ME, GETTING THOSE DAMN PARTICLES OUT OF YOUR BLOODSTREAM IS THE BEST THING THAT EVER HAPPENED TO YOU. NOT THAT HEART FAILURE'S EVER A GOOD THING, IT'S JUST--
YEAH, YEAH. YAY, NOW I'M "NORMAL." A THIRD HEART AND LIKE A MILLION BLOOD TRANSFUSIONS LATER, MY LIFE GETS TO BE JUST AS BORING AS EVERYONE ELSE'S.
"FORMERLY A SUPER HERO...
"FORMERLY AN AVENGER...
"FORMERLY COOL."

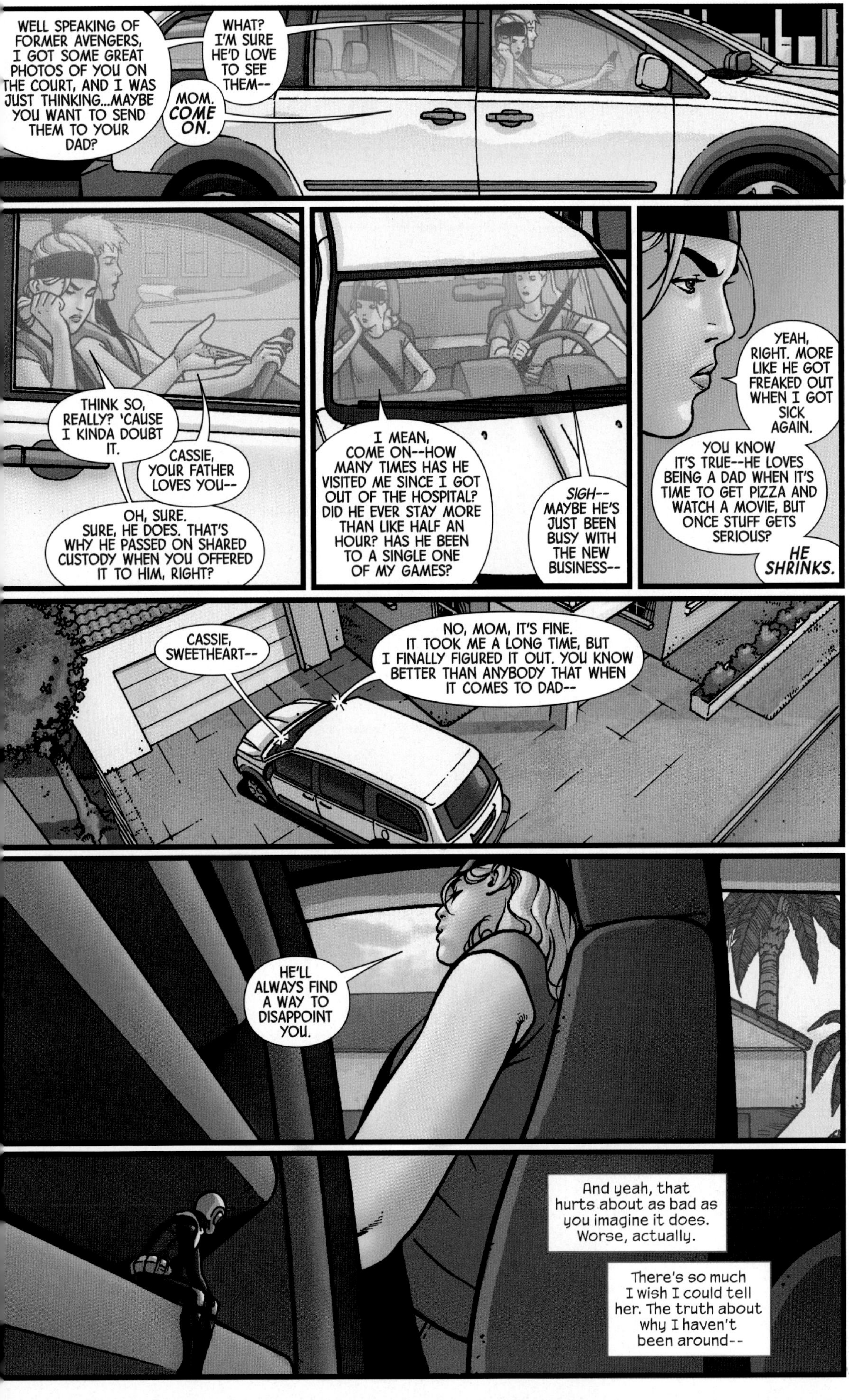
WELL SPEAKING OF FORMER AVENGERS, I GOT SOME GREAT PHOTOS OF YOU ON THE COURT, AND I WAS JUST THINKING...MAYBE YOU WANT TO SEND THEM TO YOUR DAD?
WHAT? I'M SURE HE'D LOVE TO SEE THEM--
MOM. COME ON.
THINK SO, REALLY? 'CAUSE I KINDA DOUBT IT.
CASSIE, YOUR FATHER LOVES YOU--
OH, SURE. SURE, HE DOES. THAT'S WHY HE PASSED ON SHARED CUSTODY WHEN YOU OFFERED IT TO HIM, RIGHT?
I MEAN, COME ON--HOW MANY TIMES HAS HE VISITED ME SINCE I GOT OUT OF THE HOSPITAL? DID HE EVER STAY MORE THAN LIKE HALF AN HOUR? HAS HE BEEN TO A SINGLE ONE OF MY GAMES?
SIGH--MAYBE HE'S JUST BEEN BUSY WITH THE NEW BUSINESS--
YEAH, RIGHT. MORE LIKE HE GOT FREAKED OUT WHEN I GOT SICK AGAIN.
YOU KNOW IT'S TRUE--HE LOVES BEING A DAD WHEN IT'S TIME TO GET PIZZA AND WATCH A MOVIE, BUT ONCE STUFF GETS SERIOUS?
HE SHRINKS.
CASSIE, SWEETHEART--
NO, MOM, IT'S FINE. IT TOOK ME A LONG TIME, BUT I FINALLY FIGURED IT OUT. YOU KNOW BETTER THAN ANYBODY THAT WHEN IT COMES TO DAD--
HE'LL ALWAYS FIND A WAY TO DISAPPOINT YOU.
And yeah, that hurts about as bad as you imagine it does. Worse, actually.
There's so much I wish I could tell her. The truth about why I haven't been around--

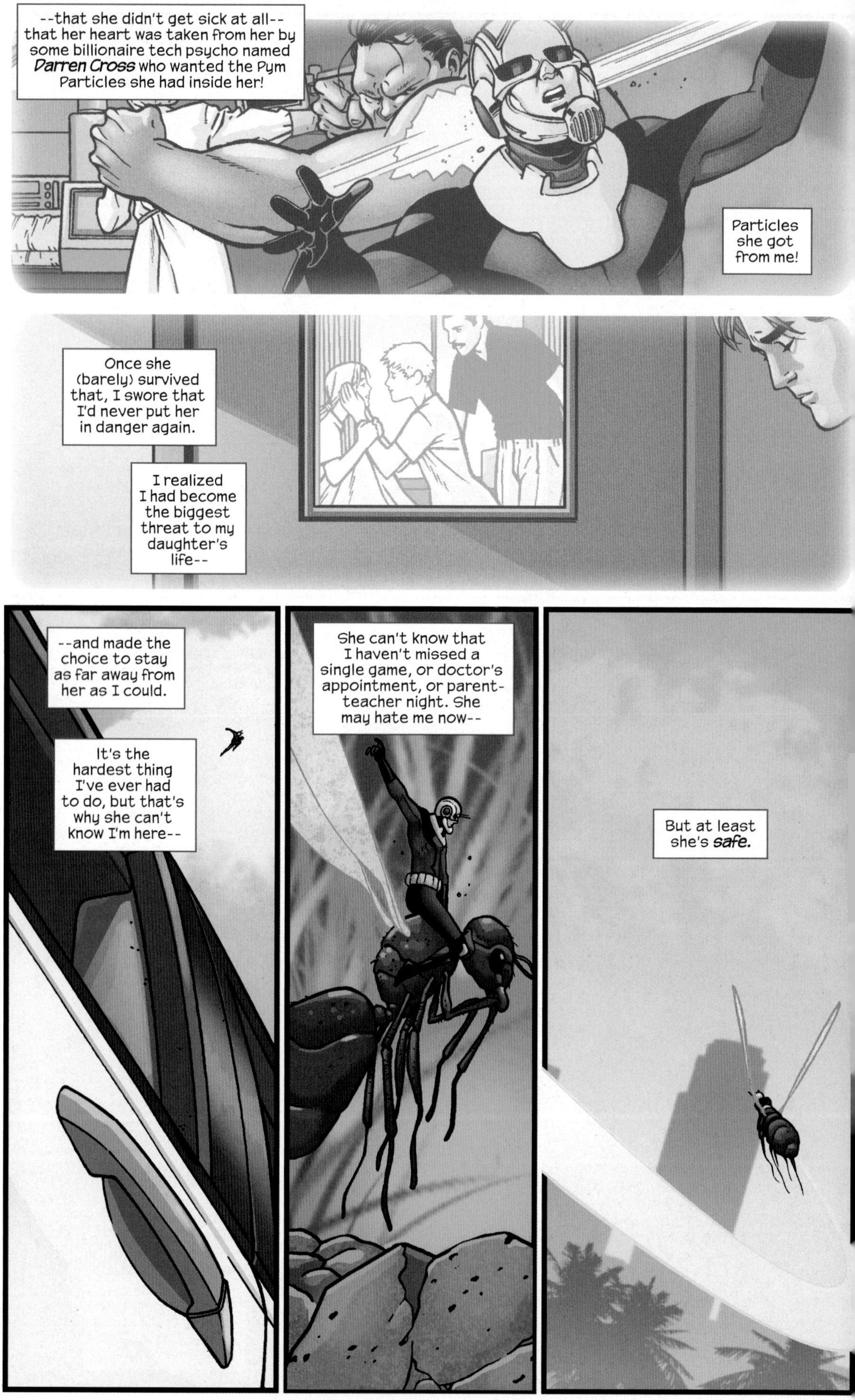
--that she didn't get sick at all--that her heart was taken from her by some billionaire tech psycho named *Darren Cross* who wanted the Pym Particles she had inside her!
Particles she got from me!
Once she (barely) survived that, I swore that I'd never put her in danger again.
I realized I had become the biggest threat to my daughter's life--
--and made the choice to stay as far away from her as I could.
It's the hardest thing I've ever had to do, but that's why she can't know I'm here--
She can't know that I haven't missed a single game, or doctor's appointment, or parent-teacher night. She may hate me now--
But at least she's *safe.*

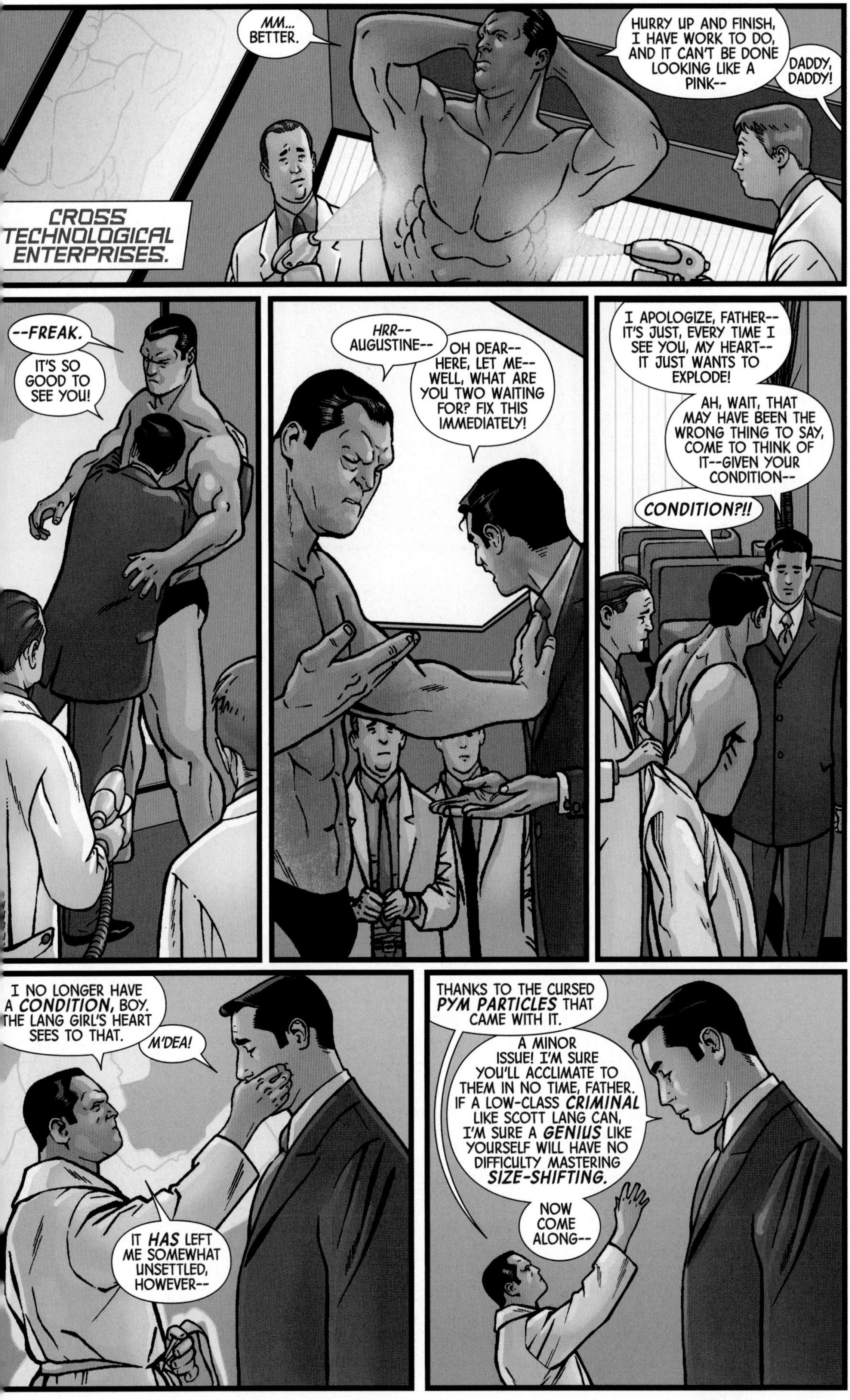
CROSS TECHNOLOGICAL ENTERPRISES.
MM... BETTER.
HURRY UP AND FINISH, I HAVE WORK TO DO, AND IT CAN'T BE DONE LOOKING LIKE A PINK--
DADDY, DADDY!
--FREAK.
IT'S SO GOOD TO SEE YOU!
HRR-- AUGUSTINE--
OH DEAR-- HERE, LET ME-- WELL, WHAT ARE YOU TWO WAITING FOR? FIX THIS IMMEDIATELY!
I APOLOGIZE, FATHER-- IT'S JUST, EVERY TIME I SEE YOU, MY HEART-- IT JUST WANTS TO EXPLODE!
AH, WAIT, THAT MAY HAVE BEEN THE WRONG THING TO SAY, COME TO THINK OF IT--GIVEN YOUR CONDITION--
CONDITION?!!
I NO LONGER HAVE A CONDITION, BOY. THE LANG GIRL'S HEART SEES TO THAT.
M'DEA!
IT HAS LEFT ME SOMEWHAT UNSETTLED, HOWEVER--
THANKS TO THE CURSED PYM PARTICLES THAT CAME WITH IT.
A MINOR ISSUE! I'M SURE YOU'LL ACCLIMATE TO THEM IN NO TIME, FATHER. IF A LOW-CLASS CRIMINAL LIKE SCOTT LANG CAN, I'M SURE A GENIUS LIKE YOURSELF WILL HAVE NO DIFFICULTY MASTERING SIZE-SHIFTING.
NOW COME ALONG--

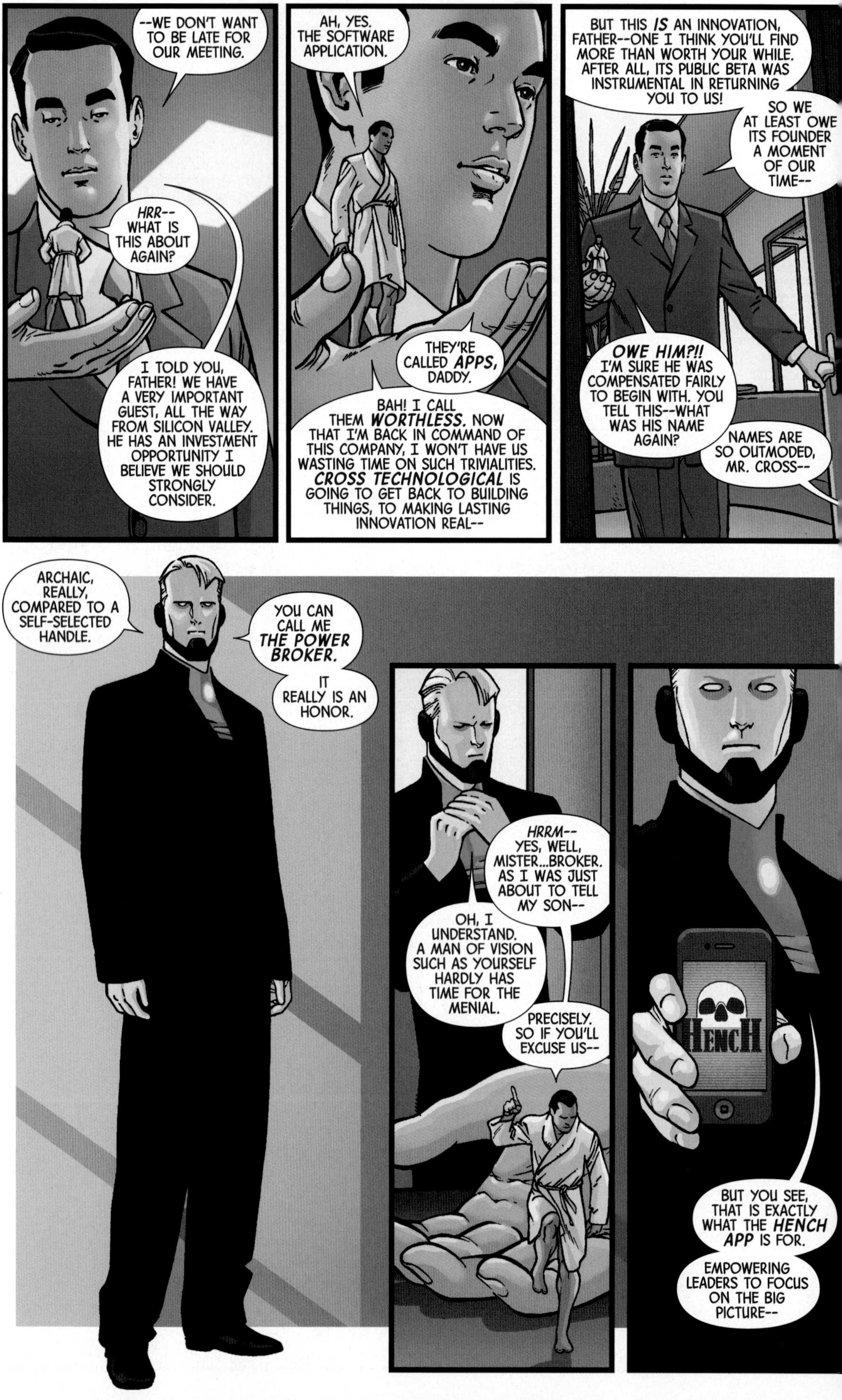
--WE DON'T WANT TO BE LATE FOR OUR MEETING.
HRR-- WHAT IS THIS ABOUT AGAIN?
I TOLD YOU, FATHER! WE HAVE A VERY IMPORTANT GUEST, ALL THE WAY FROM SILICON VALLEY. HE HAS AN INVESTMENT OPPORTUNITY I BELIEVE WE SHOULD STRONGLY CONSIDER.
AH, YES. THE SOFTWARE APPLICATION.
THEY'RE CALLED APPS, DADDY.
BAH! I CALL THEM WORTHLESS. NOW THAT I'M BACK IN COMMAND OF THIS COMPANY, I WON'T HAVE US WASTING TIME ON SUCH TRIVIALITIES. CROSS TECHNOLOGICAL IS GOING TO GET BACK TO BUILDING THINGS, TO MAKING LASTING INNOVATION REAL--
BUT THIS IS AN INNOVATION, FATHER--ONE I THINK YOU'LL FIND MORE THAN WORTH YOUR WHILE. AFTER ALL, ITS PUBLIC BETA WAS INSTRUMENTAL IN RETURNING YOU TO US!
SO WE AT LEAST OWE ITS FOUNDER A MOMENT OF OUR TIME--
OWE HIM?!! I'M SURE HE WAS COMPENSATED FAIRLY TO BEGIN WITH. YOU TELL THIS--WHAT WAS HIS NAME AGAIN?
NAMES ARE SO OUTMODED, MR. CROSS--
ARCHAIC, REALLY, COMPARED TO A SELF-SELECTED HANDLE.
YOU CAN CALL ME THE POWER BROKER.
IT REALLY IS AN HONOR.
HRRM-- YES, WELL, MISTER...BROKER. AS I WAS JUST ABOUT TO TELL MY SON--
OH, I UNDERSTAND. A MAN OF VISION SUCH AS YOURSELF HARDLY HAS TIME FOR THE MENIAL.
PRECISELY. SO IF YOU'LL EXCUSE US--
HENCH
BUT YOU SEE, THAT IS EXACTLY WHAT THE HENCH APP IS FOR.
EMPOWERING LEADERS TO FOCUS ON THE BIG PICTURE--

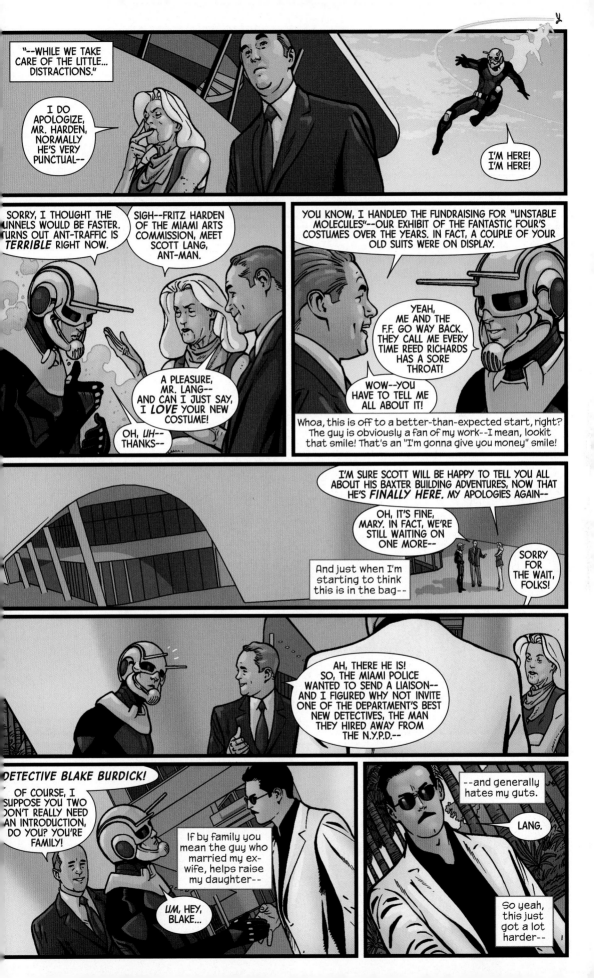

"--WHILE WE TAKE CARE OF THE LITTLE... DISTRACTIONS."

I DO APOLOGIZE, MR. HARDEN, NORMALLY HE'S VERY PUNCTUAL--

I'M HERE! I'M HERE!

SORRY, I THOUGHT THE TUNNELS WOULD BE FASTER. TURNS OUT ANT-TRAFFIC IS *TERRIBLE* RIGHT NOW.

SIGH--FRITZ HARDEN OF THE MIAMI ARTS COMMISSION, MEET SCOTT LANG, ANT-MAN.

A PLEASURE, MR. LANG-- AND CAN I JUST SAY, I *LOVE* YOUR NEW COSTUME!

OH, *UH*-- THANKS--

YOU KNOW, I HANDLED THE FUNDRAISING FOR "UNSTABLE MOLECULES"--OUR EXHIBIT OF THE FANTASTIC FOUR'S COSTUMES OVER THE YEARS. IN FACT, A COUPLE OF YOUR OLD SUITS WERE ON DISPLAY.

YEAH, ME AND THE F.F. GO WAY BACK. THEY CALL ME EVERY TIME REED RICHARDS HAS A SORE THROAT!

WOW--YOU HAVE TO TELL ME ALL ABOUT IT!

Whoa, this is off to a better-than-expected start, right? The guy is obviously a fan of my work--I mean, lookit that smile! That's an "I'm gonna give you money" smile!

I'M SURE SCOTT WILL BE HAPPY TO TELL YOU ALL ABOUT HIS BAXTER BUILDING ADVENTURES, NOW THAT HE'S *FINALLY HERE.* MY APOLOGIES AGAIN--

OH, IT'S FINE, MARY. IN FACT, WE'RE STILL WAITING ON ONE MORE--

And just when I'm starting to think this is in the bag--

SORRY FOR THE WAIT, FOLKS!

AH, THERE HE IS! SO, THE MIAMI POLICE WANTED TO SEND A LIAISON-- AND I FIGURED WHY NOT INVITE ONE OF THE DEPARTMENT'S BEST NEW DETECTIVES, THE MAN THEY HIRED AWAY FROM THE N.Y.P.D.--

DETECTIVE BLAKE BURDICK! OF COURSE, I SUPPOSE YOU TWO DON'T REALLY NEED AN INTRODUCTION, DO YOU? YOU'RE FAMILY!

If by family you mean the guy who married my ex-wife, helps raise my daughter--

UM, HEY, BLAKE...

--and generally hates my guts.

LANG.

So yeah, this just got a lot harder--

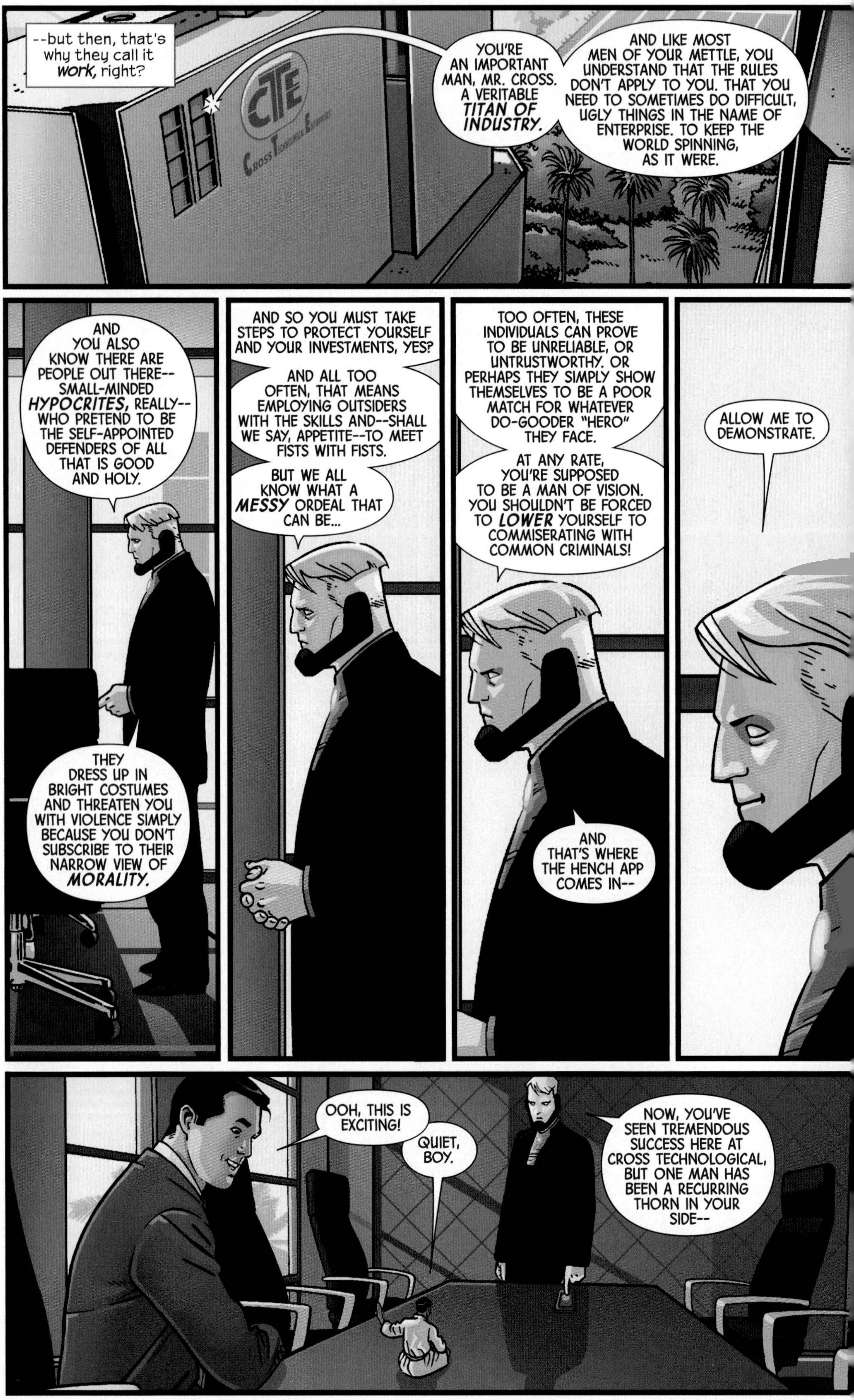
--but then, that's why they call it *work,* right?
YOU'RE AN IMPORTANT MAN, MR. CROSS. A VERITABLE *TITAN OF INDUSTRY.*
AND LIKE MOST MEN OF YOUR METTLE, YOU UNDERSTAND THAT THE RULES DON'T APPLY TO YOU. THAT YOU NEED TO SOMETIMES DO DIFFICULT, UGLY THINGS IN THE NAME OF ENTERPRISE. TO KEEP THE WORLD SPINNING, AS IT WERE.
AND YOU ALSO KNOW THERE ARE PEOPLE OUT THERE-- SMALL-MINDED *HYPOCRITES,* REALLY-- WHO PRETEND TO BE THE SELF-APPOINTED DEFENDERS OF ALL THAT IS GOOD AND HOLY.
THEY DRESS UP IN BRIGHT COSTUMES AND THREATEN YOU WITH VIOLENCE SIMPLY BECAUSE YOU DON'T SUBSCRIBE TO THEIR NARROW VIEW OF *MORALITY.*
AND SO YOU MUST TAKE STEPS TO PROTECT YOURSELF AND YOUR INVESTMENTS, YES?
AND ALL TOO OFTEN, THAT MEANS EMPLOYING OUTSIDERS WITH THE SKILLS AND--SHALL WE SAY, APPETITE--TO MEET FISTS WITH FISTS.
BUT WE ALL KNOW WHAT A *MESSY* ORDEAL THAT CAN BE...
TOO OFTEN, THESE INDIVIDUALS CAN PROVE TO BE UNRELIABLE, OR UNTRUSTWORTHY. OR PERHAPS THEY SIMPLY SHOW THEMSELVES TO BE A POOR MATCH FOR WHATEVER DO-GOODER "HERO" THEY FACE.
AT ANY RATE, YOU'RE SUPPOSED TO BE A MAN OF VISION. YOU SHOULDN'T BE FORCED TO *LOWER* YOURSELF TO COMMISERATING WITH COMMON CRIMINALS!
AND THAT'S WHERE THE HENCH APP COMES IN--
ALLOW ME TO DEMONSTRATE.
OOH, THIS IS EXCITING!
QUIET, BOY.
NOW, YOU'VE SEEN TREMENDOUS SUCCESS HERE AT CROSS TECHNOLOGICAL, BUT ONE MAN HAS BEEN A RECURRING THORN IN YOUR SIDE--

"SCOTT LANG, ANT-MAN, VERSION 2.0. A FORMER PETTY THIEF HIMSELF.

"WHERE DOES HE FIND THE NERVE, YES?"

HRRR... THE ANT.

YES, I AGREE, "HRRR." BUT WHAT IF DISPATCHING HIM WERE AS SIMPLE AS LOADING OUR STREAMLINED AND USER-FRIENDLY INTERFACE? HERE--

FIRST WE DO A QUICK *SEARCH* FOR THE HERO IN QUESTION--

THEN, OUR PATENTED ALGORITHM FINDS YOU THE BEST POSSIBLE MATCH BASED ON LOCATION, POWER SET, AND PAST CONFRONTATION HISTORY!

IT'S SEARCHING NOW...

Searching...

BOOP BOOP

Hench found!

AND WE HAVE A MATCH!

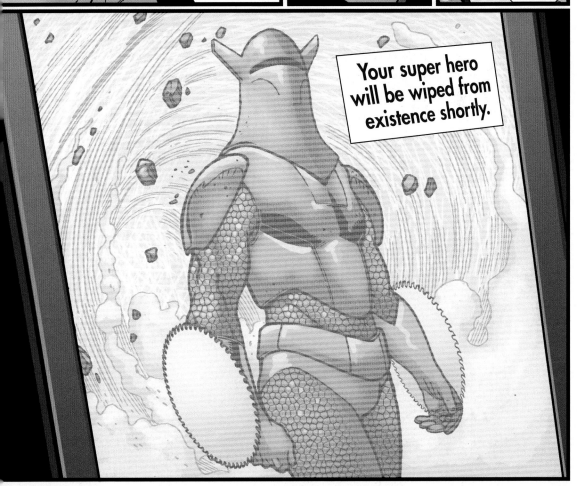

Your super hero will be wiped from existence shortly.

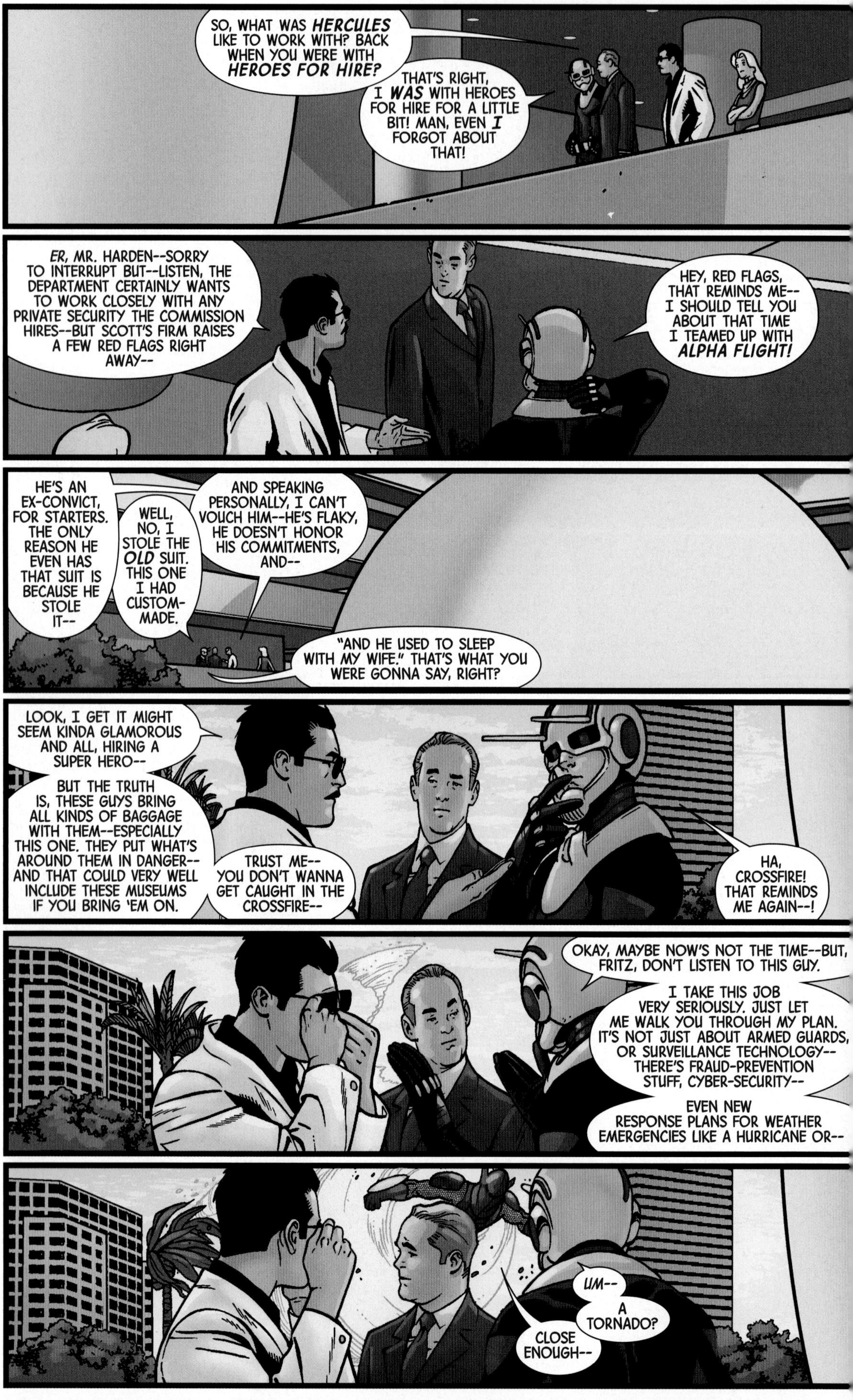
SO, WHAT WAS HERCULES LIKE TO WORK WITH? BACK WHEN YOU WERE WITH HEROES FOR HIRE?
THAT'S RIGHT, I WAS WITH HEROES FOR HIRE FOR A LITTLE BIT! MAN, EVEN I FORGOT ABOUT THAT!
ER, MR. HARDEN--SORRY TO INTERRUPT BUT--LISTEN, THE DEPARTMENT CERTAINLY WANTS TO WORK CLOSELY WITH ANY PRIVATE SECURITY THE COMMISSION HIRES--BUT SCOTT'S FIRM RAISES A FEW RED FLAGS RIGHT AWAY--
HEY, RED FLAGS, THAT REMINDS ME--I SHOULD TELL YOU ABOUT THAT TIME I TEAMED UP WITH ALPHA FLIGHT!
HE'S AN EX-CONVICT, FOR STARTERS. THE ONLY REASON HE EVEN HAS THAT SUIT IS BECAUSE HE STOLE IT--
WELL, NO, I STOLE THE OLD SUIT. THIS ONE I HAD CUSTOM-MADE.
AND SPEAKING PERSONALLY, I CAN'T VOUCH HIM--HE'S FLAKY, HE DOESN'T HONOR HIS COMMITMENTS, AND--
"AND HE USED TO SLEEP WITH MY WIFE." THAT'S WHAT YOU WERE GONNA SAY, RIGHT?
LOOK, I GET IT MIGHT SEEM KINDA GLAMOROUS AND ALL, HIRING A SUPER HERO--
BUT THE TRUTH IS, THESE GUYS BRING ALL KINDS OF BAGGAGE WITH THEM--ESPECIALLY THIS ONE. THEY PUT WHAT'S AROUND THEM IN DANGER--AND THAT COULD VERY WELL INCLUDE THESE MUSEUMS IF YOU BRING 'EM ON.
TRUST ME--YOU DON'T WANNA GET CAUGHT IN THE CROSSFIRE--
HA, CROSSFIRE! THAT REMINDS ME AGAIN--!
OKAY, MAYBE NOW'S NOT THE TIME--BUT, FRITZ, DON'T LISTEN TO THIS GUY.
I TAKE THIS JOB VERY SERIOUSLY. JUST LET ME WALK YOU THROUGH MY PLAN. IT'S NOT JUST ABOUT ARMED GUARDS, OR SURVEILLANCE TECHNOLOGY--THERE'S FRAUD-PREVENTION STUFF, CYBER-SECURITY--
EVEN NEW RESPONSE PLANS FOR WEATHER EMERGENCIES LIKE A HURRICANE OR--
UM--
A TORNADO?
CLOSE ENOUGH--

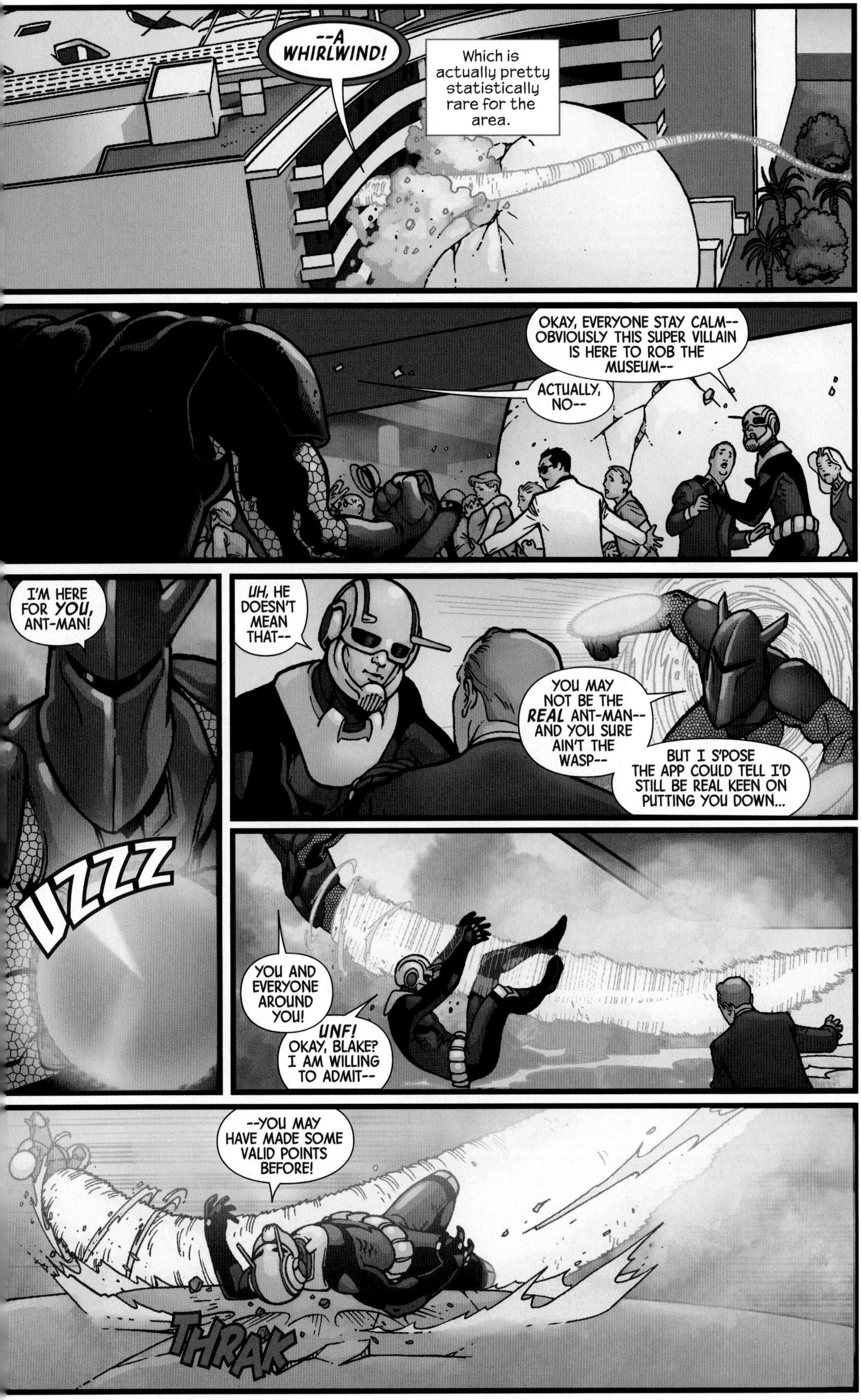
--A WHIRLWIND!
Which is actually pretty statistically rare for the area.
OKAY, EVERYONE STAY CALM-- OBVIOUSLY THIS SUPER VILLAIN IS HERE TO ROB THE MUSEUM--
ACTUALLY, NO--
I'M HERE FOR YOU, ANT-MAN!
UH, HE DOESN'T MEAN THAT--
YOU MAY NOT BE THE REAL ANT-MAN-- AND YOU SURE AIN'T THE WASP--
BUT I S'POSE THE APP COULD TELL I'D STILL BE REAL KEEN ON PUTTING YOU DOWN...
UZZZ
YOU AND EVERYONE AROUND YOU!
UNF! OKAY, BLAKE? I AM WILLING TO ADMIT--
--YOU MAY HAVE MADE SOME VALID POINTS BEFORE!
THRAK

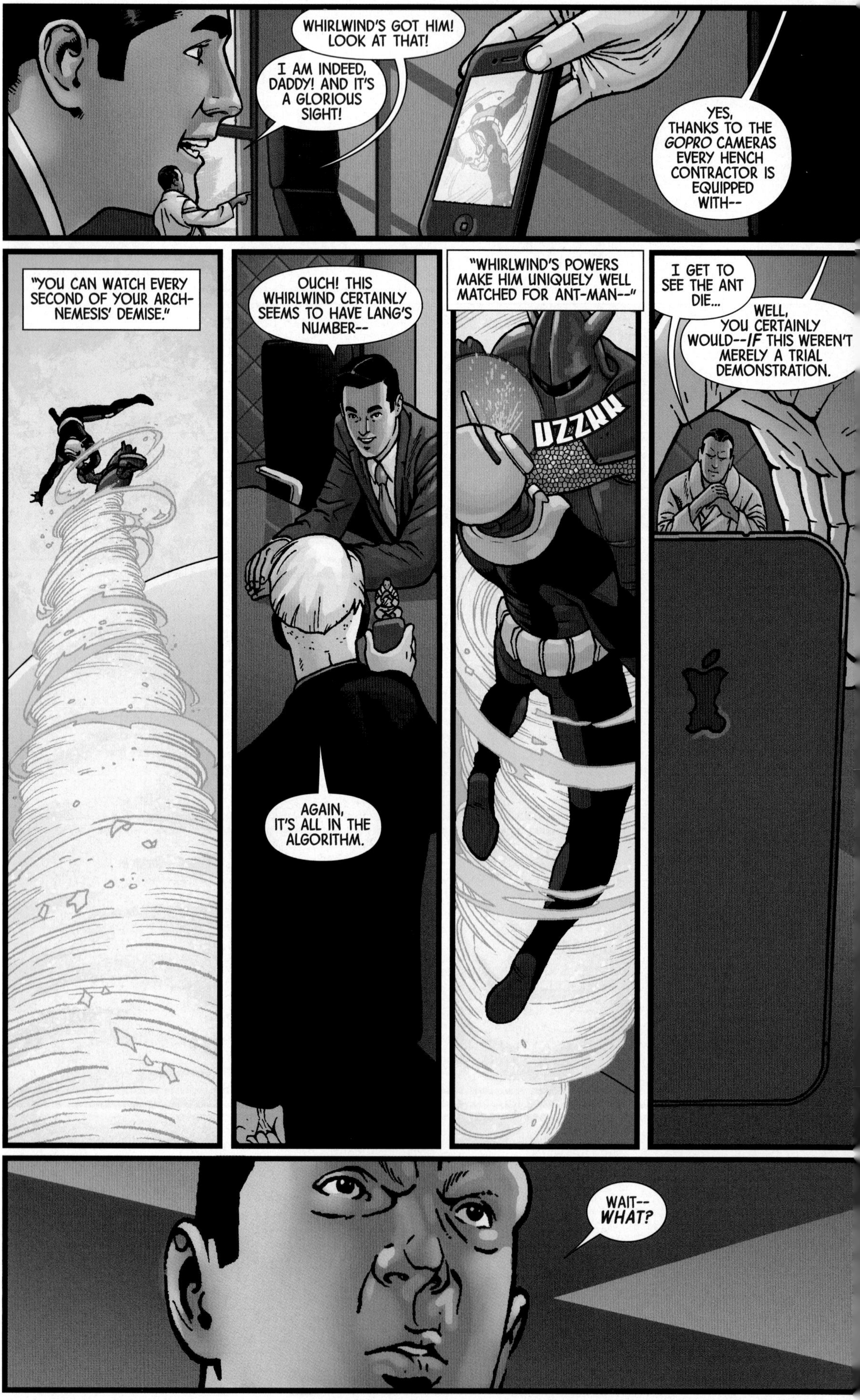
WHIRLWIND'S GOT HIM! LOOK AT THAT!
I AM INDEED, DADDY! AND IT'S A GLORIOUS SIGHT!
YES, THANKS TO THE GOPRO CAMERAS EVERY HENCH CONTRACTOR IS EQUIPPED WITH--
"YOU CAN WATCH EVERY SECOND OF YOUR ARCH-NEMESIS' DEMISE."
OUCH! THIS WHIRLWIND CERTAINLY SEEMS TO HAVE LANG'S NUMBER--
AGAIN, IT'S ALL IN THE ALGORITHM.
"WHIRLWIND'S POWERS MAKE HIM UNIQUELY WELL MATCHED FOR ANT-MAN--"
UZZKH
I GET TO SEE THE ANT DIE...
WELL, YOU CERTAINLY WOULD--IF THIS WEREN'T MERELY A TRIAL DEMONSTRATION.
WAIT-- WHAT?

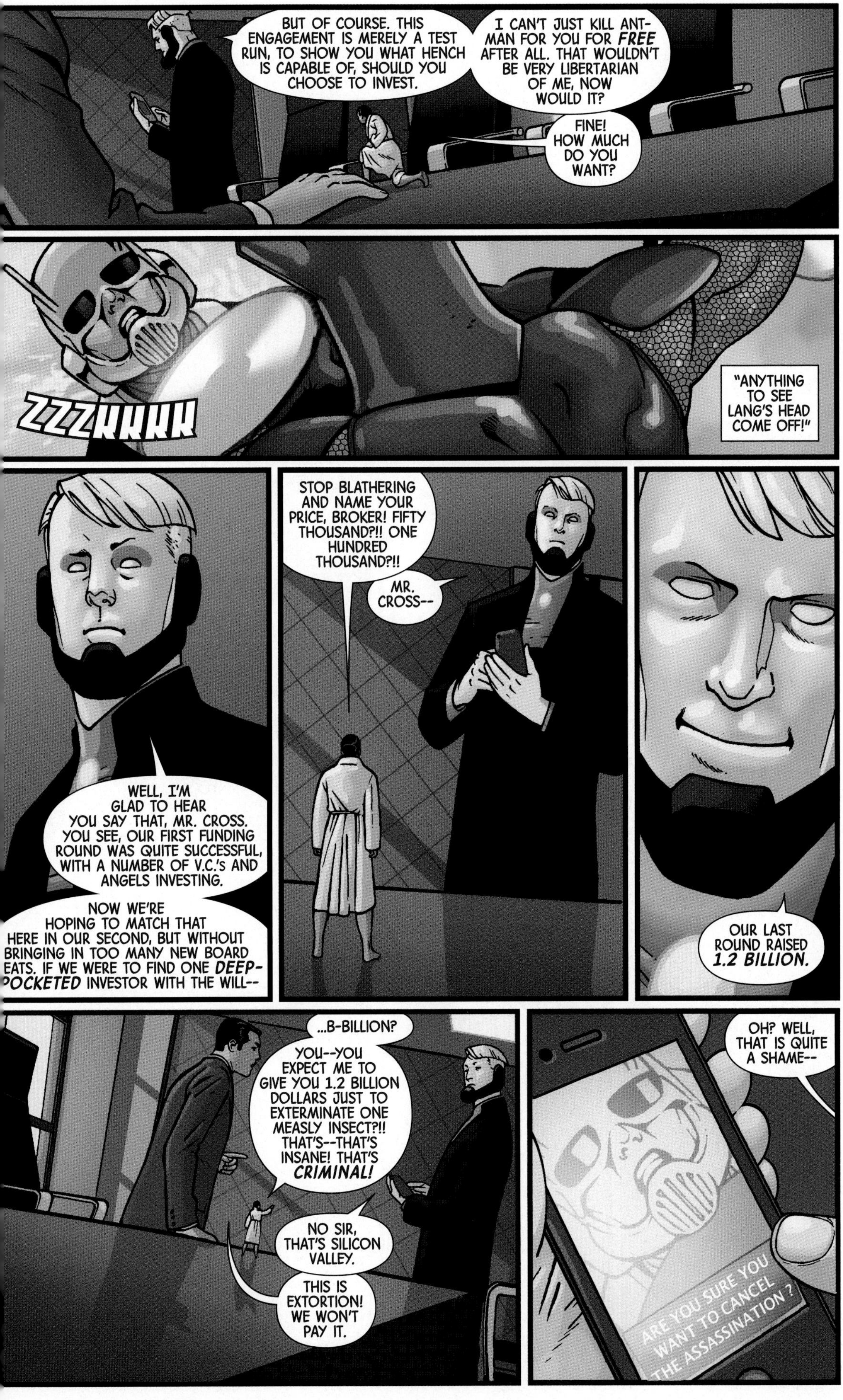
BUT OF COURSE. THIS ENGAGEMENT IS MERELY A TEST RUN, TO SHOW YOU WHAT HENCH IS CAPABLE OF, SHOULD YOU CHOOSE TO INVEST.
I CAN'T JUST KILL ANT-MAN FOR YOU FOR FREE AFTER ALL. THAT WOULDN'T BE VERY LIBERTARIAN OF ME, NOW WOULD IT?
FINE! HOW MUCH DO YOU WANT?
ZZZKKKKK
"ANYTHING TO SEE LANG'S HEAD COME OFF!"
STOP BLATHERING AND NAME YOUR PRICE, BROKER! FIFTY THOUSAND?!! ONE HUNDRED THOUSAND?!!
MR. CROSS--
WELL, I'M GLAD TO HEAR YOU SAY THAT, MR. CROSS. YOU SEE, OUR FIRST FUNDING ROUND WAS QUITE SUCCESSFUL, WITH A NUMBER OF V.C.'s AND ANGELS INVESTING.
NOW WE'RE HOPING TO MATCH THAT HERE IN OUR SECOND, BUT WITHOUT BRINGING IN TOO MANY NEW BOARD EATS. IF WE WERE TO FIND ONE DEEP-OCKETED INVESTOR WITH THE WILL--
OUR LAST ROUND RAISED 1.2 BILLION.
...B-BILLION?
YOU--YOU EXPECT ME TO GIVE YOU 1.2 BILLION DOLLARS JUST TO EXTERMINATE ONE MEASLY INSECT?!! THAT'S--THAT'S INSANE! THAT'S CRIMINAL!
NO SIR, THAT'S SILICON VALLEY.
THIS IS EXTORTION! WE WON'T PAY IT.
OH? WELL, THAT IS QUITE A SHAME--
ARE YOU SURE YOU WANT TO CANCEL THE ASSASSINATION?

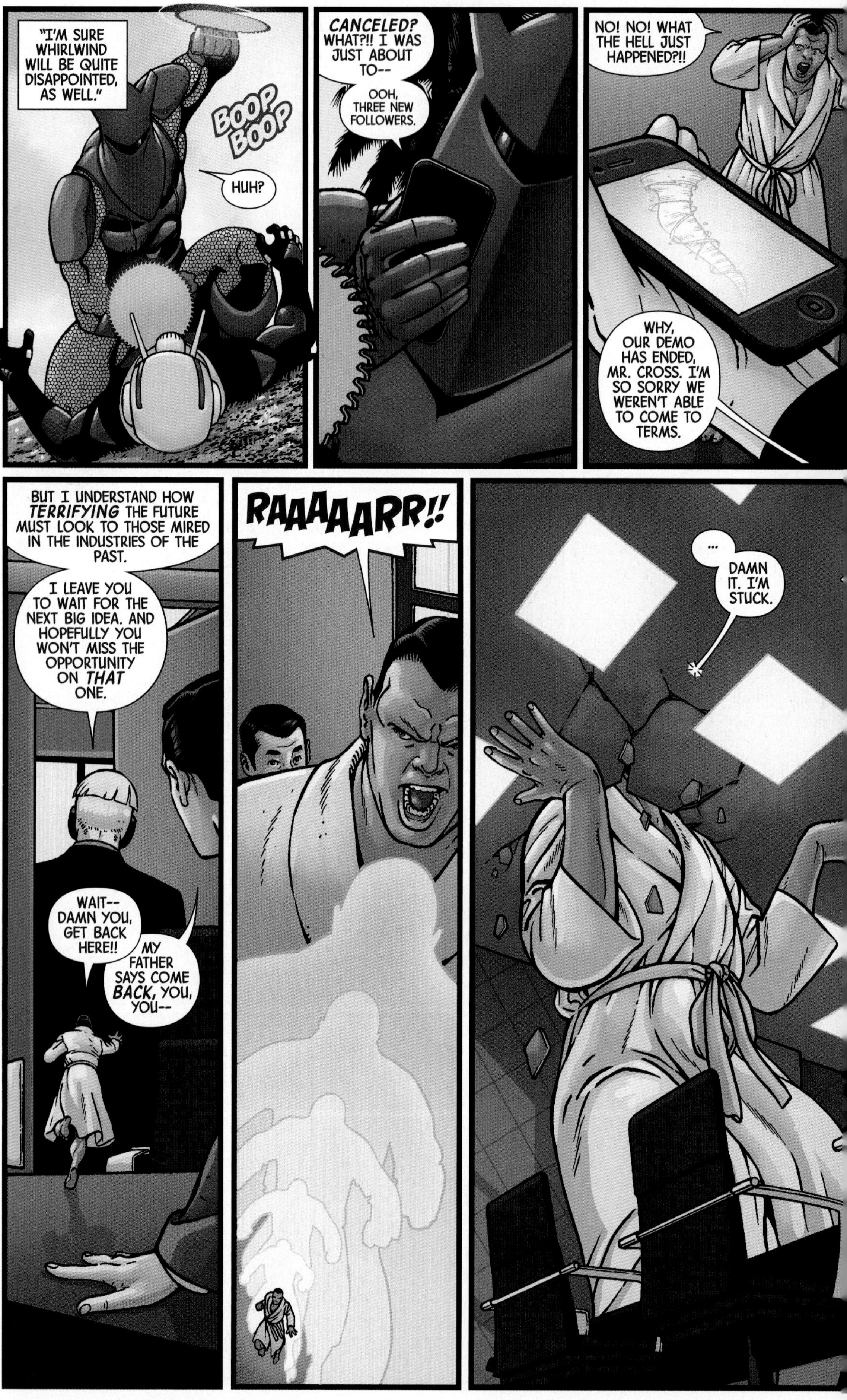
"I'M SURE WHIRLWIND WILL BE QUITE DISAPPOINTED, AS WELL."
BOOP BOOP
HUH?
CANCELED? WHAT?!! I WAS JUST ABOUT TO--
OOH, THREE NEW FOLLOWERS.
NO! NO! WHAT THE HELL JUST HAPPENED?!!
WHY, OUR DEMO HAS ENDED, MR. CROSS. I'M SO SORRY WE WEREN'T ABLE TO COME TO TERMS.
BUT I UNDERSTAND HOW TERRIFYING THE FUTURE MUST LOOK TO THOSE MIRED IN THE INDUSTRIES OF THE PAST.
I LEAVE YOU TO WAIT FOR THE NEXT BIG IDEA. AND HOPEFULLY YOU WON'T MISS THE OPPORTUNITY ON THAT ONE.
WAIT-- DAMN YOU, GET BACK HERE!!
MY FATHER SAYS COME BACK, YOU, YOU--
RAAAAARR!!
...
DAMN IT. I'M STUCK.

WELL, THAT WAS WEIRD.

SEE? THIS IS *EXACTLY* WHAT I WAS TALKING ABOUT, MR. HARDEN! TROUBLE FINDS THIS GUY EVERY TIME!

AW, COME ON, BLAKE-- THIS GUY KNOWS THE DRILL-- ISN'T THAT RIGHT, FRITZ? I BET IT WAS PRETTY COOL GETTING TO SEE A REAL LIVE SUPER HERO FIGHT INSTEAD OF JUST READING ABOUT IT, *EH? EH?*

ARE YOU KIDDING ME? NO! LOOK AT THIS PLACE! YOU DESTROYED OUR NEW PLANETARIUM!

I--I ALWAYS THOUGHT WHAT YOU DID WAS EXCITING, BUT SEEING IT UP CLOSE? PEOPLE COULD'VE DIED! WHAT IS *WRONG* WITH YOU PSYCHOPATHS?!!

WELL, I GUESS IT'S NOT FOR EVERYONE...

WE'LL TALK BACK AT THE OFFICE, LANG.

OOF. YEAH, NO WORRIES, EVERYONE, I'LL FIND MY OWN MEDICAL ATTENTION!

BOOP BOOP

HM?

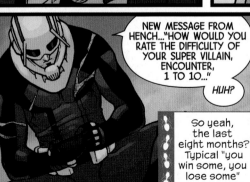

NEW MESSAGE FROM HENCH..."HOW WOULD YOU RATE THE DIFFICULTY OF YOUR SUPER VILLAIN, ENCOUNTER, 1 TO 10..."

HUH?

So yeah, the last eight months? Typical "you win some, you lose some" stuff, I guess. Beyond that, I'm drawing a blank.

MOVE... TO...SPAM.

Oh, wait, almost forgot, one other thing--

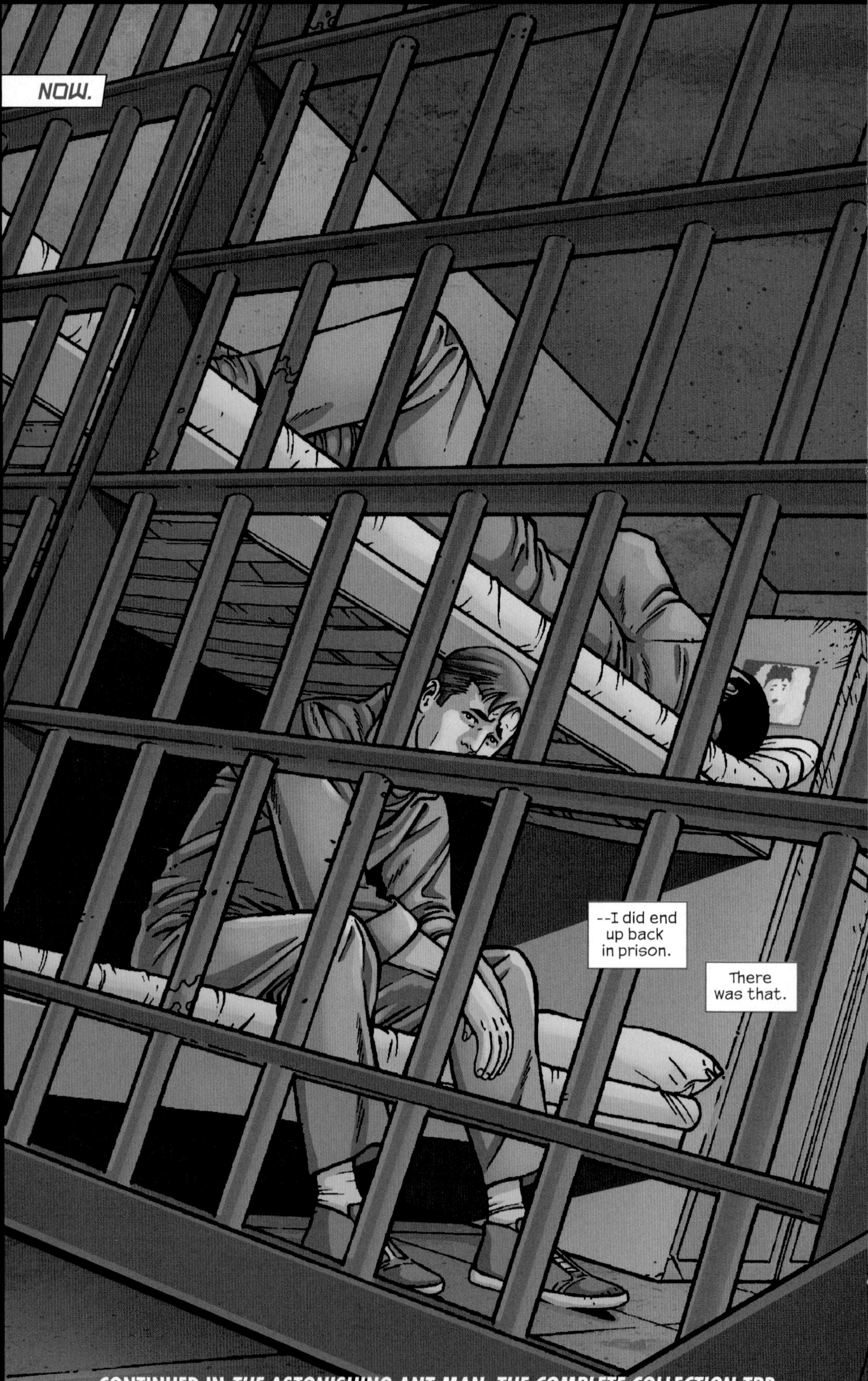
NOW.
--I did end up back in prison.
There was that.

CONTINUED IN *THE ASTONISHING ANT-MAN: THE COMPLETE COLLECTION TPB.*

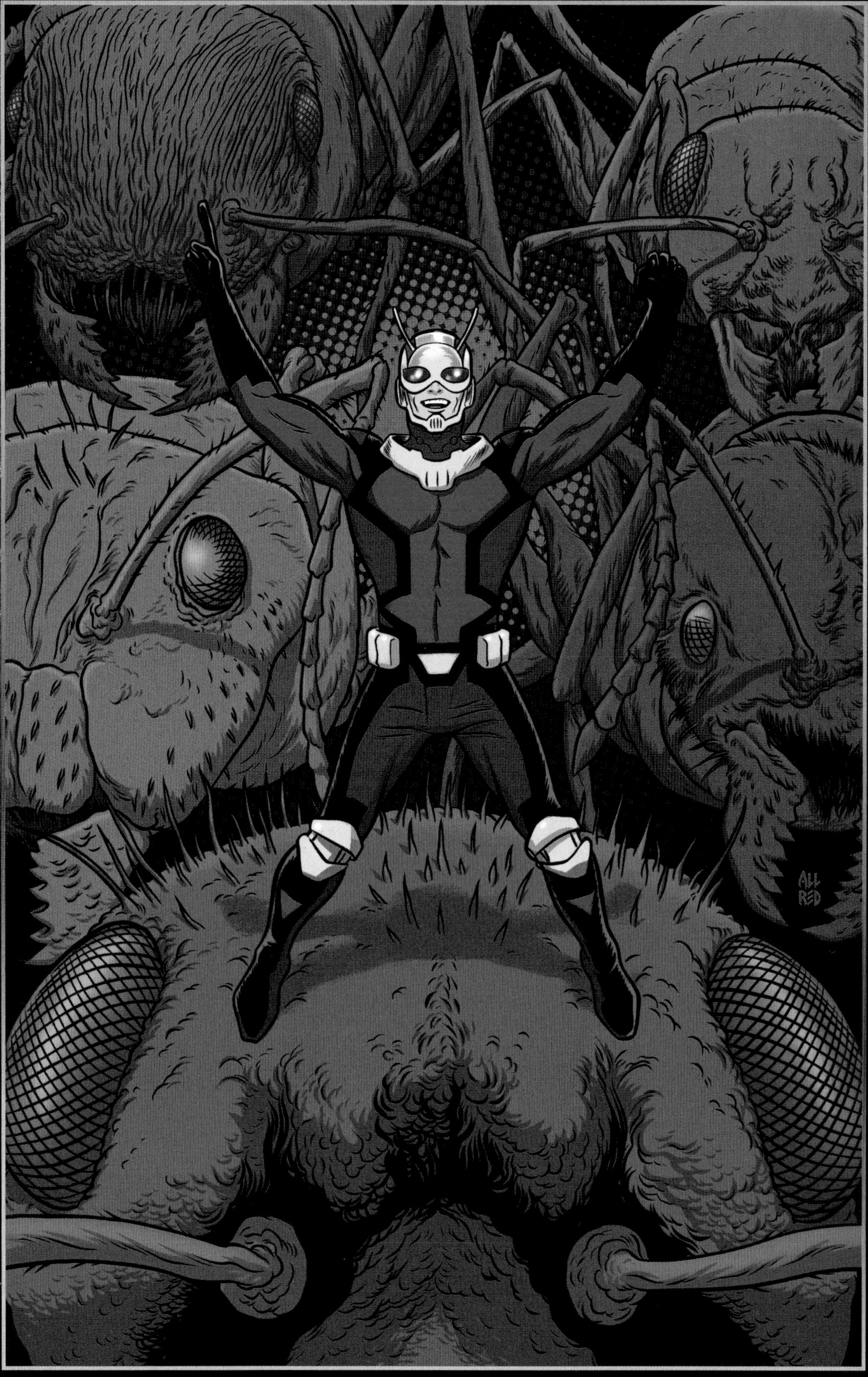
ALL RED

ART BY MIKE ALLRED & LAURA ALLRED

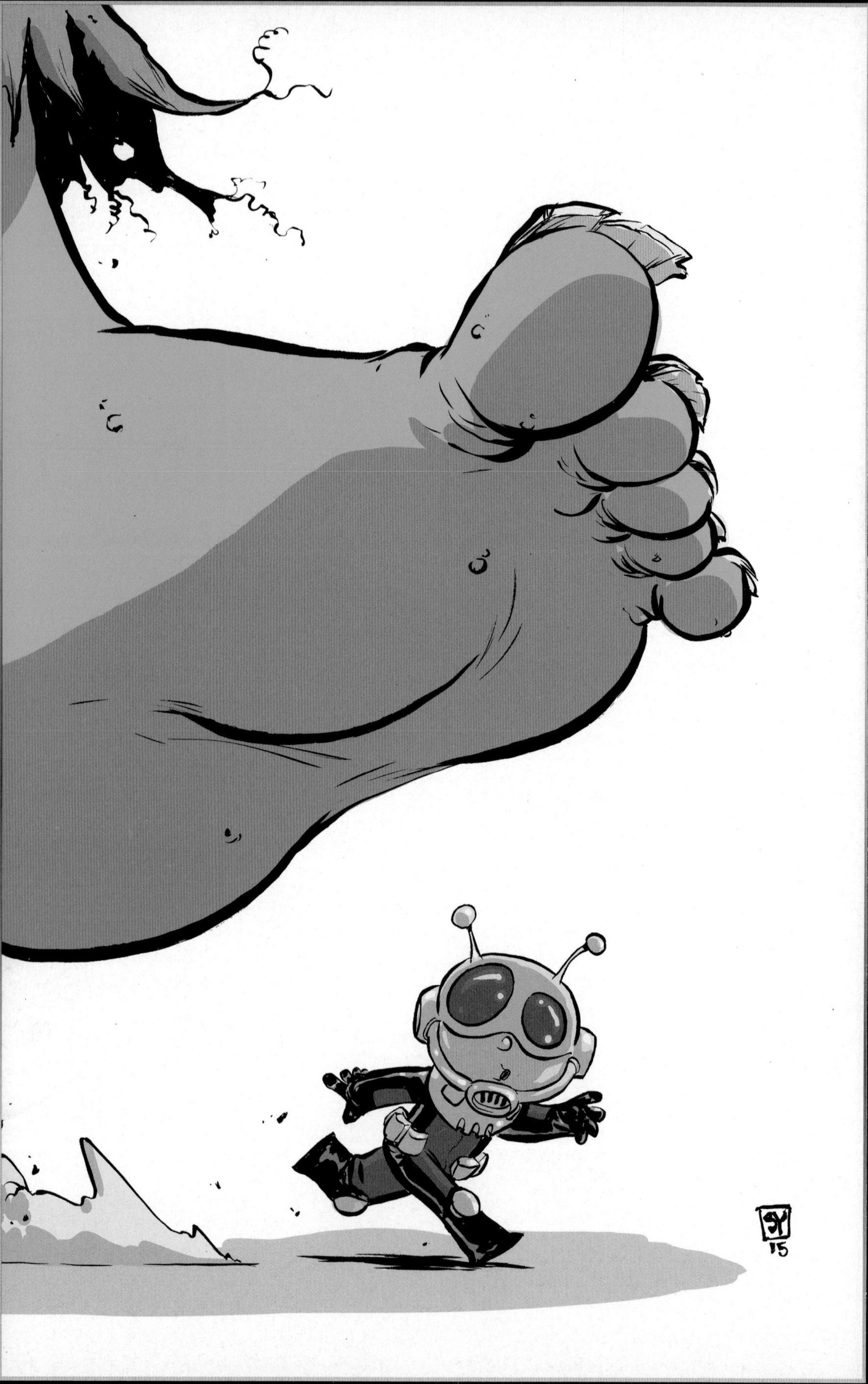
SY
'15

ART BY SKOTTIE YOUNG